# Intellectual Property Rights, Innovation and Software Technologies

NEW HORIZONS IN INTELLECTUAL PROPERTY

**Series Editors:** Christine Greenhalgh, Robert Pitkethly and Michael Spence, *Senior Research Associates, Oxford Intellectual Property Research Centre, St Peter's College, Oxford, UK*

In an increasingly virtual world, where information is more freely accessible, protection of intellectual property rights is facing a new set of challenges and raising new issues. This exciting new series is designed to provide a unique interdisciplinary forum for high quality works of scholarship on all aspects of intellectual property, drawing from the fields of economics, management and law.

The focus of the series is on the development of original thinking in intellectual property, with topics ranging from copyright to patents, from trademarks to confidentiality and from trade-related intellectual property agreements to competition policy and antitrust. Innovative theoretical and empirical work will be encouraged from both established authors and the new generation of scholars.

Titles in the series include:

The International Political Economy of Intellectual Property Rights
*Meir Perez Pugatch*

Software Patents
Economic Impacts and Policy Implications
*Edited by Knut Blind, Jakob Edler and Michael Friedewald*

The Management of Intellectual Property
*Edited by Derek Bosworth and Elizabeth Webster*

The Intellectual Property Debate
*Edited by Meir Perez Pugatch*

Intellectual Property and TRIPS Compliance in China
Chinese and European Perspectives
*Edited by Paul Torremans, Shan Hailing and Johan Erauw*

Intellectual Property Rights, Innovation and Software Technologies
The Economics of Monopoly Rights and Knowledge Disclosure
*Elad Harison*

# Intellectual Property Rights, Innovation and Software Technologies

## The Economics of Monopoly Rights and Knowledge Disclosure

Elad Harison

*University of Groningen, The Netherlands*

**Edward Elgar**

Cheltenham, UK • Northampton, MA, USA

Published by
Edward Elgar Publishing Limited
The Lypiatts
15 Lansdown Road
Cheltenham
Glos GL50 2JA
UK

Edward Elgar Publishing, Inc.
William Pratt House
9 Dewey Court
Northampton
Massachusetts 01060
USA

A catalogue record for this book
is available from the British Library

Library of Congress Control Number: 2008926570

MIX
Paper from
responsible sources
FSC® C013604

ISBN 978 1 84720 582 7

Printed and bound by CPI Group (UK) Ltd, Croydon, CR0 4YY

# Contents

# About the Author

Elad Harison obtained his BSc and his Masters degree in Engineering from the Faculty of Industrial Engineering and Management at the Technion–Israel Research Institute. In 2005, he received his Ph.D. from the University of Maastricht.

Before joining the PhD programme at the Maastricht Economic Research Institute on Innovation and Technology (UNU–MERIT) in The Netherlands, he was working as a logistic engineer and as an information systems analyst at the Israeli Navy Computing Center, where he specialized in Enterprise Resource Planning systems. His research was awarded a National Doctoral Fellowship by the Netherlands Organization for Scientific Research (NWO). The final stages of his research were supported by the Dutch Ministry of Economic Affairs.

Dr Harison completed two research projects on Intellectual Property Rights in a Knowledge–Based Economy for the Dutch Advisory Council for Science and Technology Policy (AWT) with Robin Cowan. He participated in the European Commission's Expert Group on Intellectual Property Rights Aspects of Internet Collaborations. In 2004 he visited the Copenhagen Business School as a Marie Curie doctoral fellow. Currently, he participates in the EC's study on the Effects of Patenting Computer–Implemented Inventions. He is also a member of the EC's Network–of–Excellence on European Policy for Property (EPIP). His work was presented on numerous occassions to conferences and to policy makers.

Since January 2005, Dr Harison has been working as an Assistant Professor in Business and Information and Communications Technologies at the Department of Business and Economics, University of Groningen.

# List of Figures

# List of Tables

# Acknowledgements

This book is the result of my research at MERIT, the University of Maastricht. First and foremost I would like to thank my academic supervisor Robin Cowan who helped me throughout my work on the book and during my PhD studies. Robin guided my way in the venues of academic research. He was a source of inspiration and generously shared his knowledge and experience with me. From the very beginning, Robin also helped me in resolving some of the practical aspects of scientific research: funding, organization and participation in research networks and conferences in my field. It was a great pleasure and an honour to be his student.

I am greatly indebted to Paul David, Dominique Foray, Pierre Mohnen and Ed Steinmueller who shared with me their knowledge and views on the economics of IPRs on numerous occassions and to Chris de Neubourg for his valuable comments.

I would like to thank Luc Soete, UNU–MERIT's director, and to my colleagues at MERIT, Anthony Arundel, Catalina Bordoy, Oxana Chervonnaya, Rishab Aiyer Ghosh, Hugo Hollanders, Paola Criscuolo, Geoffrey Gachino, Pedro Martinez–Lara, Nicola Matteucci, Lynn Mytelka, Herman Pijpers, Andreas Reinstaller, Bulat Sanditov and Bart Verspagen, for their support and fresh insights throughout my studies. I enjoyed the company of Müge Özman and Gottfried Leibbrandt with whom I shared long office hours and discussed new ideas and research methods. Wilma Coenegrachts, Silvana de Sanctis and Corien Gijsbers provided pleasant and efficient work environment and helped me to sort out my way within the labyrinth of university administration.

A Marie Curie scholarship enabled me to stay six months at the Copenhagen Business School and to complete large parts of the empirical study. I am grateful to Patrick Llerena, Peter Lotz and Peter Maskell for their help in organizing my stay. I would like to thank Lee Davis and Markus Reitzig who provided many useful suggestions on different parts of the thesis. A special thanks goes to Maria Theresa Larsen for her friendship and hospitality.

I also thank Egon Berghout and my colleagues at the Department of Economics, University of Groningen, for their support during the completion of this book.

Parts of this work were presented at the DRUID Winter and Summer Conferences (Copenhagen, Helsingor and Aalborg), the International Telecommunications Society Biennial and Regional Conferences (Buenos Aires, 2000; Hong Kong,

2001; Helsinki, 2003), the EUNIP Conferece (Tilburg, 2000), the METU Conference (Ankara, 2000), the ESSID Summer School (Corsica, 2001 and 2002), the ETIC Doctoral Course (Strasbourg, 2002), the 2nd EPIP Workshop (Maastricht, 2003) and the SEGERA Conference (Roskilde, 2004). I thank Maria Brouwer, William Cowan, Michiko Iizuka, Aija Leiponen, Stephen Maurer, Stan Metcalfe, Andrea Mina, Ornit and Eitan Raz, Suzanne Scotchmer, Astrid Szogs, Patrick Waelbroeck and Marc van Wegberg and the participants of those conferences for useful discussions, suggestions and comments.

I thank Judith and Kees Zijlstra for their companionship and friendship. During the period of writing this book, the Zijlstra family has become an inseparatable part of my life in the Netherlands. Judith and Kees were keen on offering me their hospitality, and help when needed. Their friendship and open heart have been a source of support and comfort throughout my years in the Netherlands.

My greatest gratitude goes to my family: To my parents, Aliza and Miron, and to my brother and sister, Barak and Avital. You fully supported me, encouraged and inspired every step of my work, while sharing with me the hardships of the distance between the Netherlands and Israel, some worries and many joys. This book is dedicated to you.

*To my parents, Aliza and Miron*

# 1

# Introduction

## 1.1 Background

The inclusion of algorithms, business inventions and mathematical formulae in the scope of patentable subject matter resulted in exponential growth in the number of software patents after the approval of the USPTO *Guidelines* in 1996. These phenomena have raised significant doubts about whether patents are granted to software inventions on grounds of sufficient novelty and contribution to the state–of–the–art of technology.

Contradicting opinions on the success of patents and copyrights to foster innovation in software technologies persist. Legal and economic scholars indicate that the present legislative regime that provides inventors with long–term, expansive rights over technology has distorted the balance between incentives to innovate and monopoly rights. Further, if a significant number of software patents are granted to minor improvements, as some scholar suggest (for example Merges, 1999), assignees are provided with wide exclusive rights over technologies in return for disclosure of relatively insignificant advances. Cosequently, in the short term low–quality patents may restrict the entry of competitors to neighbouring market niches with superior technologies.

In complex technologies, such as software which integrates a broad variety of computational elements to achieve a required functionality, patents can potentially block development of products that use one or more of the essential components (Merges and Nelson, 1990). Further, software products encompass high degrees of interoperability between the final product and other programs and between the elements that construct it. Algorithms, mathematical formulae and sub–routines are the building blocks of computer programs that accomplish particular tasks that are essential for their operation. Therefore, when invention is recognized as patentable and receives exclusive rights, patent–holders can prevent competitors from entering the market with products that use similar or improved features. Consequently, when a particular element cannot be used in computer programs without infringing legal rights and cannot be substituted, the functionality of the program might be crippled, or even not be attained at all.

In some cases software patents fail to provide a sufficient degree of knowledge disclosure in return for monopoly rights. Then, the ability of second comers to review and to learn from prior inventions and to build new inventions upon them is fairly restricted. Similarly, if patent claims (that is the potential uses of the patented invention) are general and obscure, the scope of protection is wide and covers new applications that were not envisioned by the inventors when the patent application was filed. Those domains will be excluded from other inventors in advanced phases of the technology. Moreover, if patents lack sufficient novelty and disclosure, they become "obvious" to practitioners and, hence, their quality encompasses lower levels of innovative added value and contribution to the public's welfare. Syrowik (1996) suggests that the examination of software patents by the USPTO suffers from those problems and as a result the balance between private and public interests has changed. The balance can be restored by application of a different legal scheme that limits the scope of claims of software patents to particular applications and data structures (Schumm, 1996; Witek, 1996).

Our empirical analysis indicates that the structure of ownership of software patents is highly concentrated, as every year large numbers of patents are granted to a small group of assignees, all of which are multi–national firms that operate in the electronics and ICT sectors. However, since the establishment of the *Guidelines* by the USPTO, the structure of ownership has become more fragmented as larger numbers of small patent–portfolio holders (mostly SMEs and individuals) apply for and are granted patents over their software inventions.

Granting broad exclusive rights (as defined by the patent claims) for long periods to inventions whose contribution to innovation is marginal is likely to hamper entry of new developers and firms to the market. In the long run, this scenario can lead to stagnation of the technological trajectories in the software industry. Nevertheless, those predictions could have barely been fulfilled had the market followed a different trail in reaction to software patenting.

Our findings reveal that since the 1960s the US legislation of software IPRs has lingered by more than a decade after the development of new information technologies. As a result, legislative changes suffered from two major sources of inefficiencies: First, policy adaptations were presented long after technical changes had occurred, hence applying older legislative frameworks to new technologies. Second, by the time that IPR policies were modified due to those technical developments, newer technical paradigms were introduced to the market, hence creating another source of inefficiencies. Consequently, the quality and the innovative value of software patents gradually deteriorated during the 1980s and early 1990s. However, since the enactment of the *Guidelines* in 1996, the quality of software patents is increasing and recent patents are more often cited as *prior art* than before.

The Open Source movement challenges the traditional IPR regimes by providing software developers with alternative incentive mechanisms that are based on reputation rather than on exclusive rights. Open Source development is based on disclosure of the source code and on removal of ownership rights to enable further development of applications. Open Source projects attract growing numbers of programmers and many firms adopt it as their favourite mode of development, even though their creative outputs are disclosed at a zero price tag. The book presents the dynamics of Open Source communities and elaborates whether policy–makers should integrate the Open Source mode of development as a substitute or as a complementary approach to IPRs.

## 1.2 Outline of the Book

Chapter 2, *The Economic Rationale of IPRs*, reviews the economic objectives of IPRs and their impact on the market in terms of fostering technical change. The chapter presents various legal–economic theories through which the structure of the legal regime and the public and private benefits that it provides can be analyzed.

Chapter 3, *The Role and Performance of IPRs as Knowledge–Propelling Regimes*, proposes a conceptual framework for analyzing the role and functionality of IPRs. The frame of analysis is based on insights from the evolutionary economics literature discussing the effects of technical knowledge and disclosure on innovation and technological development.

Chapter 4, *Revealing Obscure Sources: The Paradoxical Evolution of Software Appropriation Regimes*, discusses how software IPRs evolved *vis-à-vis* the development of information technologies. We elaborate the role of patents and copyrights in protecting software and assess whether software IPRs have formed an over- or under-protective regime. We also discuss the success of the Open Source movement to establish an alternative regime that is based on removal of IP claims from the source code, as well as the dynamics of online communities of developers.

Chapter 5, *Benefiting from Intellectual Property and Free Disclosure*, aims at revealing the economic rationale underlying Open Source development and how this mode can strategically be used by firms to enhance their profits. By constructing an analytical model of the market, we identify the optimal share of source code that should be disclosed and developed as Open Source to maximize profits and how this share is affected by the pricing decisions of the firm.

Chapter 6, *Designed for Innovation: The Structure of IPR Regimes and the Evolution of Information Technologies*, constructs a dynamic model of the software market that explores the links between different structures of the patent regime and the market dynamics and technical change. The chapter provides insights on the relations between patent duration and the novelty criterion and the degree of competition and the performance of technologies.

Chapter 7, *Owning Technology: The Structure of Intellectual Property Ownership in Software Technologies*, studies the structure of ownership of US software patents and how it was affected by major changes in IPR policy. Further, the chapter evaluates to what extent the quality and the innovative value of software patents have been influenced by legislative changes and reveals the links between software patenting and the emergence of Open Source projects.

Chapter 8, *Proposed Framework for Analyzing IPRs in the Knowledge-Based Economy*, discusses the economic nature of software and computational processes. We compare between the schemes of IPRs that were established for protecting computer programs and those that protect their physical equivalents (that is, computational machines). Then, we propose a new conceptual framework for legal and economic analyses of software products and technologies.

Finally, Chapter 9 provides conclusions and policy implications.

# 2

# The Economic Rationale of Intellectual Property Rights

## 2.1 Introduction

IPRs are long–living institutions that were enacted centuries before the emergence of digital technologies. Copyrights were initially constituted in the 15th century by the city council of Venice to provide incentives for authors and to prevent free rendering of their works. The roots of the patent system also evolved during the same period when rulers in England and Venice granted inventors with letters of monopoly rights over the production of their inventions.[1]

The *raison d'etre* of IPRs and the objectives to be attained by establishment of those regimes have virtually not changed since then. Patents provide economic incentives to inventors (individuals or firms) by granting them monopoly rights for limited periods over improvements of present techniques or breakthroughs in technology.[2] The procedure of patenting new inventions involves submission of patent application to the patent office, evaluation by a professional referee ("patent examiner") and approval of a patent grant if the invention is found novel and exceeds a *minimal inventive step* in technological terms.[3] In return for property rights

[1]Machlup and Penrose (1950) and David (1993) provide detailed reviews of the evolution of IPR regimes. Granstrand (1999; pp 28–31) presents historical chronology of their development.

[2]Patent protection is granted for 20 years from filing an application in the US and in the EU. Copyrights are obtained for the author's lifetime plus 70–90 years *post mortem autoris*.

[3]There are no legal standards for *inventive step* or *non–obviousness* of inventions.

over patented technologies, inventors are required to disclose to the public domain the technical know–how for which they are awarded protection. The knowledge is organized by the patent office according to pre–defined categories (and search criteria) and it is completely accessible to the public. Although the rationale behind patents and copyrights is similar, literary and artistic works differ from technical inventions, as they are automatically included in the scope of copyright protection when published and they do not require any examination process to be considered as intellectual property.[4]

IPR regimes aim at protecting diverse genres of knowledge, products and works and consist of different legal means, among which patents and copyrights are paramount from both judicial and economic standpoints.[5] For long periods IPRs were considered as efficient regimes for fostering innovation and technical progress, embracing economic incentives for innovative individuals and firms. Nonetheless, IPRs, and patents in particular, faced continuous attempts to curtail the privileges which inventors were granted by Law.

The solicitations of the anti–patent movement finally won a victory when the patent system in the Netherlands was abolished in the late 19th century. After cancelling the patent regime no noticeable changes in innovative and technological output were experienced by the Dutch economy. Whether any foreseen benefits associated with complete abolition of patent protection eventually happened remains unclear (Lerner, 2000). However, it was the only achievement ever won by patent opposition movements, and it was short–lived, as the Netherlands had to revise its policy less than 40 years after the changes took place in order to comply with the Paris Convention whose terms were adopted by many other nations at the same period.

Although complete removal of IP protection did not prove useful for the society, petitions against wide and long–lived patents are continuously heard up to the present. Their nature, however, has turned from general opposition rejecting all forms of patents to controversy over specific technologies, mainly those that have

---

Both definitions are open for wide interpretations by patent examiners and by Court. However, those terms represent qualitative measures for significant improvements beyond the state–of–the–art of technology for which inventions are recognized patentable.

[4]Registration of original works in the Copyright Office is optional but not obligatory to obtain copyright protection over them. Yet, the procedure is inexpensive and can prove helpful in legal disputes.

[5]Trademarks and industrial designs are other mechanisms of IPRs, but they play a less significant role in affecting the evolution of technologies.

recently developed. ICT and biotechnology exemplify expanding opposition to patents on practical grounds of assuring stable patterns of technological evolution and free access to knowledge, or on ethical grounds demanding wider allowances for low cost production of patent–protected drugs and medical equipment for domestic use in poor countries. The economic benefits and perils beyond the policies of legal protection as intellectual property of a single yet a dominant technological field – software products and information technologies – stand at the core of this book.

While common analyses of IPRs compare the level of legal protection granted by variety of national regimes,[6] the contribution of the legal regime to development of stable technological trajectories and innovation can be measured through different features of the system and via historical analysis of appropriation mechanisms. For example, the assessment of the enforcement of property rights by national authorities and by Courts was conducted by analysing patent litigation cases in the 19th century in the US The analysis of those early US cases reveals positive correlation between effective reinforcement of Patent Law by the juridical system and effective patterns of technical change. However, a more efficient approach that does not only include the revenues of patent–holders but also considers broader economic effects of legislation on innovation and competition in technological markets was taken by Court in the late stages of forming the US patent system through the reforms of the 1850s. Being aware of the delicate balance between social and private interests in patent litigation lawsuits, Court considered the effects of patenting on social welfare and avoided the already–prominent approach by which the public generally benefits when inventors are granted broader monopoly rights (Khan, 1995).

Those empirical observations are supported by the conclusions of a growing body of analytical models, which evaluate the links between the strength of patent rights, imitation by rival firms and the motives of patentees to embark on legal proceedings against the infringers of their patent rights. However, the success of patent–holders to recover their damages from unauthorized reproduction of the

[6]Ginarte and Park (1997) define an index of patent rights to measure changes in the level of legal protection in 110 countries worldwide over a period of 30 years. The index is based on the scope of patent protection, membership in international patenting organizations and agreements, provisions for loss of protection, enforcement mechanisms and patent duration. Ostergard (2000) assesses global changes in the degree of protection of various IPR regimes between 1988–1994 on the basis of enforceability, administration, international treaties and the relative significance of each regime for applicants through three different indices (Rapp and Rozek, Sherwood and Seyoum).

protected inventions is not guaranteed and depends on Court's recognition that rival products fall within the scope of protection of living patents. Therefore, the decision of patent–holders to engage in a *patent litigation game* and to submit a lawsuit against an infringer may prove unworthy. Yet, the possibility to prove infringement increases as wider protection of intellectual property is granted to innovators and hence the probability of failing in Court decreases as the patent regime becomes broader (Waterson, 1990). A primary finding is that if the legal costs of patent litigation increase, rivals are deterred from releasing product versions that fall within the scope of patented inventions. Following this conclusion, stricter measures of jurisdiction and enforcement can reduce the loss of social welfare that results from (deadweight) litigation costs.

Though different IPR regimes have existed for centuries, legal and economic scholars did not start analysing systematically their effects on markets and economies until the 1950s.[7] Since then, studies on IPRs have become an integral part in evaluating national innovation systems, policies and legal mechanisms designed to enhance economic growth through innovation and technical change in constantly–changing markets and technological landscapes.

A prominent concern shared by policy makers, academicians and industrialists is whether IPR legislation indeed succeeds in preserving the necessary balance between the interests of the public, that is knowledge disclosure, and those of inventors, that is monopoly over creative output, to maintain stable patterns for developing new technologies. Further, misapplying ill–defined policies of IPRs may result in opposite effects than meant, hampering both innovation and technological progress.

The second section of this chapter discusses the mainstream body of legal–economic studies, that is *reward theory*, by which monopoly rights, granted by IPR regimes, provide incentives to innovate. Particular references to the dimensions of the patent regime are made. The third section elaborates the function and role of the patent regime from the *prospect theory* perspective. We devote a special discussion to copyrights and their economic significance in the fourth section. Finally, the weaknesses of those neo–classical models are discussed, highlighting the need for an alternative framework for evaluation of IPR regimes from the

[7]Important contributions in the first stages of economic research on IPRs were made by Penrose (1951) and by Machlup (1958); path–breaking analyses of patents in various industrial sectors were carried out by Schmookler (1950).

bird's–eye perspective.

## 2.2 Do IPRs Reward Innovation? Economic Outlook on the Dimensions of the Patent System

### 2.2.1 Background

Patents, along with copyrights, are major institutional means employed to obtain legal protection for intellectual endeavours.[8] Patents are used to protect inventions arising from technological advances in processes and products.

Three criteria define minimal measures to judge whether new inventions are patentable:

- Utility: the technical know–how disclosed in the patent file must enable its further exploitation, either in applications that are explicitly mentioned in the patent claims, or in new products that can *potentially* be developed by the industry.
- Novelty: a patent is granted for an invention that carries a required level of originality over the existing body of technological knowledge in the particular field *worldwide*.
- Non–obviousness: invention is recognized as patentable if it entails a minimal, non–trivial inventive step that is approved by a 'person skilled in the art' (official examiner who has the necessary knowledge and skills).

If all those three criteria are satisfied, a patent is granted for the invention.

Intellectual property rights are essentially based on a balance between two sources of value. Public welfare is furthered when new knowledge is disseminated and widely used, both in production of goods and in generating further knowledge. Private incentives to innovate are high when the inventor is able to reap the rewards from his efforts. On the one hand, the inventor is granted a temporary monopoly over an invention and its derivative applications, thereby gaining

[8] Licensing and trade secrecy are additional features of IPR regimes that are treated by a separate body of the economic literature (see for example Friedman et al., 1991). They serve different roles: the former increases the rents accruing to an inventor without reducing his property rights, the latter prevents intellectual property from spilling out of the firm, for example via employees moving to rival firms. Unlike patents or copyrights, both of them are implemented through bilateral contracts either between firms or between a firm and its employees.

protection against unauthorized exploitation of his technical know–how and, consequently, a strong incentive to innovate. On the other hand, if the technical knowledge were disclosed for public use, its accessibility would stimulate the generation of knowledge spillovers and transfer of know–how throughout the economy. Accordingly, IPR legislation aims at optimizing social welfare and striking a balance between monopoly rights and knowledge disclosure.

The economic effects of different designs of the patent regime may largely vary, as firms respond in different ways to different market conditions and strategic considerations. Firms' decisions to imitate existing products or to create new technologies, to invest in R&D activities or to license the rights to apply inventions and technical know–how that are legally protected by other firms, to compete in technological markets or deter rivals from entering them, are largely affected by the design of IPR regimes and by the opportunities to use them for their own benefits. The following section reviews the various dimensions of the patent system and their influences on innovation and research activities. The section also includes a critical overview of the concepts and boundaries of constructing analytical models of the patent regime and its influence on economic activities.

### 2.2.2 Economic Representation of the Patent Regime

Illustrated in a stylized way, patents can be represented via a three–dimensional structure of monopoly rights over segments of the technological realm and over time. The patent regime can be described and assessed according to its *length* (duration), *breadth* (scope) and *height* (a measure of disclosure or a "minimal inventive step" over the state–of–the–art of scientific and technical knowledge). Following this view, much of the economic research on IPRs is geared toward the assessment of direct effects that are caused by marginal changes in one of the dimensions of the regime.[9]

*Patent length* determines the duration of legal protection (and the duration of monopoly rights). In the US and in the EU patent protection lasts for 20 years. In contrast to breadth and disclosure, which are both qualitative dimensions that may significantly vary among patent offices and examiners, patent lifetime is an absolute measure and therefore it can serve as a 'pure' attribute in economic anal-

[9]This section reviews the attributes of the patent regime, but the structure of the copyright system can be illustrated in a similar way.

yses of patents. Consequently, setting new patent length and evaluating the effects on activities of firms and on innovation are relatively simple and straightforward.

Nordhaus (1969; Ch. 5) was the first to highlight the significance of the design of the patent regime by examining the links between the length of patents (as a measure for the degree of protection granted to inventors) and the consequent incentives to innovate. His synopsis was later expanded (and criticized) by Scherer's work (1972). Both works aim at recognizing the nexus between patent length, firm's profits and innovation, whereas innovation is illustrated by the *invention possibility function (IPF)* that represents productivity or innovative output as a function of R&D inputs.

The model is straightforward and its dynamics are explained as follows: Assume that technical inventions reduce the production costs of existent goods.[10] However, if an invention is patented, it can be used only by its inventor. Consequently, only the patent–holder is able to apply the new technology and to reduce his costs, whilst other firms are unable to compete in price (patent infringement and unauthorized use are assumed not to exist). The inventor dominates the market and charges a monopoly price, which is lower than the competitive price that was present before the discovery of the new technology (prices will decrease to a new competitive level when the patent expires). Therefore, firms are able neither to adjust their prices to the price charged by monopolist nor to adopt the new technology and so will be driven out of the market by price competition during the patent lifetime (assuming that no other non–infringing invention will take place in this period).

The dynamics of the model are illustrated in Figure 2.1. Initially, the cost of producing one unit of product is $\overline{c}$. After a cost–reducing invention is made, the cost per unit falls to the price level $\underline{c}$. Two conclusions emerge from this graphic presentation of the market pre– and post–introduction of a patented invention. First, the deadweight loss (denoted $DWL$ in the graph) increases when the elasticity of demand increases.[11] Second, the patent–holder controls the use of the new technology and sets the monopolistic price, $c_m$, higher than the new, (potentially) competitive price level and lower than the pre–invention competitive price, hence

[10] Quality improvements and product differentiation are not included in this stylized form of presentation.

[11] This result implies low royalty fees to minimize the deadweight loss as a result of patent rights. Implications of this finding regarding compulsory licensing policies are further discussed in the next chapter.

$\underline{c} < c_m < \bar{c}$. During the patent lifetime the patentee becomes a sole producer and obtains a considerable share of the market.

A major assumption of the model, upon which both works base their findings and even conclude upon the optimal length of patents, refers to the correlation between R&D expenditure and innovation (defined as the *invention possibility function* by Nordhaus). What are the terms in which innovative output should be signified and what is the precise relationship between R&D expenditure and innovation are both the subjects of fierce controversies among economists.

Nordhaus (1969) represents innovative output by reduction in unit production costs as a result of implementing a new invention. The volume of the R&D investments made by the firm is therefore associated with cost–savings. Furthermore, Nordhaus assumes a convex invention possibility function with diminishing returns to R&D expenditure at any point.[12] Scherer (1972), on the other hand, does not revolutionize those views (for example by differentiating between industrial sectors in assessing this puzzling link), but rather relaxes some of Nordhaus's assumptions by solving the model for a number of variants of the basic R&D–cost reduction curve. The first is characterized by an inflected function with increasing returns in lower levels of R&D expenditure and diminishing returns in higher degrees of investment ("S–curve"). The second introduces discontinuity in cost reduction for a threshold level of R&D ("stair–step" function). In a reply, Nordhaus (1972) suggests that for a continuous IPF (finite) optimal patent life exists when the elasticity of cost reduction with respect to R&D is greater than 1. Further, he rejects the feasibility of the latter case, stating that "to my knowledge, there is no firm evidence on the degree of curvature of the IPF" (p. 429). Interestingly, the possibility of negative correlation between R&D and innovation (mainly in high degrees of R&D investments) has never been mentioned in innovation studies. This phenomenon is far from being an academic exercise and it was previously identified in other economic fields where the organization of the R&D process largely affects its output.

From the perspective of the innovative agent who follows the assumptions of those models, longer patent lifetime is desirable, since patent protection stretches the time in which her technology is novel in the market beyond the product lead–time. Hence, patent–holders can generate revenues over longer periods, without

[12] Traditionally, the invention possibility function is defined as: $Q = \beta \cdot (RD)^{\alpha}$, where $\alpha < 1$ and $\beta > 0$ are constant (Nordhaus, 1969; pp. 22–26).

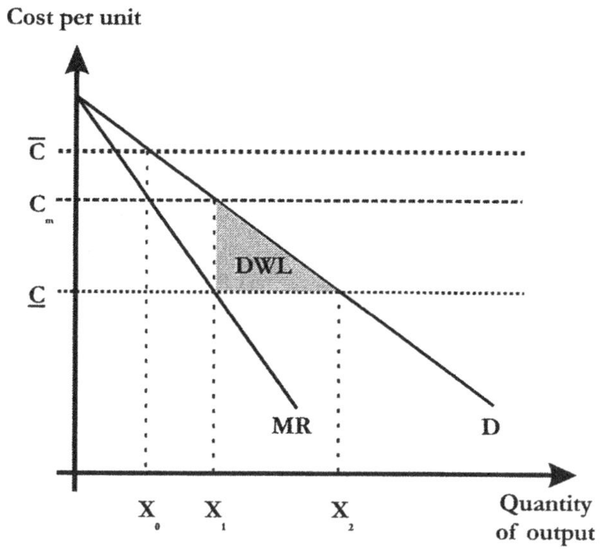


**Figure 2.1.** Market prices, firm's profits and deadweight loss at the presence of cost–reducing technology (based on Scherer, 1972).

being threatened by imitation and introduction of rivals goods in the technological environment of their patented inventions.

While Nordhaus and Scherer study the behaviour of a monopolist inventor and the modes in which his profits are affected by different patent durations, the conclusions regarding the behaviour of firms dramatically change in the competitive environment. Firms that decide to invest in R&D in such an environment face two sources of uncertainty. First, the risk of failure in accomplishing the development project successfully and the consequent loss of financial resources. Second, the competition against rival inventors is characterized as a *patent race*, in which monopoly is granted to the "first–to–patent" firm, hence pre–empting rivals from commercial exploitation of similar inventions, even if those were successfully completed by them. In this "winner–takes–all" competition between firms, longer patent life influences the firm's decision to increase its R&D expenditure. Consequently, the increased investment in R&D will enhance the firm's know–how and will curtail (with probability) the period of discovering new inventions, thus enhancing the innovative output of the firm (Kamien and Schwartz, 1974).

When the development process is positively correlated with R&D expenditure (that is, technical progress increases and development time decreases with R&D), firms increase their R&D expenditure (Chou and Shy, 1993). When R&D expenditure is taken as a fixed share of the revenues, long–term patents can improve the terms for investment in R&D by ensuring a stable stream of income during the patent lifetime and by generating ongoing innovative efforts. Hence, not only inventors but also innovation is rewarded by longer patent duration. However, results opposite to the conclusions of those models may dominate markets with high R&D intensity. Long duration of patents may restrain the development of new inventions and hinder the establishment of new firms, as inventors would prefer purchasing monopoly rights of existing technologies and guaranteeing themselves a secure and stable stream of revenues, rather than investing in new and risky R&D activities. Further, when inventors regard their patent rights as a "milking cow" and do not re–invest in R&D, longer patent duration would not stimulate establishment of new firms and development of new technologies, thus retarding innovation and economic growth in the long run.

In an attempt to strike the balance between social and private benefits in diverse technological and economic scenarios, Arditti and Sandor (1973) propose to revolutionize the patent regime by implementing a *variable patent duration.* However, from the legal standpoint, this solution seems to be infeasible and its implementation would entail considerable juridical, administrative and enforcement costs. Moreover, successful implementation is difficult, since determining the desirable patent duration depends on precise estimation of the rate of return from each patented invention *ex ante.* A potential solution for the problem of estimating the social value of patents can be achieved by calculating the average rate–of–return on patent and R&D costs of existing inventions in similar technological classes. However, this policy tool method proves inappropriate and even misleading while judging the value of patent applications in order to determine the granted duration, as inventions have to be sufficiently novel and significantly different from existent products to obtain a patent. Moreover, inventions may differ in their nature, varying from improvements of present technologies to technological breakthroughs. Therefore, a versatile patent policy that determines the unique duration of patents by interpolating the value of granted patents may result in large biases in the case of new technologies.[13]

---

[13]Diversification of IPR regimes by policy makers, applying *sui generis* legislation to protect different genres of products, has been implemented mainly in the EU. Yet,

In comparison to patent duration, the definitions of breadth (scope) and disclosure are inconclusive. Therefore, suggested modifications in both dimensions and assessment of their impact on the market are difficult to attain.

*Patent breadth* (scope) refers to the coverage of subjects that can be patented and then protected from introduction of rival goods that are similar or close to the invention. Patent breadth is determined by the technical know–how disclosed in the patent description and by immediate and potential applications that are described in the patent claims. The technical knowledge includes background on the invention, description of the blueprints and detailed discussion of the invention and its operation method.

For example, US patent no. 6,697,960 describes the "method and system for recovering data to maintain business continuity" that are based on configuration of local and remote disks and eliminate the need to use magnetic media for backup of digitally–stored data. The patent builds upon (and cites) US patent no. 6,446,175 on storage and retrieval of data by a tape backup system. Although the purposes of both inventions are similar (data backup in remote business sites, as described in the background sections of both patents), the method and system applied in patent no. 6,697,960 are significantly different from the description and the claims of earlier patents (such as those mentioned in patent no. 6,446,175) and therefore do not fall within their scope of protection.

Inclusion of advanced ways to exploit the invention, as mentioned in the claims, is extremely important for inventors, as this section provides them with property rights over anticipated applications of the patented knowledge. Wider breadth permits inventors to obtain dominance in larger market shares by excluding rivals from implementing the patented technology in a wider variety of products and by collecting royalty fees from more users of the protected technology.

As development of new products influences the structure of technology markets, patent breadth closely affects innovation. When other dimensions of the regime remain unchanged, extension of patent breadth implies higher rewards to innovators, as exclusive rights are granted to inventors over wider technological domains.[14] However, an opposite effect of wider breadth is an increasing difficulty

---

considering the unpredictable manners in which technologies evolve, those policies are open to periodical re–assessment and revision.

[14]The breadth of patents can be expanded by Court's decisions in specific cases or by Patent Offices taking a more liberal approach towards applications that in the past were not recognized patentable. For example, mathematical algorithms officially became

to receive a patent. Wider coverage of patent protection expands the ownership rights of patent holders and therefore introduces more constraining conditions to new patentees.[15]

Generally, when wider patent breadth is put into practice, product variety decreases, as patent–holders pre–empt introduction of similar products or variants of protected inventions. Apart from reducing product variety, increasing breadth directs consumers' preferences to a smaller range of goods and enables patent–holders to charge monopoly prices for those products by pre–empting introduction of clones and goods alike bearing a competitive price–tag. Those aggregate effects increase the consumers' deadweight loss and the producers' surplus.

*Patent height* defines the minimal degree of technical knowledge that should become available to the public when patented. Height is associated with the degree of novelty and non–obviousness of patents and it distinguishes patentable subject matter from marginal improvements of existent patents. As intellectual property is revealed when patent applications are submitted, rivals can improve their products and establish new technologies on the basis of the information disclosed in patents and would be able to compete with the patentee with superior products. Hence, firms aim at disclosing the minimal degree of know–how that satisfies the patent examination guidelines in order to achieve a profound position in the market. By contrast, policy makers aspire to increase the level of overt know–how that becomes available for public use. When patent height is relatively low, there is a small difference between innovation and firms' behaviour in free markets and in patent protected regimes. Surprisingly, application of intermediate degree of height generates the opposite effect than expected. Rivals increase their R&D expenditure to exceed the required degree of novelty and to enter the market. Yet, their products are sufficiently close to the patented technology to compete with it in the same class of products, and hence they reduce the revenues of the patentees. Therefore, from the innovator's standpoint patenting becomes a desirable practice only when relatively "high" patents are granted (Van Dijk, 1996).

The legal definitions of patent breadth and height are somewhat vague and

patentable in the US in 1996 (USPTO, 1996). Business methods could be patented in the US since 1998 (*State Street Bank and Trusted Company v. Signature Financial Group*; 149 F.3d 1368, Fed. Cir.).

[15]In most cases, inventions are characterized by sequential improvement upon existent technologies, rather by breakthroughs. Therefore, extension of patent breadth forces new inventors to license technological domains that previously were considered public, hence reducing their bargaining power in front of incumbent firms.

depend mostly on the expertise and on the judgement of every patent examiner. Therefore, modifications in the "size" of breadth and length and the evaluation of their effects on innovation and on behaviour of firms are difficult to accomplish. Hence, the main economic literature on IPRs typically estimates the impact of patent breadth and height on innovation and on diffusion of new technologies by constructing conceptual framework of analysis (Merges and Nelson, 1990) or by illustrating the links between the patent system, R&D investments and technological markets through analytical models (review of the literature on the design of IPR regimes is provided in Tirole, 1988; Ch. 10).

### 2.2.3 Trade–offs in the Structure of Patents and Social Welfare

An optimal structure of the patent regime that aims at maximizing social welfare of consumers and innovators can be measured by minimal deadweight losses that originate from two major sources:

1) Advances in technology are protected by patents that enable inventors to introduce them to the market at a higher (monopoly) price. Consumers may choose to adopt a new technology or to purchase at a competitive price low grade technologies that are already present in the market and are not protected by patents. However, if consumers are sensitive to price, they would prefer technically inferior substitutes outside the scope of patents of the advanced technology which, had it not been protected by IPRs, would have been offered at a competitive price.

2) Patents oblige consumers to purchase protected products at a monopoly price and prevent them from acquiring low cost substitutes that fall within the scope of patents. As a result, broader patents narrow down the variety of products from which consumers can choose a preferred technology and enable patent–holders to introduce their goods at higher prices than the competitive price.

Klemperer (1990) concludes that narrow, infinitely lived patents are desirable when preferences of consumers are indifferent among variety of patented and unprotected products (that is, this type of inefficiency is marginal), while wide and short–lived patents are more desirable when consumers' decisions whether to purchase one of the products or none of them are equally important. Between those poles lies an infinite range of designs of the legal regime, in which longer patent duration substitutes for narrower breadth, and *vice versa* to maintain a similar degree of incentives. Finally, a particular patent structure that optimizes social welfare is chosen.[16]

Those findings persist when imitation is costly (Gallini, 1992). Setting sufficiently broad patents that increase imitation costs prevents rivals from "inventing around" existent patents and from introducing minor improvements of protected technologies to avoid infringement. The optimal length is sufficiently short to deter imitators from implementing patented know-how during the patent lifetime and provides inventors with a predetermined level of rewards. Curiously, setting longer patent duration provides higher incentives to innovate. However, firms that are pre-empted from using patented technologies for long periods may enter the market by developing new non-infringing and competitive products, therefore capturing shares of the monopoly revenues.[17]

Gilbert and Shapiro (1990) share similar notions with Klemperer, investigating the trade-off between patent breadth and length and demarcating the structure of the legal regime that minimizes deadweight loss and sustains a predetermined reward. Their work focuses on identifying the optimal breadth of infinitely-lived patents. Infinite duration is justified as the optimal length of patents that maximizes social welfare (represented by the summation of inventors' profits and consumers' surplus). The model introduces social welfare in terms that are equivalent to the second source of inefficiencies in Klemperer's model. Nonetheless, product differentiation and choices of alternative products by consumers (creating the first source of inefficiencies) are not included within their model. Therefore, in the model, increasing patent breadth is associated with larger deadweight loss, as consumers avoid purchasing the patented product at a non-competitive price.

However, Gilbert and Shapiro's model is restricted to an extent and addresses only a limited sphere of real-life scenarios, as the effects of patent breadth on the cost of products and the liberty of consumers to choose among alternative goods of the same class are not included in their interpretation. The model suffers another major shortcoming, assuming negative correlation between inventors' profits and welfare at any given degree of the profits ($\frac{\partial W(\pi)}{\partial \pi} < 0$). Presumably, this rela-

[16]Technically, Klemperer (1990) identifies the breadth that minimizes the ratio of total social costs to profits, $\{\bar{w}|Min_{\bar{w}}s(w)/\pi(w)\}$ and devises the corresponding patent length $\bar{L}$ for which the innovator obtains steady incentives, $V(\bar{L},\bar{s})$

[17]Under those circumstances, inventors would charge licensing fees that are lower than imitation costs, precluding their rivals from developing non-infringing substitutes and from generating a secondary stream of revenues.

tionship seems straightforward if social welfare is only limited to the benefits of consumers. However, if the definition of social welfare includes both consumers' well–being and inventors' profits, as Nordhaus (1969) and Scherer (1972) follow in their analyses, broader patents balance the decrease in consumers' welfare (higher deadweight loss) by increasing the producer surplus of inventors, thus maintaining the level of social welfare in the market. Therefore, and in contrast to Gilbert and Shapiro's work, finite–life patents produce higher societal value than long–living ("infinite") patents.

Analysing the trade–off between length and breadth of patents is far from being trivial, as some of those models suggest. First, the reward of inventors (or the planned incentives) cannot be accurately predicted, but rather be determined *ex post*. The expected incentives to innovators affect, in turn, engagement in R&D projects and successful accomplishment of inventions as well as their patentability. Second, sectors are characterized by different modes of innovation (that is, discrete, cumulative, chemical and science–based inventions) and may react diversely to changes in the patent regime and, therefore, require further theoretical and empirical investigations on the links between incentives to innovate provided by legal means and innovation (Merges and Nelson, 1990).

Models that measure the trade–off between different dimensions of the patent system follow the essence of reward theory. They analyze how changes in patent length and breadth are applied simulteneously to maintain fixed revenues (also interpreted as firm's incentives to innovate) at the lowest possible social costs. Other models assess the correlation between the various dimensions of patents and identify trade–offs and alternative designs of the regime. However, patent breadth and height are imperfect substitutes, embodying diverse purposes and market responses when both are simultaneously modified. Where patent breadth characterizes the range of features of a given technology that can be imitated, height defines the improvement that is recognized patentable and non–infringing. The effects of those dimensions on the market are essentially different, as the expense of improving technology (by conducting R&D at some degree) is typically higher than the costs of imitation. Further, in terms of product variety, breadth is associated with horizontal product differentiation, while height measures dissimilarities of products along a similar *quality ladder* (Van Dijk, 1996).[18]

---

[18]Although Van Dijk mentions the feasibility of a combined model of patent breadth and height, it seems that the order of biases in representing the trade–off between both

Where stylized models reflect a simplified image of a complex reality, empirical findings provide a supplementary view to affirm indications that otherwise would remain within the limited boundaries of a theoretical exercise. The first challenge that economists face while analysing the dimensions of IPR regimes is to assess the effects of patent breadth and height on innovation, market structure and on adoption of new technologies by applying quantitative methods. Trajtenberg (1989; 1990) employs patent citations to measure the "magnitude" of inventions and applies this method to evaluate the links between patenting and innovation in tomography scanners.

A second challenge is to define empirically the state–of–the–art of technology and to provide a measure for patent height, in order to avoid granting patents to technologies that are already present or to minor improvements in existing technologies. Bibliometric methods applied to explore and to measure the intensity of co–publication in scientific research by analysing citations of scientific papers in patent records (Mairesse and Turner, 2005) may be further exploited to assess the novelty and the non–obviousness of the technical know–how disclosed in patents. Lerner (1994) assesses the elasticity of patent breadth and the value of firms in the biotechnology sector by employing the number of subclasses under which a patent is classified as an indicator for its breadth. His observations stand in one line with the findings that were brought in the theoretical literature earlier (in particular with the results of Klemperer's model). Significant correlation was found between increase in the breadth of patents and higher valuation of the patent–holding firms. Those results support the arguments that stand at the basis of the incentive theory: The stronger IPRs protection is (that is, through granting broader patents to inventors), the higher are the incentives to innovate (as reflected by the value of the firm). Lerner also concludes that relatively broad patents were granted by the USPTO in early stages of development of biotechnology and later, since 1988, the breadth of patents was significantly narrowed. The results suggest that the value of intellectual assets increases with wider breadth, not necessarily due to the potential to develop variety of commercial applications on the basis of patented inventions but due to the ability of patentees to pre–empt inventors from entering broader technological areas in the legally–protected sphere of their patents. A

dimensions is significant. Inevitably, his analysis is restricted to adjusting the height and the effects on the structure of the market and on social welfare, ignoring other aspects of the patent system.

second important result that Lerner's analysis produces is the link between patent breadth and the "uniqueness" of patents. Wider breadth of patents becomes more valuable in the mature stage of technological trajectories, when technological fields are massed with a multitude of competing firms that own broad portfolios of patents. The explanation of this result is almost straightforward. Large numbers of patents may emerge in any technological domain that accommodates a high concentration of firms that perform R&D. As a result, the possibility to dominate larger technological vicinities by broader patents increases. Nevertheless, technical markets in which large numbers of firms operate and many patents are awarded bear a high degree of risk for new entrants and innovators from incumbents that already own core technologies in the form of intellectual property. Consequently, wider patent breadth may encourage new entry in the short run and will mitigate competition in the long term.[19]

Through controlling the length, breadth and height of patents (separately or altogether), agents take rational and therefore uniform decisions on their patenting behaviour, introducing aspects of R&D expenditure, imitation, invention strategies and licensing terms between patent–holders and licensees.

### 2.2.4 Assumptions Embedded in the Neo–Classical Analysis of Patents

Comparative benchmark of the literature on the patent regime, its dimensions and proposed optimal design reveals that the models of IPR regimes share a common frame of reference and follow several fundamental assumptions:

1) **The economic aims of IPR regimes**

The neo–classical approach recognizes IPRs as legal mechanisms that are geared to prevent *market failure* as a result of under–investment in R&D: Firms are deterred from allocating financial resources for development of new technologies unless their inventions are safe from reverse–engineering, rendering and duplication by rivals (Arrow, 1962). Consequently, neo–classical studies on the function of

[19] Patent breadth may be changed in particular cases by applying the *doctrine of equivalents* in Court. The doctrine enables the extension of legal coverage beyond the breadth of the claims on a case–by–case basis "if two devices do the same work in substantially the same way, and accomplish substantially the same result, they are the same, even though they differ in name, form, or shape" (*Machine Co. v. Murphy*, 97 US 120, 125; 1991). Analysis of the history of the doctrine and its legal implications in the *Festo* decision are presented by White (2002).

IPR regimes as means to enhance economic growth typically aim at discovering optimal designs of the patent system that maximize social welfare (summing up the inventor's profits during the patent duration and the consumers' surplus in the following period) and minimize social costs in terms of deadweight loss from monopoly rights and R&D investments.

Following those arguments, industrial policies that aim at providing an environment in which innovation advances at a rapid and stable pace through implementation of IPR regimes do so by constructing a regime that satisfies the optimal degrees of the length, breadth and height of patents and maximizes social welfare in the short and long term. However, most analyses neglect the inter–dependencies or the substitution between the three dimensions of the patent system.

The assumption of market failure that stands at the basis of the reward theory advocates the use of extensive exclusive rights (for example monopoly over patented inventions) where other incentive mechanisms fail, thus contradicting the principal aim of knowledge transfer and diffusion of new technologies, leading to a quasi–efficient regime.[20]

**2) Stability of market over time**

The assumption embedded in the basis of neo–classical models of the patent regime is that markets reach stability at a certain equilibrium point in which economic terms remain unchanged. The final state of the market is predictable and can be determined *ex ante* by social planners if the actors and links underlying the economic system are well known. Further, if the economy reaches the desirable equilibrium, it will not deviate from it. Following this argument, in theory policy makers can steer the market towards a long–term stability at a desired optimum by identifying the structure of the market, its initial conditions and setting the magnitude of the various dimensions of the regime. Consequently, the level of social welfare can be maximized *ex ante* by determining the optimal structure of the legal regime.

**3) The essence of innovation**

Innovation is described as a sequence of discrete inventions that do not relate to each other from any technological or economic aspect. Typically, the economic benefits of inventions are associated with reduction in the unit production costs

[20] The *Fair Use* doctrine attempts to resolve the imperfections of the patent regime by defining exemptions to exclusive rights over inventions for scientific, educational and non–profit use.

and, under the assumption of homogeneous economic goods, product diversity does not exist. Although recent models consider product diversity as the relative positions of goods on the *quality ladder* and, consequently, invention reduces the costs of "climbing up" along it (see for instance Horowitz and Lai, 1996), this analytical representation of technologies reflects reality only in part, leaving out the diversity of tastes and preferences whilst matching consumers and products. The introduction of new inventions tends not to include further effects in the scope of analysis, such as fostering introduction of new products and technologies that build upon existent goods, development of new product varieties and quality improvements. However, Scotchmer (1991) describes innovation as *cumulative* in essence. Both technical improvements and breakthroughs are achieved through continuous and gradual construction of new know–how upon previous inventions. Hence, technical progress is typically achieved when innovators are "standing on the shoulders of giants".

The two ways in which innovation is characterized, either as a process that compounds discrete technological improvements or as a sequence of inventions, reach beyond the purposes of academic discussion. Understanding the emergence of the innovative process may largely and positively affect the course of IPR policies. In particular, the structure of exclusive rights granted to early inventors and to their followers may influence the market organization of core inventions and that of their technological offspring. If innovators are granted weak protection for their discoveries and technological breakthroughs, firms would prefer investing in improving existing products over entering into research and development of new technologies that can easily be rendered by others. However, if early inventors are provided with wide exclusive rights over their inventions, their followers would be preempted from introducing advanced products and improvements. Consequently, late stage development may be hampered by the legal regime. Scotchmer (1996) examines the division of profit between inventors of basic technology and "second–generation" applications (and the incentives of firms to engage in basic or applied R&D). She concludes that IPR policies that favour granting stronger exclusive rights to basic technologies and restrict patent rights granted to second–generation inventions would increase the profits of early inventors (for example by licensing out their patents to a larger number of developers).

4) **Homogeneity of agents**

The economic actors that operate in the market, including users, developers and distributors of technologies, are identical in their preferences, technical capabilities and knowledge. Therefore, they share similar decision–making mechanisms and economic rationale, leading to the formation of an anticipated market equilibrium.

5) **Homogeneity of technologies and products**

Most of the analyses assume that technologies share similar merits and hence they are identical in their market behaviour. The neo–classical body of literature largely looks at "generic" technologies, which are similar in their diffusion patterns, efficiency of R&D investments and innovative trajectories. Clearly, though, the nature of innovation differs between technologies and industrial sectors and so does the use of patenting by firms.[21]

6) **Insignificance of knowledge externalities from patenting**

The neo–classical approach typically assumes insignificant knowledge externalities from patenting that bear only minor effects on innovation and technical change. R&D expenditure and accidental inventions are perceived in the majority of patent models as the fountainhead of innovation, while the role of knowledge disclosure through patenting in the innovation process is excluded from the scope of most of the analyses, including those of knowledge transfer between firms and other actors, for example universities, public research and strategic collaborations. Horstmann et al. (1985) elaborate the signalling effects of patents in a multi–stage game and conclude that the *equilibrium propensity* of firms decreases when the profitability of competitors increases due to further exploitation of the disclosed know–how. More recently, Verspagen and De Loo (1999) measure knowledge spillovers from patents between sectors and Maurseth and Verspagen (2002) assess their impact on the economy.[22]

If the market indeed behaves as a homogeneous and stable system, as described above, application of a *uniform legal regime* would be sufficient to achieve a sustainable trajectory of innovation. A straightforward conclusion is that a single,

[21] Empirical studies on the links between innovation and appropriation reveal significant differences between sectors in the propensity of firms to protect their inventions by patents: while the majority of pharmaceutical firms would have not developed or introduced new products in the absence of patent protection, abolition of IP protection in other sectors, such as office equipment, vehicles and textiles, would have only minor impact on the behaviour of firms (Mansfield, 1986).

[22] The effectiveness of patents as sources of knowledge at the firm's level is discussed in Chapter 2.

"optimal" patent system that adequately addresses the needs of a wide variety of technologies would be sufficient to maximize social welfare through innovation.

This commonplace perspective on IPR regimes emphasizes the role of patents in promoting investments in research and development in firms and in enhancing the level of social welfare by sustaining the propensity of inventors to innovate. However, opponents of wide IPR provisions often comment that originality and creativity exist regardless of any economic incentives. Novel endeavours are initiated even under difficult economic terms, as anecdotes in technical and artistic fields demonstrate (one may think for example of the Open Source movement and its equivalent phenomena, permissive sharing of music and books, mainly those that are published by new artists). Yet, a stable stream of profits from patent–protected products along the duration of the patent provides a continuous source of expenditure for R&D activities and, consequently, development of new products and technologies.

## 2.3 Appropriating Innovation on Creative Grounds: IPRs and *Prospect Theory*

A widely accepted perspective on the economics of intellectual property, which differs from the neo–classical standpoint, is the *prospect theory.* The theory explains national policies that aim at producing social benefits by granting rights over public property to individuals and firms, in return for royalties and private investments in development and exploitation of public resources. In many nations governments are not interested in or are unable to exploit public resources and prefer to transfer the property rights to private firms in return for licensing fees, royalties, investments in domestic industries and regional development (general review and analysis of the theory of property rights appears in Barzel, 1997). Kitch (1977) draws parallels between the right to use public resources to generate profits in defined manners within a certain geographical area (for example, rights over mining or operating fishery boats) and the provision of intellectual property rights to inventors (that is, the right to exploit commercially the "technological prospects" that they discover). Kitch argues that patents allow inventors to discover and to produce technological advances within a particular field and hence to develop it without risking their R&D investments. Their competitors are forbidden from duplicating the patent–protected inventions and producing rival goods.

Beck (1983) criticizes the rationale of Kitch's interpretation of the patent system on various grounds: Property rights over prospects (for example land) are exclusive rights granted not only for the physical asset but also for any future use of the prospects that later are developed by the right owners. In comparison to property rights, patents grant exclusive rights over present inventions and do not provide patentees with any control over future applications of their technologies. If patent claims are very broad, Courts may limit their scope and enable release of new inventions that build upon existing patents. Hence, succeeding developments within a technological domain can also be accomplished by new entrants, other than the owners of existing patents. Further, if future development of a technological prospect can be accomplished during the patent lifetime only by the patent–holders, as prospect theory suggests, other inventors would be prohibited from entering (or "trespassing") this field. Following this argument, we may assume that patenting technologies in their early stages provides patent–holders with monopoly not only over their own inventions, but also over some of the technological advances that follow them. Consequently, other inventors would not participate in R&D on the basis of existing patents, unless their efforts are coordinated with patent–holders and they obtained a "right of entry" from them. However, this view does not comply with reality or with the objectives of the patent system.

Kitch's analysis suffers weaknesses similar to those mentioned for the reward theory. First, the rights over prospects are bounded by both geographic borders and use. For example, a mining license is restricted to a certain zone and cannot be expanded geographically or to other types of use of the land, such as agriculture or construction. However, this is not the case in innovation. Whereas the value of a mining area is determined by a given amount of prospects underground, the significance of inventions and the value of patents may dramatically change in various stages of the diffusion of technologies, on the basis of their commercial success, licensing and citations by other patents, as well as by exploitation of the technology in new and unexpected ways.[23] Second, both the prospect theory and the reward theory relate to the role of market failure and under–investment in innovation, as a result of the difficulty to protect revenues from technical knowledge, which is a non–rivalrous good. On these grounds, Kitch highlights the common-

[23] For example, it is hard to imagine that anyone, including the patentees, had fully recognized the commercial potential and the value of patents on the Cohen–Boyer process of recombinant DNA at the beginning of the 1970s. Those patents became a major keystone in the evolution of the biotechnology industry.

alities between the uncertainties of generating economic benefits from developing physical resources and the inability to predict whether investments in R&D in a technological *terra incognita* would truly fulfil the expectations and would become profitable.

In an attempt to analyze the patent system and to assess to what extent the current regime fosters innovation and technological advance, Kitch (1977) suggests a path breaking analogy of property rights over intellectual endeavours and rights granted for physical prospects, such as land use or fishery. Although both regimes are based on provision of (temporary) exclusive rights as incentives offered for development efforts, this doctrine suffers major shortcomings due to major dissimilarities between the economic properties of prospects and those of technological know-how. In particular, prospect theory fails to reflect the cumulative nature of innovation. Patenting technologies in their early stages can largely be interpreted as a barrier for development of new inventions, rather than as exclusive rights that protect the claimed applications and the disclosed know-how.

## 2.4 The Role of Copyrights in the Economy

Different from patents, copyrights aim at protecting artistic and literary works, such as books, photographs and phonograms. Copyright legislation worldwide is based on the guidelines of the Berne Convention. The Berne Convention defines a minimal term for protection of the author's lifetime plus 50 years, which can be extended when rules are written at the national level.[24] The (non-limiting) scope of coverage by copyrights includes not only literary and artistic works but also the derivatives of copyrighted works, such as translations and adaptations. The derivative artefacts enjoy copyright protection equal to the terms of protection of the original works. The Convention also enables optional protection for official, legislative and administrative texts, lectures, folklore works and even mailing addresses (WIPO, 1998).[25]

The incentive mechanisms underlying copyrights are not less complex than those that are at the basis of the patent system. Since generation of artistic and literal works differs in essence from technical inventions and does not encompass similar degrees of investments in R&D as technologies require, the insights of re-

[24]Copyrights are granted for author's lifetime plus a term of 70 years in the EU and 90 years in the US.

[25]US jurisdiction has not followed this extension, as the *Feist* doctrine demonstrates.

ward theory that justify long–term monopoly rights to elevate the scales of *art production* do not necessarily apply in the case of cultural goods. Towse (1999) interprets the economic function of copyrights as a risk–sharing mechanism between publishers and authors: publishers invest in distribution and promotion of creative works and share an agreed part of the profits with the authors in return to rights to reproduce their works. The model may explain the rationale of copyrights in cultural industries, in which creation and dissemination are carried out separately by the authors and producers. Yet, this model can hardly be characteristic of software development, where most of the applications are developed within firms and marketed by them.

From a moral standpoint, copyrights are indeed another form of appropriation mechanism, which provides "incentives to create" new artistic works to authors and creators of other cultural genres, such as choreography and photography. However, a major conflict between copyrights and the nature of artistic and literary works is emphasized by the nature of those products. Property rights emerge when scarcity of resources exists and when investments in developments may prove insufficient.[26] Copyright–protected goods do not seem to suffer from any source of scarcity: written books or composed music are generated by their creators under a wide range of market terms. Therefore, economic theory should be giving a higher weight to the rationale of rewarding authors' creative efforts *ex post*.

In a seminal paper on the economics of copyrights, Landes and Posner (1989) highlight the distinction between (abstract) *ideas*, which are excluded from the legal scope of copyrights, and the tangible *expressions* for which legal protection is guaranteed on the basis of originality. They state:

> Since the costs of developing a new idea are likely to be low in most cases relative to the potential reward from licensing the idea to others, there would be a mad rush to develop and copyright ideas ... with minimal expression. [Consequently,] although the development of new ideas would be accelerated, the dissemination of ideas might not be. (ibid.)

Looking at the impact of changes in the design of legal regimes on technology markets, scholars identify only minor benefits to the society from extended term

[26] In the case of patents, problems associated with scarcity of resources can emerge from under–investment of firms in R&D. The patent regime aims at providing exclusive rights to inventors to prevent such a market failure in new products and technologies (Arrow, 1962).

of copyrights, at the expense of high social costs. A critique of the extension of the duration of copyrights by 20 years was submitted to the US Supreme Court by a group of legal and academic scholars, stating that the modified doctrine encompasses only marginal incentives for authors and creators, but significantly increases the social costs of monopoly. Hence, the extended term may hinder innovation by limiting for a longer period the right to use earlier material in new works (Akerlof et al., 2002). Common opinions suggest that the protection of different genres of creative endeavours is fundamentally divided between patents or copyrights. Analysing IP doctrines that protect a certain technology or a product jointly by patents and copyrights, Reichman (1994) argues that integrating both regimes to protect different technical functionalities and merits does not necessarily guarantee complete protection and even appears to be under–protective in some cases. However, under other market conditions, the dual protection creates an overlap between both legal blankets, covering a similar *subject matter*, which may be overprotective in favour of market incumbents, providing them with excessive ownership rights over technologies. Since the publication of his work, an increasing variety of legal regimes that merge patent and copyright protection or adopt selected aspects of each system, were established by legislators (for example in several EC Directives on knowledge–based industries). Alternatively, firms design *public licenses*, custom–built to the characteristics of new products, to maintain wide and rapid diffusion of their technologies and products.[27]

## 2.5 Further Considerations

The "traditional" faculty of the economics of IPRs[28] concentrated on studying the immediate and short–term effects of legislative frameworks, mainly that of patents, on innovation and technical change. Innovation is analyzed in most cases as a single–period process, where sequential contributions and breakthroughs and different genres of technology are evenly treated. However, in reality, innovation is a dynamic process whose effects are not limited to selected markets but diffuse

[27] Bessy and Brousseau (1998) find positive correlation between the diversity of licensing agreements, as appropriation mechanisms additional to the use of IPRs, and higher levels of technical knowledge acquired by licensees in various industrial sectors. In the particular context of information technologies, Perens (1999) proposes a model of public licensing strategies to enhance the diffusion and use of software applications.

[28] Here, I notably refer to the special issue of the *RAND Journal of Economics* from January 1990.

to other technological domains and mushroom new products and technologies in neighbouring technical fields to that of the invention.

The development of new products and technologies is indeed a puzzling process, whose underlying mechanisms are, to a large extent, obscure. What are the sources of innovation and the inputs that may enable the foster of creativity and do technological breakthroughs emerge in laboratories and research units are issues whose solutions are still far from being completely understood. The pace of innovation, that is, the technical progress that a single invention produces and contributes to fostering later stages of research, is unpredictable and cannot be easily associated with exogenous parameters, such as R&D expenditure or one of the dimensions of the patent system.

Innovation is typically characterized by a wide variety of products with increasing quality and decreasing price–tags. Diffusion of advanced technologies and products into daily use signifies an increasing social welfare, as households purchase similar or technically–improved goods at lower prices. Similarly, firms that are authorized to implement the state–of–the–art of technology can generate further inventions and technological progress. Yet, most studies identify social welfare benefits with minimizing deadweight loss or draw causalities between R&D, innovation and reward within a static frame of analysis. This body of literature hardly refers to the dynamics of the technological diffusion process. Indeed, enduring the application of stronger IPR regimes and granting innovators increasing levels of monopoly rights may consequently increase their rewards from successfully–commercialized inventions, but in the long run it may hamper the pace of innovation by restricting the use of progressive techniques in research and development of new products.

# 3

# The Role and Performance of IPRs as Knowledge–Propelling Regimes

## 3.1 Introduction

The economic role of IPR regimes and their impact on technological markets are broadly discussed in the previous chapter. However, the complexity underlying the economics of IPRs, the ties between legislation and innovative output and their application within the strategies of firms call for systematic evaluation of the role of IPRs in the economic system. Further, the impact of IPR regimes on knowledge disclosure is not necessarily restricted to provision of direct incentives for innovators to disclose their know–how, but also generates a wider array of effects that stem from knowledge spillovers and from their contribution to technological learning in firms. Whether there is a need for governing emerging technological markets by enacting new IPR rules and by extending the scope of present doctrines or should economies be left unregulated to the market powers and to the "invisible hand" are among the main concerns that policy designers confront. Issues of policy changes should be assessed within an adequate framework that includes short– and long–term goals of economic policies, major inputs and outputs and reference to institutions that are involved in the innovation process. Hence, technologies and markets influence different forms of institutions and regulatory frameworks, as well as being affected by them, to an extent.

The impact of long duration of monopoly rights on innovation and on the market goes beyond momentary effects as the many neo–classical economists suggest. Economies and markets usually react to legislative changes in different ways after long periods, due to the different diffusion phases of the technology. For example, the consumption behaviour of early adopters of new technologies differs from the behaviour of consumers of mature technologies. Consequently, strategies of firms that are based on IPRs (for example strategic patenting) may significantly be altered as the technology evolves. The impact of marginal changes in the design of IPR regimes (such as extension of the duration of patents or their scope of coverage) on innovation and on the market can be properly assessed *ex post* after a long period from the implementation of new policies, rather than through analysis of a momentary situation.

Evaluating the effects of IPRs on technological markets, mainly those of knowledge and information goods, requires application of a new conceptual framework that differs from conventional economic insights. This chapter draws a frame of analysis that builds upon several major observations adopted from evolutionary economics. The first is the perception of the economy as a dynamic system, whose responses to external stimuli (for example changes in regulation) should be assessed in a wider perspective than through their impact on the "return on invention" and on the R&D investments of firms in a given period. Instead, markets, institutions and technologies co–evolve over time and may closely (or loosely) interact with each other. If regulation, for example, is altered, firms and technologies would react in an adaptive way, often with a time lag from the introduction of the altered policy. Similarly, markets and policies are not static and respond to advances in technology, either by modifying strategies of firms and the behaviour of consumers or by dictating new rules.

Second, the dynamics of knowledge formation and their links to innovation and to the development of new technologies are highlighted in the evolutionary economics literature. Our analysis aims at identifying the prevailing dimensions of IPR regimes that affect the formation and the mobility of technical knowledge and, in turn, influence the pace and the patterns of innovation and development of information technologies. IPRs may contribute to technological progress, but their misapplication impede technological advances in the long run. Therefore, IPR policies should consider the relations between the structural factors of the legal regime and the processes of innovation, introduction of new products and creation of novel know–how.

Generic laws of IPRs that apply general legislation to a wide variety of technologies and products are favoured by policy makers and practitioners over *sui–*

*generis* laws that are especially formed to meet the unique needs of each technology. From the social welfare perspective, the costs of administrating and enforcing IPRs and the expenditures on training attorneys and examiners are lower in the case of a legal doctrine, due to similarities in legal procedures that regulate a large variety of technologies. However, when a general doctrine is applied to information technologies, it may suffer significant shortcomings, granting over– and under–protection to various components. The ratios of knowledge disclosure and novelty to the degree of monopoly rights are of major importance, as they affect the stability of innovation patterns and competition. In particular, negative effects of overprotective IPR regimes may result from strong monopoly rights over creative endeavours. Under those terms, firms may acquire competitive advantage via legal practices, rather than through innovation and creativity, thereby dedicating additional resources to legal procedures rather than to R&D. Further, as IPRs are mostly enacted as a generic set of rules that address a wide variety of technologies, they are rarely tailored to fit the needs of specific technologies. The adequacy and the weaknesses of the regime to assure a prominent development of technical knowledge and advanced products are discussed in the following section.

## 3.2 Disclosure vs. Exclusion: Implications of Mobility and Ownership of Technical Know–How

### 3.2.1 Background

Evolutionary economics emphasizes the role of distribution and disclosure of knowledge and dissemination as principal devices in fostering the innovative and technological virtues of firms. Knowledge creates further knowledge and opens new avenues for introduction of new products through a process of cumulative improvement of existent technologies: "Most inventors stand on the shoulders of giants, and never more so than in the current evolution of high technologies, where almost all technical progress builds on a foundation provided by early innovators" (Scotchmer, 1991).

Entrepreneurial and innovative output usually takes the form of incremental improvements on the basis of prior innovation, though seldom breakthroughs and accidental discoveries occur. Technologies commonly emerge from long and systematic processes of research and development from technological learning, by which the capabilities of the firm are gradually constituted (Dosi, 1988). Firms are able to recognize the value of new information (either externally acquired or developed in–house), and then assimilate it and exploit it in their products only when they already possess a sufficient degree of similar technical capabilities that enable them to process and to synthesize it into their organizational knowledge base. This ***absorptive capacity*** of firms is greatly affected by the present levels of their competences and technical know–how (Cohen and Levinthal, 1990). If firms acquire essential knowledge and capabilities earlier, they are able to compete more efficiently in the market and to "catch–up" with advanced technologies that their rivals own. However, in the extreme case, if the firm lags behind competitors in possessing and assimilating knowledge assets, it cannot implement recent technical advances and will fail to compete in quality and price.

Another important property of technical knowledge is that it is transferred and evolves in an "epidemic" manner. The exposure of firms to new technologies expands as ***knowledge spillovers*** occur within and among different sectors. Knowledge spillovers are generated also by the mobility of labour between firms, reverse engineering of rival products, imitation of existing technologies and from scientific and technical publications.[1]

Disclosure of know–how to the public domain expands the population of firms that apply it in their products. Information that has previously been kept secret within companies is published and other inventors are capable of experimenting with new techniques, consequently enhancing their technological competences and raising their innovative output. The provision of property rights over inventions provides firms with incentives to do so. IPRs assure the safe exposure of trade secrets and protect their applications by Patent Law. Had other products that sufficiently differ from the technology of the originating firm been developed by other inventors, they would have been recognized as non–infringing and patentable by themselves.

Further, the preparation of patent applications forces firms to organize and to present their knowledge in a standard and rigid format. This process of ***knowledge codification*** encompasses substantial benefits for firms, including substantial reductions in the costs of business processes and higher organizational efficiencies and perfomance, as follows (Cowan and Foray, 1997; Cowan et al., 2000).

First, acquisition of particular know–how may turn out to be unnecessary if

[1] Different forms of legislation, for example trade secrecy and Fair Use doctrine limit the free flow of technical know–how to protect inventors from cloning their products.

shares of the information have already been augmented and can be easily retrieved. Knowledge can be transferred and communicated within organizations through explicit forms of representation. By codifying know–how, firms are able to enhance the capabilities of their employees and to reduce transaction costs that are associated with the acquisition of knowledge. However, the accessibility of employees to know–how becomes possible only if it is disseminated in an "explicit" format, such as in a form of patent records. Hence, investments in re–acquiring knowledge that already exists can be spared or re–allocated to R&D activities, thereby enhancing both the efficiencies of firms and social welfare.

Second, codification reduces the effects of asymmetric information and increases coordination within and among firms. For example, when knowledge that was previously kept by technical personnel is distributed to other units of the firm, workers may utilize it in different ways, such as initiating new projects and evaluating plans and operations. In a similar way, firms cooperate in order to integrate their own technological competences with different sources of knowledge to develop advanced products.[2]

Third, codification of knowledge that previously existed in a tacit form enables easier commodification and commercial exploitation of it in final goods. This knowledge is not kept anymore within the domain of individuals and can be used by others, regardless of any personal or professional properties of its previous owners. By transforming knowledge that previously was based on personal experience of workers to routines, firms can standardize organizational processes and control them, thereby increasing their volume of production and the quality of their products (Nelson and Winter, 1982; Ch. 5). For example, identifying the "right conditions" of temperature and moisture of paper mash was an essential skill of machine operators in paper mills, which remained tacit for many years. By measuring (that is, codifying) the parameters of the chemical process firms were able to develop sensor–based equipment that dramatically increased the efficiency, quality and stability of paper production.[3]

Knowledge codification is a costly process that requires investments in working hours, capital resources and information technologies. it is carried out by the firm only if it is economically justified (Cowan et al., 2000). The decision whether to

[2]Review of inter–firm research collaborations in a variety of industrial sectors is presented in Hagedoorn (2002).

[3]By codifying the tacit knowledge of machine operators, similar processes fostered the development of advanced production methods in the fast food industry.

codify specific knowledge prospects is not necessarily driven by motives of transferring knowledge from a tacit to an explicit form simply for the sake of easier representation, but it involves economic considerations of the costs and benefits of the codified know–how. Nevertheless, the process can be accomplished successfully if the organizational environment of the firm supports efficient sharing, storage and retrieval of knowledge.

As this argument goes, IPRs (and patents in particular) may be perceived as mechanisms to promote codification and approximation of state–of–the–art, tacit know–how, which otherwise would be kept in secret by its creators. More generally, patents provide firms with a framework for representing their tacit knowledge (as well as measuring the efficiency of their R&D teams). Hence, learning from patents has become easier than ever before, as patent records include detailed descriptions of the inventions, blueprints and claims that are browsable online by any interested person.[4]

The application of information technologies for accessing patent databases and retrieving information on particular inventions is very beneficial from a social welfare perspective, as the new tools have significantly reduced the search costs of patentees, patent attorneys and firms. Further, the publication of technical details in patent records reduces information asymmetries and uncertainty, thereby assisting the formation of joint ventures between firms and the efficient allocation of investments in R&D projects. Nevertheless, patenting embraces substantial societal costs: the use of know–how is restricted for long periods by law and firms are usually prohibited from applying what they learnt from the *knowledge base* of patented inventions.[5]

While *reward theory* and *prospect theory* indicate that the major aim of patents is to provide "incentives to innovate", *evolutionary theory* suggests that its primary goal is to provide inventors with "incentives to disclose" know–how on novel inventions that otherwise could have remained within the firm's domains.

Cohendet and Meyer–Krahmer (2001) suggest a different perspective on the

[4]During the last years patent offices worldwide have made significant investments in digitization of patent databases and in construction of Internet–based interfaces to access their contents online. See, for example, the USPTO website in: www.uspto.gov.

[5]Following *Roche Products, Inc. v. Bolar Pharmaceuticals Co.* (733 F.2d 858, Fed. Circuit, 1984), testing the feasibility of producing patented inventions when those patents are still valid (in order to enter the market when they expire) was recognized infringing. See Grossman (1990) for review of Fair Use of patented inventions vs. the Experimental Use exemption.

links between IPRs and innovation, emphasizing the role of patents in knowledge production processes. The existence of trust between collaborating firms is perceived as the primary motive behind the decision of firms to apply patenting as a preferred appropriation method. Inventors rely on patent protection to safeguard their intellectual assets while sharing them with others. If the level of trust and cooperation between business partners of the venture is low, specialized know–how can easily be acquired from other parties. However, when higher levels of trust between parties exist, business partners benefit from reciprocal exchange of knowledge. Patents function as "access rights" to codified information and serve as a signalling device for the value of inventions or as indicators of reputation and innovative qualities of potential partners. Although trust seems to be a key factor in patenting decisions, the motives of firms are affected by far more complex considerations that are geared towards obtaining market dominance and technological leadership by implementing legal means. However, trust itself cannot be used as a criterion for determining the design of IPR regimes. It is notoriously difficult to quantify and to measure trust (even on an approximate scale) and therefore it imposes further uncertainties and abstraction into a system which is already complex enough. Nevertheless, trust can provide new insights on the merits of IPR regimes and their links to the business environment, but it can hardly be used to establish any measures for articulating new policies.

Paradoxically, although IPRs aim at fostering knowledge disclosure and innovation on the basis of the patented know–how, IPRs limit other parties from freely exploiting it. To some extent, patents even restrict new inventors from introducing advanced technologies that build upon disclosed know–how, by providing the first innovators and authors monopoly rights over their creative endeavours. Preserving the balance between knowledge disclosure and its exclusion from being freely used is the primary challenge of policy makers and regulators.

### 3.2.2 Structural Considerations

The legal realm of intellectual property rights offers various means for protection of novel technological and artistic artefacts. On the one hand, patents, copyrights and trade secrecy are different methods that are used for protecting intellectual endeavours, and on the other hand, licensing, Fair Use doctrine and anti–trust laws foster information flow and utilization of legally protected know–how.

Legal and economic scholars are concerned with different aspects of IPR regimes.

The present length, breadth (and less often the height) of patents are often criticized as overprotective and as pivotal encumbrances for developing technologies (see the discussion above). Industrial organization studies, the chief body of economic literature on the design of IPR regimes, apply static analyses to evaluate how marginal changes in the determinants of patents and copyrights affect the market and the behaviour of firms and what is the optimal magnitude of each dimension of the regime under different market terms. However, IPR regimes are not uniformly shaped across nations and industries and may vary in their systematic attributes. Therefore, a closer look into patent regimes worldwide reveals further policy considerations beyond the three–dimensional structure of each regime, which stand in the scope of international harmonization efforts.[6] Other attributes of the patent system (that is, the structural factors of the regime, such as the ownership of a patent by the "first to file" or by the "first to invent" among competing inventors), which are second in importance to length, breadth and height, are far from being administrative fine–tunings and can significantly affect the strategic behaviour of firms.

A major difference between the US patent system and other international regimes refers to the ability to challenge monopoly rights that were granted to patent applicants. In Europe and Japan, the "first to file" patent applications obtains patent rights, whereas US patents are granted to the "first to invent". What seems as a minor variance in legal definitions is in fact a meaningful difference that influences the risks of innovators and the introduction of new technologies (and consequently their adoption patterns). According to non–US patent laws, if a patent were approved, the first to apply for it would receive ownership rights over the protected invention. In the US, the first to develop a patented invention can regain the rights over it, even if the patent has already been granted to the earliest applicant. Therefore, in the EU and in Japan the validity and the novelty of patents can be challenged by other parties, but ownership rights of applicants cannot be put to question. In comparison, US patents can be pended within a year from issuing if another applicant proves that she preceded the patent–holder

[6]Some of the aspects of the following discussion may apply also to copyrights. However, the structural and legislative properties of the copyright regime significantly differ from those of patents. Following the characteristics and the goals of each regime, it is reasonable to assume that the impact of modifying the configuration of patents on innovation and technical change would be far more significant than equivalent changes of the copyright regime.

in developing the litigated invention (even though she was late in submitting her patent application).

The impact of the US legislation on the patenting decisions of firms can formally be described as a non-cooperative game between patent applicants and rival developers with asymmetric information. Assuming that the applicants cannot obtain information about the R&D operations of rival firms, rivals are able gain knowledge on new patent applications from the USPTO databases virtually at no cost. Consequently, inventors would avoid revealing information on their technologies in their early stages of development and would prefer trade secrecy over patenting, unless patent applications over the very same inventions are submitted by rival firms.

Some developers would prefer delaying their patent proceedings due to strategic reasons until another applicant receives a patent over the same invention. Then, they would submit a "first to invent" appeal and obtain the patent rights, regardless of their position in the *patent race* as followers of the earliest applicant. By appealing to the USPTO after firms have already been granted patents and made substantial investments in production facilities and in R&D, inventors are able to suspend the introduction of new products by their competitors and to aggravate their losses in the first phases of commercializing a new technology. Consequently, the risk of patenting in the US is significantly higher than in other countries, and firms often delay the submission of their patent applications. Ordover (1991) concludes that European and Japanese innovators, having to follow the first-to-file doctrine, are persuaded to apply for a patent earlier than US applicants, as a failure to submit their patent applications before competitors do so results in loss of (potential) monopoly rights over their inventions. Theoretically, the US policy may result in a lower scale of social welfare than in other states, as inventors may delay their patent applications, as well as the disclosure of technical know-how and the introduction of new technologies, to avoid the risks of engaging in patent litigation with competing firms. Therefore, the competitive behaviour of firms and their rivals in Europe and in Japan typically follows the dynamics of *patent races*, while the decisions of US firms involve other considerations, such as the technological level of their competitors and the risks of imitation, and often result in some form of a *waiting games* (Dasgupta, 1988).

A second structural difference between the Japanese regime and the US and European patent systems refers to the outline of patent records and to the structure of the specified claims in particular. The US and European legislative frameworks enable patentees to include multiple claims within a single patent and therefore to protect a broad range of present and future applications of an invention within a single patent. The Japanese system requires submission of separate patents for every component of the invention or for each particular application of it. The structure of the US and the European patent systems provide inventors with broader legal coverage than that of the Japanese regime (even when inventors apply for multiple–patent protection, following the orders of the Japanese Patent Law), as patent records in the US and in the EU are far more open for legal interpretation of their scope, while Japanese applicants are required to "anticipate" and apply for patents for all the beneficial and particular uses of their inventions (Brueckman, 1990; Karjala, 1990). From an economic standpoint, the Japanese Patent Law exhibits a more restricted form of exclusive rights by granting exclusive rights to smaller shares of technological domains, while the US and the European doctrines "fence out" wider technological areas. Therefore, the Japanese patent system applies a munificent approach towards dissemination of technical know–how and towards the diffusion of new technological advances over the interests of patent–holders. Nevertheless, from a social welfare perspective, setting up appropriation policies that build upon the Japanese patent system may suffer significant shortcomings. Single–claim patents involve higher legal costs for the firm and for the patent office. Moreover, when the breadth of patents is narrower than in other international patent regimes, the risk of disclosing largely applicable technical know–how increases, and may result in lower propensity of firms to protect their inventions by patents.

Although the European and the Japanese patent systems do not significantly differ from the US regime, both regimes propose alternative standards and should be considered as a basis for future reforms in the US patent system. Application of narrower patent claims or even single–claim patents and in–depth examination of the minimal inventive step of new patents are likely to foster the entry of new firms into technological markets that previously were dominated by patent–holders. By implementing policies that modify those legal measures, new entrants would be able to compete more easily with incumbent firms by introducing new products based on advanced knowledge that sufficiently differs from the patented inventions.

### 3.2.3 IPRs and Anti–Competitive Behaviour of Firms

The legal framework of anti–trust laws had been formed to ensure free competition to provide legal means for assuring that entrepreneurs can develop and distribute rival technologies and products. Anti–trust authorities attempt to guarantee that monopolization of a market does not hinder competition either in the market or via introduction of new technologies. Contrary to the anti–trust doctrine, patents and copyrights provide monopolistic power to inventors of technologies and to creators of artistic and literary works for relatively long periods. Ownership of a technology is guaranteed to the holders of the rights with no constraints, as in most countries no legal guidelines for compulsory licensing of patents or copyrighted works exist. Further, in most of the countries, jurisdiction had declined to state that refusal of patent holders to license patented technologies violates the anti–trust doctrine, even when patent–holders deliberately rule out any use of their technologies by other firms. Although patents and copyrights are often criticized as inappropriate means for fostering innovation and technical change (in the case of patents), as well as other sorts of creative output (in the case of copyrights), both regimes are still the most dominant institutional frameworks for protecting intellectual property. This issue is amplified by the views that patents and copyrights are overprotective and provide excessive degrees of monopolistic power over inventions in new and core technologies and to works in cultural industries, hence impeding innovation and competition in those markets.

It is indeed striking how fundamental prospects of IPRs are inconsistent with the main characteristics of competition law, as the two legislative systems are long–living regimes. Anti–trust policies aim at preventing the formation of monopolies and their influence on consumer choices and on competition, thereby assuring the emergence of new, inventive entrants in the market. IPRs, in turn, function in quite different motion. They aim at securing sufficient incentives to innovate by granting monopoly power over technological fields, and thus appear to be in a conflict with the objectives of competition law. Being aware of this conflict for a long time, the US Supreme Court stated that "since patents are privileges restrictive of a free economy, the rights which Congress has attached to them must be strictly construed".[7]

Yet, the relations between competition law and intellectual property rights

[7] *United States v. Masonite* (Supreme Court, 1942).

are not as straightforward as it seems. Gallini and Trebilcock (1998) suggest that it is possible to reconcile the two regimes by perceiving competition laws as promoting inventions by ensuring free competition and market entry in the long run, while IPRs offer monopoly rights over technological advances to encourage innovation in the short run (hence providing inventors with incentives to innovate). However, this conclusion has to be treated carefully. A closer look at the evolution of technologies suggests that monopolistic market structures and the consequent pricing of products reduces the demand for technology in the short term and deters both technological diffusion among users and effects of learning–by–doing and learning–by–using in firms (Arrow, 1962; Rosenberg, 1982). Consequently, lower scales of technological learning, which are significant for generating technical advances, may slow down the pace of innovation in the long run.

Typically, anti–trust authorities prohibit mergers and acquisitions that create technological monopolies to avoid formation of high barriers for entry. However, under particular circumstances, monopoly over technology is permissible by anti–trust laws. The case of the acquisition of Wellcome by Glaxo demonstrates the efficiencies of monopoly in developing new technologies. The firms received FDA approval for a new migraine treatment with oral application. The acquisition of Wellcome by Glaxo was denied in its first stages by competition authorities in the US to prevent monopoly in migraine–treating drugs. However, this decision was revised and the acquisition was finally approved when Glaxo successfully proved that its rivals performed only marginal R&D activities in this technological field and had no tangible basis to enter the new market (Tom, 1998). The high costs of R&D for development of pharmaceutical drugs create high barriers for entry, such that technological monopolies are within the natural structure of the industry. As this acquisition was not going to tip any competition over this market segment, and since regardless of whether the acquisition took place other firms were unlikely to enter this market (due to the high R&D costs), the acquisition was allowed to proceed.

Although the tension between anti–trust laws, deterring monopolies over technological markets, and IPRs forming monopolies over technological fields has not been resolved, both EU legislation and the US Law avoid application of compulsory licensing. The European Court of Justice stated that "refusal to grant a license, even if it is the act of an undertaking holding a dominant position, cannot in itself constitute abuse of a dominant position".[8] The US Court has expressed a similar opinion that refusal by patent holder either to license or to use its patent is not an anti–trust case. The degree of complexity to which the tension between anti–trust legislation and IPRs has evolved is amplified when the technologies of the New Economy are considered. Software technologies, Internet–based communications and accessibility to database contents applied by vast numbers of users via the Internet or massively distributed, generate wide scale *network effects.* The resulting "lock–in" to a single technology and its implementation as a dominant market standard (Arthur, 1987) questions the role of competition authorities in markets in which technological merits (and not necessarily business strategies of firms) lead to a monopolistic position.

Policy makers, aspiring to encourage knowledge spillovers between inventors and other firms, have faced opposite opinions about IPR regimes and enforcement of Competition Law when core technologies are dominated by monopolies. How variations in the patent regime, such as those presented above, contribute to innovation satisfy the goal of economic growth is still a puzzling affair. Although Ordover (1991) supports the implementation of structural changes that typically follow the design of the Japanese regime in the US, the legal and administrative costs involved in modifying the patent system might exceed the benefits of those changes. However, some of the structural attributes reviewed above should not be instantly ignored and should be considered while forming new IP policies or revising the present legislation. The application of some of those structural changes in the existing regimes can foster knowledge disclosure and competitiveness in markets that were previously dominated by monopolists. Finally, further inquiry is needed to determine the motives of firms that initialize a litigation process in order to stop patents from being granted to rival firms. Therefore, further empirical inquiries of litigation cases and opposition to patents are necessary to broaden our legal and economic knowledge on the ways that firms apply to utilize the less–spotted prospects of the patent system as strategic means.[9]

---

[8] *RTE & Anor v. Commission of the European Communities* (1995).

[9] A leap forward in the study of patent litigation and objection processes was made by Graham et al. (2002), studying the re–examination of patents in the US and in Europe. However, their analysis is concerned with different issues than those mentioned here, such as the rate of opposition and the outcomes of patent re–examination by the patent offices in various industries.

### 3.2.4 Compulsory Licensing: Enabling the Use of Patent–Protected Inventions

Systems of IPRs are commonly perceived as major institutional tools in innovation policies, fostering disclosure of technical know–how that otherwise could have remained within the domain of the firm. Interestingly, scholars highlight alternative means to promote innovation and knowledge disclosure. Public procurement, prizes granted to the first–to–invent an essential technology (for example discovering medical drugs) and public research contracts are common examples (Wright, 1983; Dasgupta and David, 1994; Davis, 2004). Another mechanism that is inherent in the patent system is *compulsory licensing.* Wide implementation of compulsory licensing is advocated on occasion as a balancing instrument against excessive monopoly pricing of inventors. However, in practice, compulsory licensing was enforced only in a small number of occasions worldwide.[10] Compulsory licensing is closely associated with *anti–trust policies* and their legislative framework, also known as *Competition Law,* which is discussed above.

The enactment and enforcement of compulsory licensing raise legal and ethical difficulties, questioning the rights of patent–holders to own intellectual assets for long periods and the legitimacy of governmental intervention. However, from an economic standpoint, the benefits of implementing compulsory licensing may overcome the drawbacks in a variety of market conditions and technological spheres.[11]

Compulsory licensing provides regulators with flexibility to intervene in patent policies. Via particular exemptions that restrict the practice of patent rights by their holders when the balance between monopoly rights and market power is heavily distorted. By applying compulsory licensing, substantial welfare losses (that is, deadweight loss) and slower adoption of technologies, due to a non–competitive structure of the market, can be avoided. The "neo–classical" deadweight loss results from granting inventors excessive exclusive rights over the technology. When compulsory licensing measures do not exist, inventors are able to protect their monopolistic position by strategically patenting a wide range of applications and

[10]The TRIPs agreement permits compulsory licensing in cases of "national emergency or other circumstances of extreme urgency or in cases of public non–commercial use" (Article 31b), for example production of low–price, generic versions of anti–HIV drugs for developing countries.

[11]This section elaborates the economic aspects of compulsory licensing. Ethical, moral and political aspects of the compulsory licensing are left outside the scope of this discussion.

later by charging monopoly prices for them. However, if inventors are obliged to share their exclusive rights in return to royalty fees, the market can become more competitive and the prices of goods are likely to be lower than the monopoly price. Consequently, the profits of inventors having to compete with other firms would decrease in some degree. However, under compulsory licensing, revenues are generated from both royalty fees and the mark–up $\rho^*$ on the price of goods that are produced at the cost of $\underline{c}$ (Tandon, 1982).[12]

A second social benefit from compulsory licensing is the rapid diffusion of new technologies, as more firms are able to introduce competitive products at a lower price without infringing the rights of patent–holders (as long as royalty fees are paid by them). In order to prevent situations in which patentees charge expensive royalty fees to preserve their monopoly, compulsory licensing should be accompanied by other anti–trust measures, such as public control over the royalty rates.[13]

Further, compulsory licensing prevents abusive use of monopoly rights by patentees. Inventors are granted rights ownership over core technologies and standards for long periods and are free to license them at any cost. Consequently, patent–holders do not dominate only the protected technology, but also wider scope of downstream products. Compulsory licensing removes the monopoly power of single inventors and opens new opportunities for developing the technology by other firms. Yet, innovators are rewarded for their efforts by royalty payments from licensees.

Licensing out core inventions with low royalty fees may prove a desirable strategy for inventors. If patented inventions become accessible to a wider population of firms, the technology will diffuse rapidly and will become a market standard, broadly used by both consumers and firms. In the long run, if the technology becomes successful, the innovating firm will occupy large market shares and will generate higher revenues from royalty fees. Alternatively, the firm can grant exclusive rights over patents to a small group of licensees at high fees per firm. It is difficult to predict *ex ante* whether licensing patents to a small group of firms, to many licensees or keeping the technology proprietary is more profitable. However,

[12]Formally, $\underline{c} \cdot (1+\rho^*) < c_m < \bar{c}$, where $\bar{c}$ is the pre–invention market price, $c_m$ is the monopoly price and $\underline{c}$ is the post–invention competitive price. $\rho^*$ denotes the royalty fee per product unit determined by the regulator ($\rho^* < 1$).

[13]Compulsory licensing is positive from the perspective of firms' learning, enabling them to develop in–house capabilities that build upon patents without infringing them.

when an invention becomes widespread as a core technology or produces strong network effects, low rates of royalty fees will assist its widespread adoption and will increase the total profits of the firm.

The case of Cohen–Boyer patents exemplifies the advantage of applying a licensing scheme that is based on inexpensive royalty fees. In 1973, Stanley Cohen of Stanford University and Herbert Boyer of the University of California discovered the process of recombinant DNA, a first keystone for the new scientific field of biotechnology. The first patent application was submitted by Stanford University in 1974, and in 1976 Cohen and Boyer founded Genentech, which became the first biotech firm. Since the submission of the Cohen–Boyer patent applications, licensing agreements have generated more than $140 million in royalty fees. The successful implementation of *non–exclusive licensing* terms, which strengthened the evolutionary path of the biotechnology industry by charging (relatively) low royalty fees for the Cohen–Boyer process, helped to establish new trajectories that continue to implement this scientific knowledge. Three particular characteristics distinguish the recombinant DNA as a technological and commercial success story. First, the invention was at that period a unique technology, having no competing methods to conduct similar processes and products. Second, the technology that was presented was inexpensive to use and easy to implement. Third, and most importantly, the Cohen–Boyer process was a core technology that served as the foundation of a wide range of applications and opportunities for developments in the established field of molecular biology (National Research Council, 1997). Further, the licensing strategy of the Cohen–Boyer patents emphasizes the importance of assessing the elasticity of technological diffusion with regards to royalty fees, mainly in core technologies. If high fees behave as barriers for entry of firms to markets of developing technologies, the variety of applications and use would be more limited in relation to markets in which innovators charge lower royalties. When low royalty fees are charged, patented technology spreads more rapidly and widely.

## 3.3 The Role of IPRs in Developing New Technologies: Empirical Findings

### 3.3.1 Background

The social value of IPRs and their rationale are based on promoting knowledge production and diffusion of new technologies, as technical advances have a central importance in economic development and growth. A question that is often heard in this context, yet remains unsettled, is how important are IPRs for nourishing innovation and technical change?

The sources of innovation and the links between institutional and organizational factors that are involved in research and development of new technologies and the innovative yields of firms were explored since the beginning of the 1980s in a series of innovation studies. Von Hippel (1982) studies the impact of appropriability and R&D expenditure on innovation empirically. Levin et al. (1987; hereinafter referred to as the "Yale Survey") examine the reliance of firms on IPRs as a method of acquiring better protection for their technical know-how and observe that firms prefer safeguarding their intellectual property by applying strategic and contractual methods, such as trade secrecy and lead times, over legal means. Arundel compares the preferences of American and European firms to use various appropriation methods (that is, secrecy, lead times, patents, and so on) to protect their intellectual assets. His findings are consistent with those of Von Hippel and Levin et al. Lead–time and secrecy together are more important as means to protect property than patenting. They are from 10 per cent (Switzerland) to 120 per cent more common than is patenting in Western European and Irish companies.[14] Moreover, firms stated that superior sales and services, learning curves of new technology and lead times were the most preferred means for appropriation against competitors. Patents were among the least common methods in use (see Figures 3.1 and 3.2).

The second goal of IPRs is to encourage the diffusion of knowledge. Put in a different way, "if new innovations are not widely used, the system will be less beneficial than one with less creativity, but where the materials created are more broadly disseminated" (Besen and Raskind, 1991). Patent documents enter the public domain and become "transparent" to anyone who searches for novel tech-

[14] The results of studies conducted in Japanese firms were similar to those presented here.

nical information and ideas. Nonetheless, there is a strong tendency among firms, particularly among SMEs, *not* to use patents as a source of technical knowledge.[15] Hence, a second important issue in the examination of IPR regimes refers to the significance of patents in technological learning of firms and whether patents and copyrights live up to the expectations of policy makers as a major source of know–how.

Comparing the contribution of various information sources to the process of innovation, high technology firms rely on knowledge acquired from patent records and (copyright–protected) publications only as a marginal source (McFetridge, 1995). Earlier innovation surveys by Von Hippel (1982) and Levin et al. (1987) found that firms retrieve technical know–how mainly through recruited employees, affiliates, trade shows, conferences and professional literature. Patents have taken a lower position as firms' channels of learning (see Figure 3.3). Arundel (2000) strengthens their conclusions grading knowledge disclosure via patent records as the least important source of information for innovative activities in European firms after customers, suppliers, trade fairs and competitors. Moreover, firms prefer to protect their intellectual assets by applying other means than IPRs, such as lead–time and trade secrecy. Low and medium technology firms give higher importance to patents and copyrights than high technology companies, but in both cases firms give lower priority to their use as appropriation methods (McFetridge, 1995; see Table 3.1). The results of recent innovation surveys conducted by Arundel (2000; 2001) in European ICT sectors and by Hanel (2002) in Canadian firms affirm the conclusions of earlier studies, that is, firms apply IPRs to dominate substantial segments of evolving markets and technological trajectories in their initial stages of development.

The importance of using various appropriability mechanisms by firms may considerably vary among different industries, between firms in similar sectors and even between product and process inventions at the same firm. Therefore, firms usually implement IPR strategies that are based on combination of different appropriability methods that serve various purposes. For example, a firm may protect various components of a chemical product by patents, while keeping essential substances undisclosed to prevent their rivals from inventing around them substitutes that are analogous in their technical functions and sufficiently–diverse to be non–infringing and patentable. Industries commonly rely on combination of various

[15] *Innovation & Technology Transfer*, Vol. 1/00, January 2000, p. 15.

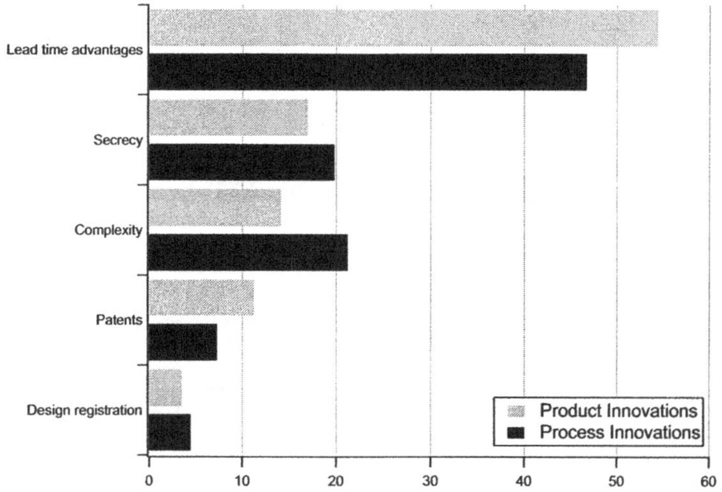


**Figure 3.1.** Major appropriation methods in European firms (Source: Arundel, 2001).

appropriability mechanisms, such as applying both secrecy and lead–time for the same products. When some of those mechanisms are jointly implemented, they generate unique "appropriability strategies" that are especially formed or adapted to the technological environment and to the conditions that are present in the market. Secrecy and lead–time are implemented among large populaces of firms in many different industrial sectors, whereas other appropriation means are less widespread and are applied only in particular sectors.

### 3.3.2 The Strategic Use of Patenting

Patents are among the less preferred appropriability mechanisms that are used by firms, as they involve considerable legal costs.[16] Nevertheless, during the last decade patent statistics in the US shows stable growth in the number of patents in "traditional" classes and dramatic increase in recent technologies (see Figure 3.5). Those dynamics of the patenting behaviour indicate a rising propensity of firms to protect their intellectual endeavours by patents.

[16]The average cost of patent application is about 6,900 dollars (www.invention.com). To compare, the average filing cost in the EPO is around 8,000 Euros (EC's IPR Helpdesk).

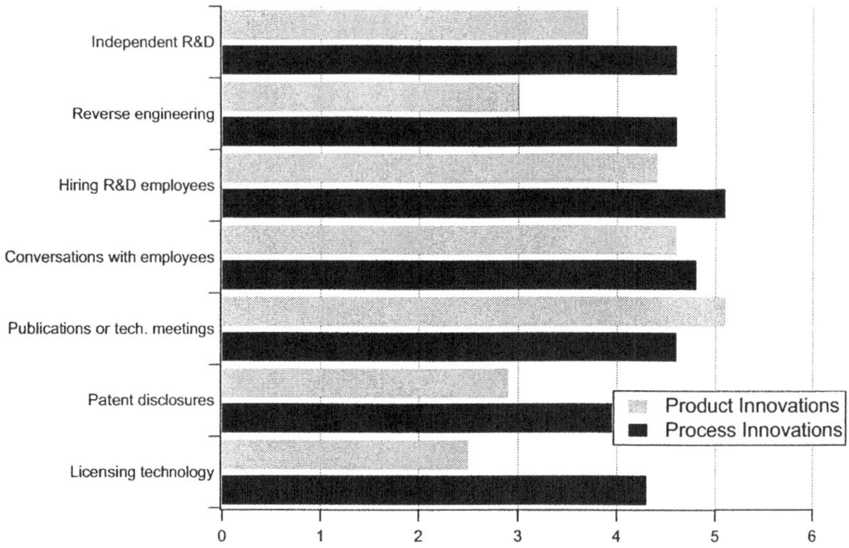


**Figure 3.2.** Firms' channels of learning (scaled by importance) (Source: Levin et al. 1987).

| Source | High Technology Firms (%) | Medium/Low Technology Firms (%) |
|---|---|---|
| Affiliates | 71 | 100 |
| Trade shows and conferences | 70 | 56 |
| Literature | 68 | 46 |
| Discussions with other firms | 32 | 26 |
| Reverse engineering | 8 | 1 |
| Copyrighted material | 3 | 7 |
| Industrial designs | 3 | 7 |
| Plant breeder's rights | 3 | 1 |
| Patents | 2 | 13 |
| Integrated circuit designs | 2 | 3 |

**Table 3.1.** The share of firms applying various sources of information for innovation (Source: McFetridge, 1995).

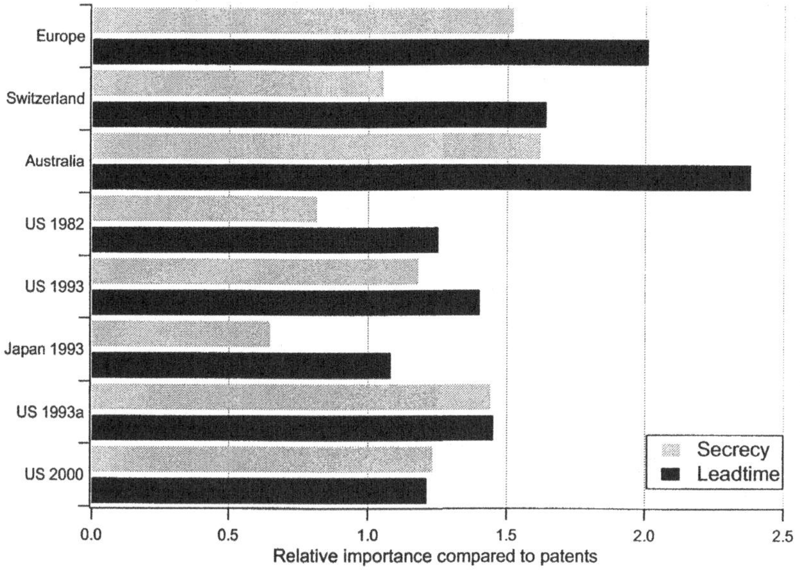


**Figure 3.3.** Relative importance of secrecy and lead–time for gaining competitive advantages from product innovation (Source: Arundel, 2000; Cohen et al., 2000).

Therefore, a presumed contradiction between the low propensity of firms to patent their inventions, as appears from the results of innovation studies, and the steadily growth in the number of patents emphasizes the following issue:

**Why do firms patent if patenting is costly and second in importance as means for appropriating their revenues?**

The link in question between the increasing number of patents and their contribution to social welfare has become a major policy concern after recent reforms in the US patent system extended the scope of protection to include recently–evolving technologies. Legislative changes have taken place despite broad public opposition and criticisms by legal scholars and economists (see, for example: Eisenberg, 2000; Gallini, 2002). Of a particular concern are the manners in which patents correspond to the original purposes of the system shaped by the early legislators "to promote the progress of science and useful arts" (US Constitution, Article 1, Section 8). However, the application of patents as a part of the business strategies

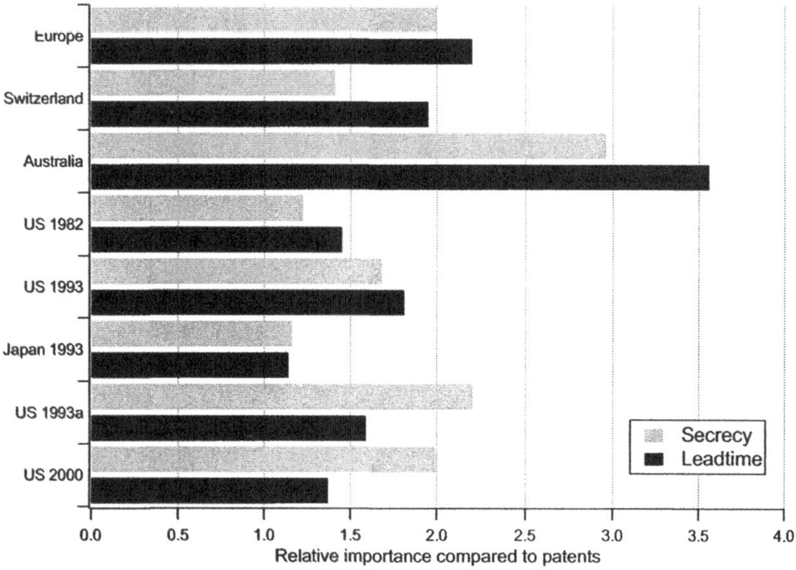


**Figure 3.4.** Relative importance of secrecy and lead–time for gaining competitive advantages from process innovation (Source: Arundel, 2000; Cohen et al., 2000).

of firms created controversy over the success of the patent system in promoting innovation in new and leading industries, such as computers, pharmaceuticals and biotechnology.

Patenting choices are not necessarily geared at securing monopoly revenues, as *reward theory* suggests. The propensity of firms to patent is influenced by many factors that relate to the general context of their business environment, such as the structure of the market, ownership of patent rights over core inventions by other firms and the nature of technology and its patterns of diffusion. Further, as this argument goes, patenting decisions cannot be distinguished from the competitive behaviour of the firm and its rivals. Generally, minimal disclosure of knowledge in return for maximal protection by patent is most desirable from the firm's perspective.[17] Empirics reveal that *strategic patenting*, methods in which firms employ

[17] By maximal protection we mean the longest duration and the widest scope of patent that can be approved by the examiners of the patent office.

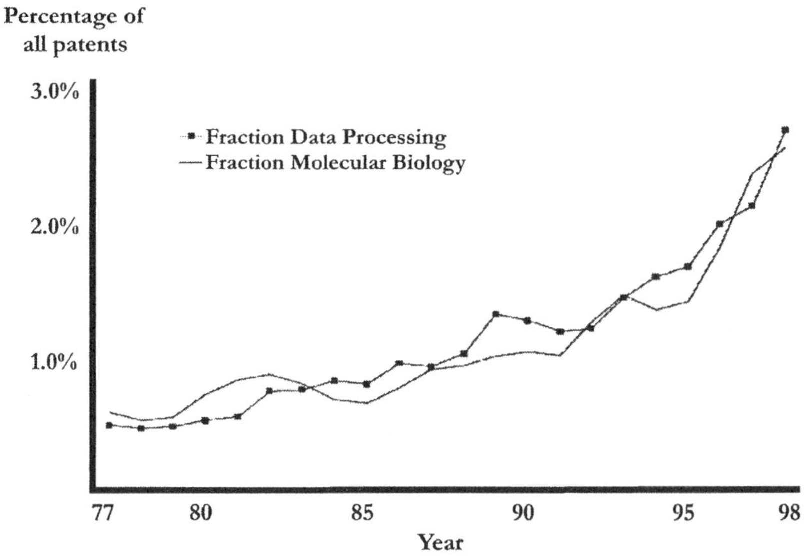


**Figure 3.5.** The share of patents in recently–evolving technologies (Source: USPTO; brought in Jaffe, 2000).

patents to gain competitive advantage against rivals and to preempt new entrants from operating in their market niches, are important strategic tools.[18]

Granstrand (1999) classifies in several categories the underlying reasons for the decision to apply for a patent:

- Pre–emption of new entrants from operating in defined and related technological fields.
- Blocking rivals from obtaining competitive advantages from being "the first to patent" (thereby reflecting *monopolistic competition* and *patent races* between firms).[19]

[18]The intensive use of strategic patenting as a part of the business strategy of the firm is a long process that requires it to adapt its culture, to conceive the present and the future value of its intellectual assets and to form links between the legal unit and its R&D and business departments that support the necessary organizational processes (Granstrand, 1999).

[19]Patent races are associated with welfare loss, as firms duplicate their R&D efforts but only one firm obtains monopoly rights over the invention.

- Building–up portfolios of the technical assets that can be traded or exchanged in cross–licensing agreements with complimentary technologies.
- "Signalling" investors before IPOs with the potential value of the firm and its commercial opportunities to exploit the technology.

The Carnegie–Mellon survey (Cohen et al., 2000) identifies multiple reasons beyond the decision to apply for a patent: protecting intellectual assets from being commercially exploited by other firms, blocking rivals from patenting related inventions, defending the firm against patent litigation lawsuits and gaining advantageous positions in cross–licensing negotiations. Firms indicate that the primary motive beyond their patenting activities is to preclude rivals from copying their inventions. This is followed by the use of patents to inhibit competitors from protecting complement technologies ("patent blocking") and to prevent infringement lawsuits by the "first–to–apply" for a patent (thus *patent races* take the form of patent litigation practices). Therefore, firms patent to enable free use of their own technologies without being sued by other firms that were faster to patent similar technologies, and in doing so preempt the firm from its market. Similar patenting behaviour and strategic considerations are prominent in the semiconductor industry, where the increasing propensity of producers to patent (and the consequent growth in the number of patent grants) do not reflect significant changes in the R&D expenditure patterns over time.

Cohen et al. (2000) distinguish between "complex" and "discrete" inventions by the amount of patentable features that are embodied in each product. *Discrete* technologies are characterized by a small number of patentable elements. Products are relatively distinct and compound a weak degree of complementarity between different technical features. Firms that operate in markets of discrete products often base their strategies on "inventing around" leading products and developing substitutes that can compete with patented inventions without infringing them. Therefore, firms that hold patent rights over core technologies usually extend their patent portfolios to cover a wide range of applications to include product substitutes that do not fall into the scope of their original invention (that is, non–trivial inventions). Moreover, expansive IP portfolios reduce the possibilities of other firms to "invent around" patented inventions. Alternatively, firms enter the market with their own product versions after rival patents have expired. In this case, both competition and product variety are enriched after a long period, when the patents expire.

At the other pole are *complex* technologies, which are identified by integration of technologies and strong interdependence between their components and elements. The complexity of the products and the technologies rises from two different sources: First, a large number of components are integrated into the final product and lack of one of the necessary elements prevents its successful completion and production. Second, the R&D activities of the firm depend on its ability to use patented inventions that are essential for the development of new products. If patents over complementary inventions are held by different firms, separate negotiations between the firm and each right–holder are required to obtain full access to the technology. Refusal of one of the firms to license its invention would put the R&D and the production of new goods to a halt.

The case of *Polaroid Corp. v. Eastman Kodak Co.* demonstrates the concerns and the risks of firms that invest in developing complex products that require integration of various technologies, particularly when some components are already patented by rival firms. Polaroid Corporation, a leading innovator and patent–holder of numerous patents of instant photography, submitted a lawsuit against Kodak Corporation for infringing twelve of its instant camera patents. Court decided that seven of Polaroid's patents were valid and were infringed by Kodak actions (that is, by producing and marketing similar products). Consequently, Kodak awarded Polaroid over 900 million dollars in damages for infringing its patents and Kodak was prohibited from competing with Polaroid in the instant camera and instant film markets (US District Court of Massachusetts, 16 USPQ2d 1481). The results of the ruling were harmful to Kodak's commercial activities and business development, affecting them in three major areas: First, the company had to abandon its investments in R&D and production of instant cameras, hence worsening its losses beyond the damages that were determined by Court. Second, the firm abolished its plans to expand the market, thereby losing a major expected source of income, restricting its future activities and increasing its vulnerability to changes in the business environment. Third, since Kodak's products had already been available in the market for several years and the firm was prohibited from producing and supplying films for instant cameras, it had to compensate the owners of those products for not being able to use them anymore. Fourth, the ruling affected the pattern of technology development and innovation, hindering Kodak and other firms (except Polaroid) from furthering the features of the new technology and from competing with advanced products in the instant camera and instant film markets.

Following the lessons of *Polaroid v. Kodak*, firms are trying to obtain wider exclusive rights via "defensive patenting". Those rights serve both purposes of trading access rights to patented inventions with other firms (Jaffe, 2000) and establishing a basis for solid intellectual property portfolios that threaten rivals from submitting patent litigation lawsuits, as firms can initiate a counter action of the same sort against them (Hall and Ziedonis, 2001).[20] According to the Carnegie–Mellon survey, obtaining stronger bargaining power in inter–firm negotiations (for example cross–licensing agreements) seems to be less important in "discrete" industries than it is in high technology sectors, due to weaker degrees of complementarity between inventions.

Patenting to gain reputation, to establish internal measures for the performance of R&D personnel or for generating royalty revenues are motives that are less valued by firms.

Manufacturers and developers of "complex" products use technologies of their own and those whose patent rights belong to other firms. This dependence fosters cross–licensing of patent rights between firms, as technology builds upon present inventions (those negotiations are significant particularly in the electronics, vehicles and computer sectors). In case of enforcing other firms to negotiations in cross–licensing agreements, patents function as "bargaining chips", as inventions can be related one to each other as substitutes or as complementaries. When substitutes are considered, patents block competitors from being the first to acquire monopoly rights over inventions. When the technology presents a pattern of complementary inventions, patenting mainly strengthens the negotiating position of the firm.

Firms that operate in "discrete" industries (such as chemicals) are generally driven by the propensity to block competitors from patenting substantive products. Therefore, a strategy that is based on discovering and patenting substitute technologies fortifies the competitive position of the firm and weakens the dominance of its rivals. In "complex" industries (for example telecommunications), the motives to patent mainly aim at forcing rival firms to collaborate and to trade

[20] In some cases, firms find their technologies difficult to patent and choose to disclose them via professional and scientific journals, thus obtaining reputation by application of "defensive publication" that prevents rivals from patenting similar and related inventions, as the know–how has become public domain.

access rights to their inventions in return for rights to use the firm's patents. Hence, patenting large number of complementary technologies in the field enables the firm to construct patent portfolios and to create dependence of other firms on its patents, which forms a basis for negotiations over mutual licensing of patent rights.

Under particular market conditions and merits of the technology, firms prefer to avoid protecting their inventions by patents and implement other means of appropriation. In some cases, the high degree of disclosure of novel techniques required to obtain a patent enables competitors to "invent around" the patented invention with a relative ease. Hence, firms that operates in "complex" industries prefer keeping their core technologies covert, to prevent others from developing technological substitutes that directly compete with their core technologies. At the same time, patenting less significant components, which are essential for producing the goods but involve smaller degrees of knowledge disclosure, prevents other firms from competing with complementary products. However, the application of an integrative strategy of patents and trade secrecy in "discrete" industries is more complicated and in some scenarios even impossible. Consequently, firms must assess the risks of revealing their core knowledge and competences to rivals: whether their products can be easily reverse–engineered and, hence, should be patented and to what extent their know–how can be transformed into advanced products by others (thus maintaining secrecy). Other major reasons for avoiding patenting include the difficulty of proving the novelty of inventions, patent application costs and the legal costs of defending the patents in Court.[21]

Since the Yale survey in the early 1980s, scholars observed major changes in the preferences of firms that apply various appropriability mechanisms. First is the emerging use of trade secrecy, by itself or as a part of other appropriability strategies. Along with the increasing numbers of patent applications and with widespreading opposition to recent patent policies, firms have recognized the benefits of secrecy. Indeed, secrecy encompasses some risk that novel technologies would be revealed,[22] but its main advantages are minimal disclosure of advanced knowledge (particularly in firms whose unique competences and know–how are perceived

[21] The decision of avoiding patenting due to high costs of legal procedures, that is, patent applications and litigation suits, is typical to SMEs. Both types of expenditure put a heavy financial burden on the firm.

[22] The risk and the damages of unauthorized disclosure by employees can be limited, to an extent, through a contract.

as their core assets) and the low costs of enforcing it. This trend, characterized by the rise of secrecy as a prominent mechanism of appropriability of inventions is troublesome for innovation, as advances in technology are not distributed among larger technical and scientific communities and knowledge spillovers are formed. Consequently, the diffusion of technical knowledge is impeded. This may result in lower levels of innovation followed by an economic slowdown in the long run. Second, firms have shifted from *patent races* towards *patent portfolio races* that secure a wider spectrum of applications of their core inventions (that is, patenting around them) and obtain large amounts of patents in important fields that later can be traded with rivals in return to rights of using their patented inventions (that is, patents serve as "bargaining chips" in licensing negotiations). Third, firms that operate in complex technological fields are motivated to patent as many technologies as possible, otherwise they may fail to produce any goods that implement a wide range of essential inventions if patent–holders refuse to license any of them.

On the other hand, patent portfolio races may contribute to social value, encompassing two positive impacts from the social planner's perspective. The probability to successfully accomplish licensing agreements in complex industries increases when a small number of firms holds wide shares of the technology than in the case of many firms that hold patents over small fractions of the technology. Moreover, the costs of coordinating and negotiating the terms of licensing agreements increase with the number of the patentees that hold access rights to necessary technologies.

Additionally, firms are encouraged to disclose technical knowledge in the process of establishing of patent portfolio. Otherwise, if the knowledge stays within the domain of the firm, it would not be able to gain exclusive rights over it and to trade it for access rights to technologies that were developed by other firms.

Comparing the results of the Yale survey (1987) with those of the Carnegie–Mellon survey (2000) reveals only modest changes in the behaviour of firms and in their appropriability strategies, although the technological agenda and the IPR legislation, mainly in knowledge–based products, have substantially changed during the 1990s. The importance of secrecy as an appropriability mechanism has increased in all the industrial sectors and has become the second most–preferred method after lead–time (previously, learning curves were positioned after lead–time). Lead–time remains first in importance with a marginal change in the propensity of firms to implement it. Surprisingly, the relative effectiveness of patents has been extended to include new technological fields and patent records and manuals can be accessed online.

The Carnegie–Mellon survey highlights three prominent patenting strategies that are common among firms in all the sectors:

- Firms apply for "block to play" patents to prohibit rivals from developing technologies that are similar or close to those that are held by the firm and to secure their technologies from patent litigation suits by first–to–patent competitors. Consequently, this strategy enables firms to expand their technological domains and to invest in R&D without running into the risk of being excluded from exploiting their inventions in later stages. Although "block to play" patents involve unnecessary costs that otherwise could have been devoted to R&D and hamper other firms from applying patented inventions (particularly in cases of "sleeping patents" that were never used by their patentees), firms entering new technological fields are provided with suitable environment for innovation without risking their R&D investments.
- "Patent fences" do not aim at blocking other firms from obtaining a stronghold position in cross–licensing negotiations, but rather they are directed at fortifying a dominant position in the market by owning monopoly rights over core inventions and technologies in domains in which competitors may invent around firm–owned patents to legally trespass them.
- "Player" strategies refer to patenting for blocking and cross–licensing purposes with no intention to obtain royalty revenues from licensing in the course of this action. "Player" strategies are widely used in firms that operate in complex industries. They are less popular among producers of discrete products, due to the limited scope of applied technologies, and among large patent portfolio holders in most sectors, due to their ownership rights that are preferably gained via fencing out rival firms instead of negotiating access rights with them.

The use of the "block to play", "patent fences" and "player" strategies varies between firms that operate in different industries and among producers of "discrete" and "complex" products (see Table 3.1). Most firms in discrete industries usually construct "patent fences" to annex technological areas and to impede development of competing products (that is, *substitutes*), since the capability of firms to generate direct revenues from licensing is relatively weak, unless the firm holds patents over "core technologies". Cross–licensing negotiations between firms seldom occur in discrete–technology markets. "Block to play" strategies are often used by firms in other discrete industries, where patents are mainly implemented to generate monopoly rents and royalty fees during the patent lifetime with relative ease. In complex industries patents serve as *bargaining chips* to obtain an advantageous position in cross–licensing agreements and as means for generating licensing revenues. Hence, firms that own large patent portfolios choose to apply "player" strategies to preempt competitors from entering the market and to gain rights to complementary technologies, where possible.

## 3.4 Conclusions

Knowledge dissemination is a primary instrument in promoting the development of new technologies. Usually, inventors do not develop new products in a void, but gradually further prior inventions. However, empirical studies indicate that patents are widely used for strategic means (for example blocking rivals from entering the market, or as "bargaining chips" in cross–licensing negotiations), rather than as mechanisms for distributing novel know–how. Hence, the motives of firms to apply for patents are far from the goals of policy makers and from the rationale of the originators of IPRs.

The conclusions of those studies present grave concerns regarding the contribution of IPRs to innovation and technical change and their ability to maintain the balance between private interests and public benefits.

Further, the main issues over IPR regimes spawned a series of related debates. The success of IPRs to achieve sustainable development of technologies in various industrial sectors and under different market conditions by providing inventors with monopolistic position is continuously questioned by legal and economic scholars.

In addition to the traditional roles of IPRs, that is, provision of incentives for innovation and in return for knowledge disclosure, patents (and to a lesser extent copyrights) promote the codification of know–how by firms. IPRs provide incentives to transform knowledge prospects into standard formats of presentation that can be judged by practitioners for utility and novelty and can be later applied by other firms.

The technical contents of inventions can further be exploited in other products or be published in technical manuals and "cookbooks", which may be protected only by copyrights. Yet, patents provide larger economic incentives for knowledge codification and disclosure than copyrights, as their form of exclusive rights covers also technical applications of the protected technology, rather than the published description of inventions (that can be protected as a literary work by copyrights).

The findings of various innovation studies suggest that the perception of patents as an exclusive solution for issues of intellectual property ownership, technological development and innovation is misleading. The role of IPRs, and in particular the functions of the patent system, should be reviewed within a wider context that includes the behaviour and the strategies of firms, institutionally supported mechanisms of knowledge transfer and the unique properties of different technologies and industries. Therefore, any analysis of IPRs cannot be adequately accomplished without considering the market dynamics and the technology.

The empirical evidence emphasizes the use of patents by firms for non-innovative purposes, that is, pre-empting competitors from entering new technological markets by forming legal barriers around technological domains. The findings reflect major concerns whether the extant IPR regimes fulfil their primary role in fostering creativity and disseminating technical and literal endeavours or eventually hinder them. Firms may strengthen their positions in the market against entry of competitors by patenting and commencing patent litigation procedures, due to high fixed costs of juridical procedures. Indeed, those legal practices are found to be more common in large firms than in SMEs. However, the consequences of those strategies, if broadly employed by market incumbents, may prove perilous to innovation and technical change, nipping in the bud inventions that mushroom in small-size firms. To emphasize, firms have other means for commercial exploitation of intellectual assets and technical know-how and, indeed, employ them for this purpose. Patents are commonly used only as legal means to capture rents from innovation and in some industries they play insignificant roles.

Apart from following the original intents of the founders of the patenting system, that is, directly protecting inventions from being imitated by competitors and securing the revenues of inventors, firms use patents for objectives that had not been anticipated by the originators of the regime. In some scenarios, patents may even contradict their fundamental goals.

Firms that operate in discrete industries (for example chemicals) commonly use patents as strategic means by building patent fences around their core inventions. Those patents usually aim at covering a range of potential substitutes of the core inventions, which may be developed by other firms to compete with the original products by reverse–engineering their compounds. Later, if the process significantly differs from the patented procedure, a new patent is granted, although the end products are similar in their structure and function. A complete protection of market segments acquired by the firm is gained by avoiding licensing its patents over product substitutes, although sometimes those patents are not commercialized (therefore, this sort of patents is named "sleeping patents"). In other cases, patents are widely used to protect the firm and to threaten its rivals against litigation lawsuits. From the social welfare standpoint, defensive patent applications against offensive ("blocking") patenting by competitors is undesirable. Firms are engaged in costly legal processes of patent applications (which otherwise were not submitted to the patent office), litigation and protection from infringement lawsuits. Moreover, those purposes are far from the aims of the patent system and in some cases even contradict them.

Finally, comparing the results of the Yale survey with those of the CMS reveals only limited changes in the decisions of firms to use various appropriability mechanisms, although legislation has experienced dramatic changes since the 1980s (for example extensions in the scope of patents to include gene sequences, computer programs and algorithms). Recent studies suggest that the effects of structural changes in the patent system on technological development and on economic growth are fairly restricted and both goals are largely affected by the nature of technologies as well as by patenting strategies of firms.

# 4

# Revealing Obscure Sources: The Paradoxical Evolution of Software Appropriation Regimes

## 4.1 Introduction

The rise of the information society results in enormous changes throughout the economy. The "health" of information sectors is central to the future economic growth of every country. While the information sector encompasses many different industries, information goods are pivotal. Out of a great variety of information goods, the paradigm example, probably, is software. Indeed, software is now incorporated into so many "other" goods, that it may be the most pervasive sub–sector of the new economy. Its growth certainly attests to widespread diffusion – in the OECD countries in the 1990s software sales (excluding bundled operating systems) have been growing at roughly 11 per cent per annum (12 per cent if bundled operating systems are included; OECD, 2000). Besides this immense growth in sales, we also see enormous amounts of piracy. Losses of sales due to piracy are estimated to be in the neighbourhood of 11 billion USD annually (SPA, 1997, 1998; SIIA, 1999). As one can imagine, piracy of this magnitude is accompanied by claims by software vendors that it threatens the development of the industry as a whole.

Since the mid–1980s regulators have been seriously concerned with issues of infringement of intellectual property rights in relation to information goods and software in particular. The US has been leading the way in establishing a legal doctrine for protecting software intellectual property with European and Japanese legislation typically following (Karjala, 1990; Brueckmann, 1990).

A basic definition for the protection of intellectual property in the US legislation distinguishes "*ideas*" from "*expressions*". Patents are granted only for technological advances that permit the practical solution of specific problems in the field of technology and fulfil the fundamental terms of being an "*idea*", that is utilization by the application of the technical know–how in products and processes, novelty and non–obviousness of the invention. Copyrights aim protecting creative endeavours, that is, artistic and literary works and their derivatives (which are original by themselves) that cannot be technologically utilized. Nevertheless, careful examination of the US Patent Office Guidelines for Computer–Related Inventions (USPTO, 1996) leads to consideration of computer programs as *hybrid legal entities* that may warrant protection by both regimes, since on the one hand, algorithms, processes and ideas involved in a computer program can be patented, and on the other hand, other elements and concepts of software, such as interfaces, code lines and final copies of software products, can be protected by copyrights (Reichman, 1994; Nichols, 1998).

Advances in the technological frontiers of software and information systems highlight issues concerning the ability of the current doctrine to preserve the balance between the guarantee of property rights for inventors of software technologies, and economic inefficiencies that result from monopoly power.

The EU expressed particular concerns over the rise in illegal reproduction of digitized works for private use, facilitated by technical advance in communication platforms, and over their increased diffusion (European Commission, 1995). However, implementation of IPR regimes aiming at diminishing unauthorized duplications in the short run should be judged not only by their ability to protect the interests of owners of software copyrights and related rights, but also by avoiding pitfalls caused by overprotection that may lead to fragmentation of the Internal Market in the long run.

The growing medium of the Internet as a distribution channel can foster new types of infringements of intellectual property rights in many ways. The share of data communication equipment as a percentage of the total OECD IT market almost doubled in the 1990s, increasing from 2.6 per cent in 1990 to 5 per cent in 1997. The number of worldwide Internet hosts grows rapidly (37.7 million hosts in July 1998, an increase of 23 per cent over January 1998) (OECD, 2000). Additionally, the volume of core copyright industries in the US economy was estimated to have a value–added of 254.6 billion dollars in 1994, representing 3.78 per cent of the GDP. The revenues from online software sales were estimated to be 10 per cent of the total revenue of the copyright industries in 1996 (approximately 0.5 per cent of the US GDP) and were predicted to triple by the end of 2000 (OECD, 1998a). While the volume of legal distribution of copyrighted material over the Internet seems enormous, so does illegal distribution, as the Napster case shows (or is alleged to show).

The growth in development and use of software products, their contribution to the *New Economy* and the projected emergence of new software markets in electronic commerce have led policy makers and software publishers to re–assess the present regimes and their ability to cope with violation of the intellectual property of software technologies and products.

## 4.2 The Evolution of Software Intellectual Property Regimes

The legislation of software patenting and copyrights passed through several stages of modification from the early 1960s to the 1980s. Until the mid–1980s, patent applications for software–based processes and computer program algorithms were rejected, following US Patent and Trademark Office (USPTO) policy guidelines. The USPTO justified its decision by arguing that novelty measures could hardly be established in the dynamic field of software development. Further, historically, patent protection has been given to mass–marketed commodities, thus excluding computer programs that were distributed only in small volumes at that time. As a result, until the late 1970s the software industry relied mainly on trade secrecy contracts and licensing agreements (Branscomb, 1990; Samuelson, 1993).

A shift away from the perception of IPRs as germane mostly for mass–produced physical goods began with the parallel development of the personal computer and the shrink–wrapped software[1] market in the mid 1980s. Some computer programs have become mass–consumption goods, as computer applications are now distributed through a variety of channels (except for, by and large, operating systems, which tend to be supplied with hardware as in the 1960s). This reduces

[1]Software products that are physically distributed in packages and are accompanied by licensing agreements that regulate their use.

the force of the USPTO's previous rationale. Consequently, the US Patent and Trademark Office considers software goods and software–embedded products as patentable since 1986.

More recent policy guidelines, in contrast with those established in the previous period, have considered software goods (and embedded software technologies) as legal entities that are owned by their creators and can be protected through intellectual property rights. Those new guidelines have preserved the traditional distinction between an "idea" and an "expression", hence enabling software technologies to obtain patent protection as other types of technical advances do.

Table 4.1 shows the gradual evolution of the software industry in terms of the nature of software, typical users, IPR mechanisms and regulation. We can observe from this table a gradual move away from the open system of the 1950s and 1960s towards a relatively closed system that appears to be emerging in recent years.

Emerging legislation and rulings appear to be a continuation of the regime that was developed for physical goods, with analogies drawn between various elements of software and traditional technologies or artistic artefacts. This incremental approach, in which sofware IPRs have developed over time, has intensified the debate over IPR protection. Indeed, the main issue, debated but unresolved, is the ability of the current IPR regimes to address technical changes that are presented by information goods. Several suggestions have been proposed to strike the right balance between provision of incentives to innovate (thought extremely important by software industry investors) and the freedom of knowledge or the diffusion of information (thought vital for technology transfer, knowledge spillovers and further innovation). Those suggestions frequently appear when new challenges are felt by the market and they are often contrasted with inappropriate (and in some aspects archaic) economic models (Reichman, 1994).

A striking aspect of the evolution of software IPRs is that software is being treated as both patentable and copy–protected. Previous techno–economic paradigms built a dichotomy between copyrights and patents as two regulatory mechanisms that protect different sorts of subject matter. Patents apply to the ideas and the processes underpinning the inventive step of an invention, whereas copyrights apply to the expressions of creative works, basically to their literary or artistic forms. However, as noted above, the USPTO guidelines divide the protection given to software, such that algorithms and processes are patented, while interfaces, code lines and final products are copyrighted.

The legal overlap between software patents and copyrights, protecting the very same product, is claimed to be overprotective and is likely to result in a monopolistic dominance of technological know–how in software development areas.

IPR regimes aspire to promote high levels of creativity, both for "art" (copyrighted works) and "utility" artefacts (patented inventions). As new technologies present new economic paradigms, it is argued that the implementation of both regimes provides broader protection than that which IPR regimes originally meant to offer (Menell, 1989; Reichman, 1994; Samuelson et al., 1994; and others). Examination of the aircraft and radio industries in their infant stages shows that patents registered by market dominators created barriers for entry for new inventors and potential market entrants and hence slowed down the pace of innovation at a stage critical for the development of those technologies (Nelson, 1994).

Mackaay (1994) expresses some concerns regarding the effects of IPRs on the software industry. He argues that software innovation is hampered by the existing intellectual property regime that provides broad protection and does so for lower levels of creativity than are appropriate for this (relatively) new industry. He suggests that the adaptation of the legal regime lags beyond the technological changes and fails to keep up with the changing attributes of new and rapidly evolving technologies. Though developed in the context of software, this argument obviously applies to any rapidly changing industry, but it is especially strong when the industry is at the heart of a significant shift of a technological paradigm.

The following sections review legal *modus operandi* employed to protect software goods, the issues and the constraints of the existing methods for software protection.

| Period | Software Applications | User Profile | Type of Protection | Regulated by... |
|---|---|---|---|---|
| 1950s–1960s | Bundle of hardware and software for central machines | Researchers and Academics | No protection: informal exchange | No Regulation |
| Early 1960s–Late 1960s | More diverse and complex program for Central Computers | Researchers, Academics and Earlier Market | Trade Secrecy and Licensing | Fair Use Law Trade Secrecy and Contract Law |
| Late 1960s–1970s | Commercial venture software projects, based on scientific research | Industry and Academics | Trade Secrecy and Licensing; Patents and copyrights rejected | Fair Use Law Trade Secrecy and Contract Law |
| 1980s | Personal Computers (PC) and industrial processes/ equipment | Industry, Business, Academic and Home users | Trade Secrecy Copyrights Patents "Shrink Wrap" Licensing | Copyright Act[a] ("expression"), Patent Law[b] ("idea"),[c] Berne Convention |
| 1990s | Personal Computers and Internet (World Wide Web)/LAN/ WAN[d] | Industry, Business, Academic, Home and Net users | Hybrid character of software; International Copyrights and Patents Laws; New economic models (as "Sharing" and "Bundling") | EU "Green Paper" (European Commission, 1995); TRIPs Agreement (WTO, 1995); Suggested *Sui Generis*[e] Law for Software Linking, Web Caching and Browsing – *"on a case by case"* basis ruling. |

**Table 4.1.** Taxonomy of the development of software IPRs, 1950s–1990s (*Based on*: Samuelson, 1993; Reichman, 1994; Holderness, 1998; Morisson, 1999).

[a] Adapted to software IPRs by CONTU (National Commission on New Technological Uses of Copyrighted Works, 1980).

[b] A change in US Patent and Trademark Office (USPTO) policy occurred after the US Supreme Court's decision in *Diamond vs. Diehr*, 1981, by which software involved in industrial processes can be patented.

[c] See *Whelan vs. Jaslow* ("Whelan Test") for the "expression/idea" ruling.

[d] LAN – Local Area Networks; WAN – Wide Area Network.

[e] *Sui Generis*: "of its own kind", used to describe something that is unique or different.

## 4.3 Software Patents

### 4.3.1 Background

From the very first stages of computer and software technologies, US industries have dominated global software markets. This trend continues with US firms holding a share of 47 per cent of the global packaged software markets and 36 per cent of the global ICT markets (OECD, 2000). Hence, US legislation of software IPR regimes and its dominance in the global markets since the release of the first commercial applications were released have largely determined the attitude worldwide towards patent protection.

The most important event in software patenting in the US, later influencing legislation in the EU and in other parts of the world, occurred in 1986. A verdict given by the Supreme Court in *Diamond v. Diehr* found a rubber curing process involving a software element patentable, and hence approved the patent claims. The verdict was important in two ways: First, it created a precedent by permitting a piece of software to be patented. Second, it defined distinction between the patented "ideas" and the non–patentable (but copy–protected) "expressions" that are embedded in software technologies and goods.

In 1996, the USPTO wrote new guidelines to steer the evolution of software IPRs (officially in the US and *de facto* in most of the other countries). The Patent Office adopted an evolutionary rather than a revolutionary approach and so has created its software policy on the basis of existing IPR legislation and rulings. Notwithstanding, part of the examination procedure has been adapted specifically for software innovations and clearly shows an attempt to accommodate the hybrid aspect of software as both an "idea" and "expression". The procedure of the examination of software patent applications is illustrated in Figure 4.1.

In the European Union, the EU Council Directive on the Legal Protection of Computer Programs (91/250/EEC) presented guidelines for future legislation and instructions for adaptation of the national software IPR regimes of the Member States, on the basis of key principles that were adopted from US rulings. The terminology for legislation is taken from US guidelines, and a similar distinction between "*ideas*" and "*expressions*" exists.[2] According to the Directive, the legal term "computer programs" includes both the source code and preparatory designs

[2]The differences between the Directive and the US doctrine mostly relate to the broader permissions for reverse engineering allowed by the Directive.

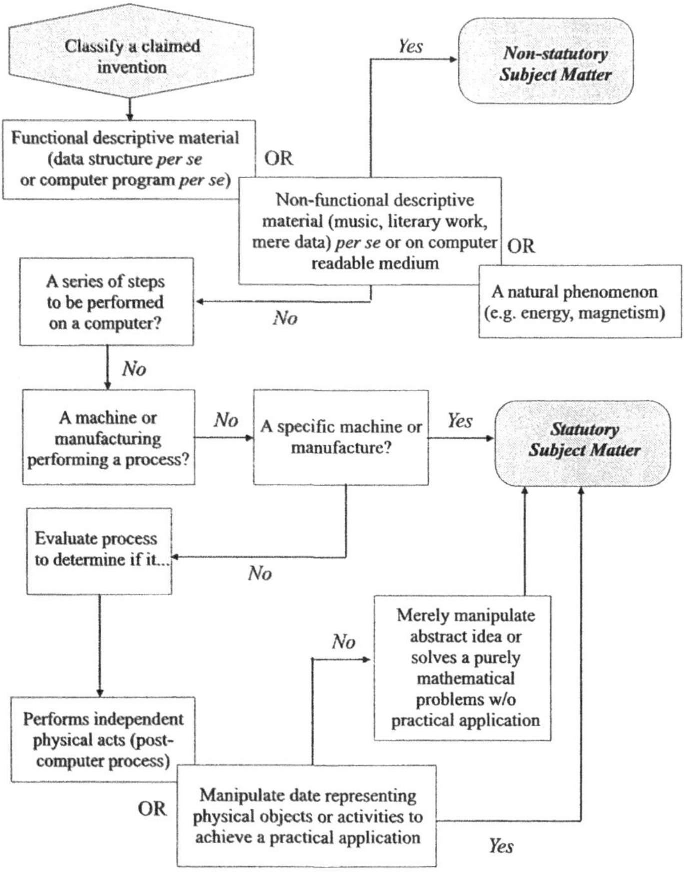


**Figure 4.1.** Guidelines for software patenting (Source: USPTO, 1996).

(similar to the *SSO principle*).[3] The aim of software patenting is to protect ideas and principles embedded in software that are not covered by copyrights (as also stated in the USPTO guidelines; see Figure 4.1). With the adoption of major parts of the US doctrine, the EU has consequently left the door open to the emergence of legislative issues in the protection of software that are similar to those that have emerged in the US (Brueckmann, 1990).

As shown in Figure 4.2, patenting has become a much more common method by

[3] The "*structure, sequence and organization*" of computer programs enjoy copyright protection, as final software products do (this is also known as the "Whelan test").

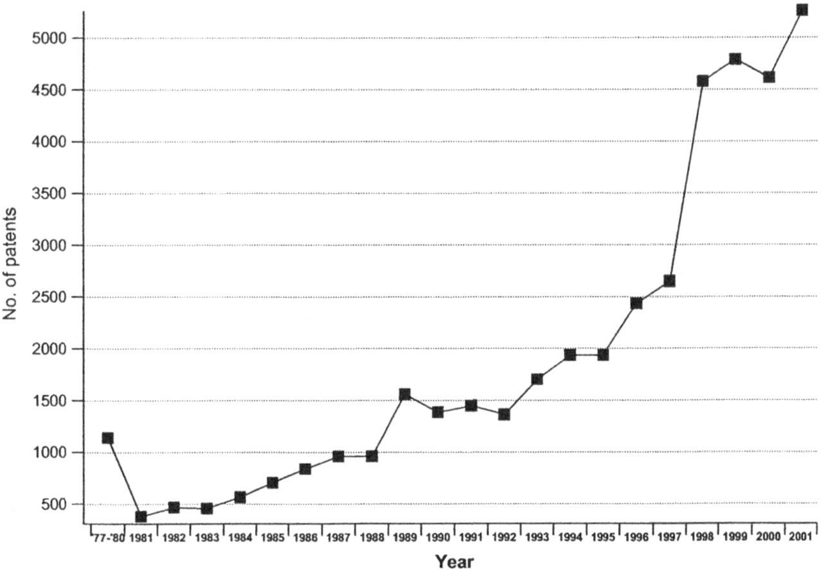


**Figure 4.2.** Number of software patents in the US, 1977–2001 (original classifications only) (Source: USPTO, 2002).

which software developers protect their technological advances. Note that numbers of software and software-related patents rapidly increased since 1992.[4] The annual growth rate in the number of patents in class 395 ("information processing system organization" – the major class for software-application patenting) between 1992 and 1999 was 33 per cent on average. To compare, the equivalent annual growth rate in the total number of US patents between 1992 and 1999 was only 6.3 per cent.

While it has been possible to patent software technologies for more than a decade, arguments for, and in particular against the present doctrine have been heard throughout this period. However, scholars differ in their opinions whether the present statutory regime is over- or under-protective and what possible consequences may be for the software industry and its trajectories of technological development. Most importantly, the debate has shifted towards what design of the

[4]Stolpe (2000) mentions that the vast majority of software publishers in Germany prefer to protect their products against unauthorized use by legal means over application of technical methods.

legal regime should replace the present legislation, in order to guarantee efficient protection and incentives while avoiding monopolistic impediments to innovation.[5] From this debate we may conclude that the drawbacks of the current overprotective regimes outweigh to some extent the advantages arising from implementation of strengthened legislation.

### 4.3.2 Are present IPRs an under–protective regime?

Advocates of strengthened IPR regimes argue that protection measures should be elevated in order to guarantee incentives to innovate (Clapes, 1993) and to protect small firms against predatory imitation by large firms (Heckel, 1992). Other arguments that are based on effective resource allocation claim that the scope of patent protection should be *broadened,* that is, a single patent should provide protection to a wider technological sphere in order to allow co–ordination between inventors and to effectively allocate resources and R&D investments, as new entrants adopt agreed technological standards for development of advanced applications (Cohen, 1999). Further, protective regimes do not only co–ordinate efforts to innovate, but also encourage firms to introduce products earlier, in order to achieve advantageous market positions as "first–movers". Therefore, firms are forced to increase their R&D efforts and, doing so, they accelerate the pace of innovation.

Even technological lock–in is seen as a reason for stronger IPRs. A lock–in to a single software platform is an advantage and contributes to standardization. Consumers' choice of a single technology from several available technologies is influenced not only by its technical merits, but also by the number of users that have adopted it. As the number of users of a particular technology increases, so does the possibility for interaction using it as a single standard ("*network externalities*"). Market standards allow "secondary markets" (that is, application developers) to devote more resources to development of a wider variety of applications for a single (standard) platform, instead of allocating resources for development of similar functionality for rival technologies, interfaces and converters (Farrell and Saloner, 1992).

Standardization is certainly valuable in creating static efficiencies, such as economies of scale in production, installed base economies and network externalities. In software, in particular, scale economies are important in production of

[5] Contrast, for example Schumm (1996) with Cohen (1999).

complementary applications. Given the possibility that a market standardizes on an inferior technology (Arthur, 1987, 1996; Farrell and Saloner, 1985), the "static efficiencies" argument is easy to justify only if "any standard is better than none". But this neglects dynamic issues and makes perhaps an unrealistic assumption that the quality of a platform technology does not restrict the technical qualities of its complementary applications.

### 4.3.3 Are present software IPRs an overprotective regime?

As innovation and diffusion both have social value, if the relative social values change, in principle the regime should be changed in response. For example, if the social value of knowledge diffusion increases, then the IPR regime should be altered to facilitate (or place fewer restrictions on) the diffusion, which would necessarily be at the cost of incentives to innovate. One can argue that in the case of software (and information goods in general) this has indeed happened.

The net benefits of diffusion increase if the costs of diffusion decrease, all else being equal. This has clearly happened with the growth of the Internet as a distribution channel for all sorts of information goods.

Software is in many ways a "general use" technology. That is, it is an input to or a component of many other technologies or goods. In particular, it is a very important input into the generation of further innovation. Thus, if software technologies were widely diffused, they would have very large positive effects on the creation of knowledge, and would reduce the costs of producing many goods.

It may also be the case that the costs of strong protection have increased. That is, while the net benefit of the monopoly given to innovators is still strong at the individual level, it is less likely to be so at the social level. The argument here is that a legal monopoly prevents entry. When a technology is rapidly changing, entry is vital in continuing innovation. An overprotective regime prevents just this type of entry that is caused by and causes rapid advance (Samuelson et al., 1994; Davis et al., 1996).

As a classic example of a general use technology with the potential to create extremely strong market power consider the merge–sort algorithm. The *merge–sort* method is an algorithm for effective classification and sorting of objects (such as records in a database). It was presented in the beginning of the 1970s, and since sorting is used in very many applications, it has become a very common and widely–used algorithm in computer science and throughout the software industry. Had its inventor registered a patent for this mathematical method of sorting, most of today's software development activities and products would have been dominated by a single person. We can easily imagine the harmful influence of a monopoly, had it been granted to a merge–sort patent, on the present development and innovation in software technologies, as no alternative method with similar efficiencies has been invented (Schumm, 1996).[6] This suggests a new test for examination of software claims. Patenting an idea or an algorithm should be accompanied by claims for the future applications of the algorithm, which would be an integral part of the patent scope. Thus, patent protection would be limited to future applications that were mentioned in the claims. Doing so, disclosure of technical know–how allowing implementation of knowledge in unclaimed fields can then be achieved. Although the proposed test does not restrict broad claims from being registered, it is an initial attempt to improve the present situation, in which wide allowances are granted to software inventions, by limiting the scope of protection to explicit applications registered in the patent claims.

This sort of arguments suggests that if it was possible to revise the present legislation, software should have had a less restrictive IPR regime than many other goods. A *sui–generis* regime may be (politically) difficult to create, but at this point in time, since the regime is now being constructed, there is an opportunity to resist calls for stronger protection or, alternatively, to demand compulsory licensing.

## 4.4 Copyrights

As in the case of patent regulation, the US is leading the way in revising its copyright regulation, fitting it to the new technologies. The rights of the owner of a copyrighted work are well defined in section 106 of the Copyright Act, which was approved by the United States Congress in 1976. Its definitions include the right for reproduction of a copyrighted work by its right holder, the right to prepare derivative works that are based upon the copyrighted material, the right for distribution of the work, and the right to perform and display it publicly. Additionally,

[6] One could argue that the presence of a patent would have prompted "working around" the invention. In this case, this seems unlikely. Given how pervasive is the use of sorting and how time–consuming it is, incentives to find efficient algorithms are very strong even in the absence of the need to work around a patent.

an eligible work must be presented on or in a tangible medium to be protected by copyrights (Diotalevi, 1998).

Copyrights are considered as a "*half baked cake*" when they are used to protect software from misappropriated use. The copyright system was adjusted in the light of the hybrid character of computer programs and in order to complete and complement the changes taking place in the regulation of patents. Nevertheless, software copyrights have not succeeded in addressing the character of the technology in general and they are frequently examined by Court on a "case by case" basis. Reichman (1994) argues that the application of copyrights to protect software products resulted in an overlap with patent ("*utility*") protection of the ideas and algorithms embodied in software, as software copyrights that are eventually legislated in most of the countries, may lead to an overprotective regime. Reichman advocates a *sui–generis* law that can be tailored to the technical characteristics of software goods and can help reducing the level of protection that software products currently enjoy.

A major juridical test was created by the precedent of *Whelan v. Jaslow.* The ruling in this case drew explicit guidelines for software copyright infringements. In *Whelan*, the Third Circuit ruled that copyright protection is made available for the "*structure, sequence and organization*" of a computer program, hence this doctrine was nicknamed the *SSO principle.* The SSO principle significantly widened the scope of software copyrights, which formerly were granted only to the source code.[7] The Court concluded that copyright protection that follows the SSO principle is essential to supply enough incentives to invest in software development. Moreover, the Whelan Test prescribes the perception of *functionality* of a module of a computer program as an *uncopyrightable* part, different from other aspects of software that are protected as "expressions" (Samuelson, 1993).

Criticism published after the ruling regarded the decision as overprotective. It was argued that the monopolistic dominance over patented technical know–how contrasts the incremental evolution of the software industry, largely based on knowledge transfer and technological spillovers. The term of copyright protection was also regarded as unnecessarily outstretched, compared to the average life–cycle of software applications (Menell, 1989). Indeed, interpretation of the ruling led to the conclusion that a new computer program, applying what are by now relatively

[7]The statements and instructions that a programmer writes to create a program.

common procedures and user interface design, such as word processor fonts[8] and methods for real–time data input[9] may violate the SSO principle. Thus, owners of rights may not only dominate software *technologies* by obtaining patents, but also software *designs* for elongated periods by copyrighting.

In the EU Member States, legislation is applied nationally, under a uniting legal framework supplied by WIPO's Berne Convention.[10] For example, the Dutch law is based on the Copyright Act (1912), which was modified in 1985 according to the Paris Act of Berne Convention.[11] Although the Directive for Legal Protection of Computer Programs contained explicit guidelines for adaptation of national regimes (software copyright regimes, in particular), there are substantial gaps in policy implementation which have slowed the legal harmonization among Member States. Two examples of such gaps seen in the Dutch case illustrate the tension between national legislation and the "*Fortress Europe*" regime.

A report on the Implementation and Effects of Directive 91/250/EEC on the Legal Protection of Computer Programs, submitted to the European Commission (COM (2000)199), found that the Dutch policy of software IPRs differs from the instructions of the Directive by prescribing a wider scope for "expression" (European Commission, 2000). The explicit definition by which ideas and principles embedded in software do not enjoy protection by Copyright Law has not been clearly defined and consequently the formal distinction between "idea" and "expression" appears to be somewhat vague in the Dutch legislation.

The second gap concerns the differences between the Directive and the Dutch law in placing restrictions over de–compilation of software goods.[12] Article 4 in the Directive includes the following limitations on de–compilation of computer programs:

> 1. *The permanent or temporary reproduction of a computer program by any means and in any form, in part or in whole. Insofar as loading, displaying, running, transmission or storage of the computer*

[8] *Adobe Systems vs. Southern Software* (Federal District Court, 1998) – fonts were approved to be copyrighted subject matter.

[9] *Interactive Network vs. NTN Communications* (California Court, 1995) – "real–time data feed" methods were approved to be protected by copyrights.

[10] WIPO – World Intellectual Property Organization; WTO – World Trade Organization.

[11] *Staatsblad* no. 307 (30.5.1985).

[12] Notice that the Directive has an extremely broad definition of "de–compilation".

*program necessitates such reproduction, such acts shall be subject to authorization by the right holder.*

[This would include, for example, making a second copy on a hard drive.]

2. *The translation, adaptation, arrangement and any other alteration of a computer program and the reproduction of the results thereof, without prejudice to the rights of the person who alters the program.*

[This would include, for example, translating the dialogue boxes from English to Dutch.]

3. *Any form of distribution to the public, including the rental of the original computer program or of copies thereof. The first sale in the Community of a copy of a program by the right holder or with his consent shall exhaust the distribution right within the Community of that copy, with the exception of the right to control further rental of the program or a copy thereof.* (European Commission, 1991)

[This would include, for example, re–selling a piece of software if it were previously installed, even if it is now completely uninstalled.]

However, Article 6 of the Directive makes an exception aimed at increasing innovation and product development: de–compilation of computer programs is permitted if the purpose is to achieve interoperability of the software with other applications (a process that is prohibited by US law). The Netherlands did not validate this exception, thus restricting the scope of software de–compilation. However, it is worth mentioning that the report considers the overlap between software copyrights and patents as non–problematic, since it is mostly concerned with provision of a broad scope of protection for software goods (European Commission, 2000). Hence, the authors of the EC's report on the implementation of the Directive on the Legal Protection of Computer Programs hold an opinion that expansion of software IPRs by application of a more protective copyright regime, despite the overlap in the protection that patents and copyrights provide, is the favoured decision.

## 4.5 The Creativity Paradox: How IPRs are Challenged by the "Open Source" Movement

The rapid development of the Internet accelerated in the 1990s and confronted software users, developers and authorities with a wide variety of issues. The IPR regime, developed in an era in which physical goods dominated the economy, was in some ways not in keeping with the new realities of intangible, information goods, the ease of their reproduction and the ease and geographic scope of their distribution enabled by the Internet. One aspect of the evolution of software, and information goods in general, has been the attempt to commodify them in such a way that they fit into the old IPR paradigm. Therefore, one movement has been towards applying strong property rights, such as patents, in this area. The natural evolution would seem to favour the development of "closed" software platforms, offered to the market with absolutely minimal disclosure of the embedded knowledge. As we have seen, software patenting both as a means of protecting property and as strategic means to preempt new entrants has become more and more widespread.

By contrast, though, since the beginning of the 1990s we witness a significant increase in the development of Open Source systems, which are offered publicly with a free–use license (for example Linux, Apache and Sendmail). Why do software developers and software firms offer their creative output at zero price, even though the current legislation allows software developers more means to claim property rights over their products than ever before?

Software IPRs have been developing in an evolutionary rather than a revolutionary manner, thereby tending to force the technological agenda to fit to the outmoded legal patterns of IPRs. Even the current resolution, extension of the "idea/expression" doctrine to include computer programs and algorithms in its scope of protection, attempts only to modify existing IPR regimes by providing developers with a dual protection scheme, that is, patenting embedded *ideas* and copyrighting final products. Like any other type of patents, software patenting aims at promoting innovation and knowledge disclosure by granting exclusivity over inventions to their creators, "fencing off" new algorithms and techniques from the public domain. Yet, legal scholars, economists and even programmers themselves, continuously criticize the current regime as jeopardizing further developments in ICT.

As a good, software continuously challenges the current IPR regimes. In addition, new modes of software production, for example Open Source, do not fit well either. A growing body of empirical literature and anecdotal evidence implies that Open Source may be extremely effective as a production technology.[13] The stability of Open Source software, and the speed with which developers respond to needs and problems argue that Open Source as a mode of production has many advantages. However, whereas properties of software production are complex and not entirely known, Open Source development has brought to the fore far more complex issues that challenge current IPR policies and legal paradigms. Open Source development is an approach that explicitly eschews traditional notions of intellectual property rights, as it relies on a free disclosure and reciprocal exchange of technical know–how, ideas and code lines within a virtual community, fully accessible for distribution and use by all. The Open Source community rejects patents and copyrights in favour of its own parallel "regime", which is based on variants of public licenses that differ in their terms of distribution, use and obligatory disclosure of advances in the source code (for example Copy–left, MPL and the BSD licence). Yet, Open Source treats innovative output relatively as a public good, available to be used by whomever sees value in it.[14] In the case of Open Source, traditional means of appropriating value from innovation by formation of monopoly rights do not apply. Rents cannot be extracted through the market for the good itself, as it appears from the usual innovative process. Similarly, traditional means of control of the technology do not apply. If the core of the technology is within the public domain, the locus of control has necessarily to be created and maintained in some non–traditional ways. Therefore, the challenge is to develop a new system in which the values of openness are maintained, but in such a way that incentives can remain, and in which control of the technology is not usurped by those that feel threatened by it.[15]

---

[13]See, for example, the exponential growth of websites using the Apache server and the success of the Open Source community in continuously providing its users with technical support (Lakhani and von Hippel, 2003).

[14]In many cases, Open Source licenses protect themselves from modification of terms by applying copyrights for this purpose; see Perens (1999) for a review of primary Open Source licensing methods.

[15]For example, imagine what could happen if Microsoft decided to create "its own version" of Linux.

## 4.6 From IPR Protection toward Communal Benefits

Since the mid–1990s, two major trends in software economics have arisen. The first supports strengthening intellectual property rights for software and information goods, whereas the second approach presents a progressive attitude, commonly known as Open Source, by which legal *modus operandi* to protect software goods and innovation should be only minor. In order to understand the background for the emergence of those two approaches, the technological evolution that led those changes should be first introduced.

Issues of intellectual property rights, copyrights and patent protection for software–embedded processes and later for software goods appeared after the verdict in *Diamond vs. Diehr* (Supreme Court, 1986), in which software elements were recognized as patentable. During the beginning of the 1990s, the US Patent Office (USPTO) decided to examine its guidelines for protecting software goods. The result of its efforts defined progressive and tolerant allowances for patenting.

The main change in the USPTO policy is the ability to patent algorithms that enabled the patenting of advances in software technologies (the "idea") as a part of developed software. In addition, the *final product* is protected by the Copyright Act (the "expression") (USPTO, 1996). Hence, since the Court's verdicts and legal guidelines determined legal methods for protection of software–based ideas, processes and algorithms have come to be protected by patent law. Consequently, the number of patents in the category of "information processing" (the major classification for software application patenting) has rapidly grown since 1992.

The other approach, the Open Source movement, was established in order to integrate and to coordinate the aggregation of skills of computer developers. While this movement evolved in the 1970s in academic institutes and public laboratories, the extensive diffusion of the Internet has dramatically changed the scope of the movement and has involved larger parts of the population in Open Source development. This model involves the full life–cycle of software development in a cumulative and communal manner and is nicknamed the "Bazaar model" after the way in which programmers are openly invited to take part in projects at any time.[16] The model is named to contrast with the prevailing methodology in the software industry – "the Cathedral model", in which "closed" development teams

[16]The stages of the model include: development of the source–code, debugging, testing and quality assurance, documentation, version release and a continuous development of related features (as software "patches").

have well-defined areas of responsibility coupled with structural processes and procedures for testing, debugging and non-frequent releases of versions (Raymond, 1999). The "Bazaar model" allows communities of users and developers to create a dynamic process in which products are opened to changes, freely implemented and frequently updated, mastered and enriched by their users. In order to assure that programmers disclose their advances back to the community, and those are shared as public domain, unique schemes of "public licenses" were formed (GPL, MPL, GNU and others).

The number of Open Source applications has been growing exponentially since the beginning of the 1990s. The technological diffusion of the Internet has fostered the creation of programming teams via discussion groups and message boards and has orientated talent toward joint development of network-based applications. To illustrate, the Open Source Apache, the leading platform for Internet communication servers, is estimated to have captured 57–60 per cent of the market for Internet hosts.[17]

The success of the "Bazaar model" to attract skilful programmers that prefer to devote their time, efforts and original developments "with no reward" to a virtual community is still puzzling. The rise of the Open Source movement is far more impressive when one considers the potential rewards that Open Source developers could have acquired during the Internet gold-rush of 1995–1999[18] by commercial exploitation of their source codes and by using the new legal guidelines to protect them from being "stolen" by others.

Economists and social scientists have recently begun to examine the rationale behind the "altruistic" behaviour of software developers, sharing their intellectual and professional output at "no cost" with other users. Initial conclusions classify the contributors to Open Source projects into three groups:

- *Participants* in Open Source communities are involved mainly in software documentation and testing via regular use of the applications. Their incentives include satisfaction and expertise in state-of-the-art software technologies.

[17]Based on estimations of Inktomi and the NEC Research Institute (http://www.inktomi.com/webmap/); Netcraft (http://www.netcraft.com/); E-Soft (http://www.securityspace.com/s_survey/data/index.html).

[18]The "Internet gold-rush" turned out to be an "Internet bubble": a frenzied runaway of investors from high technology stocks and the crash of many software firms, between March and December 2000.

- *Programmers* develop source code of Open Source applications. They benefit, to a large extent, from adoption of relevant procedures and algorithms by other projects in which they are involved, and from the relationships with other actors in their professional circles. Their incentives also include "learning by doing", that is, gaining expertise from development of new software and from knowledge spillovers from other programmers in their communities.
- *Project leaders* initiate development of new Open Source applications, mostly as a "call for solution" of engineering problems that they confront in commercial projects (for example, development of unique email protocols as a part of a communication project). Later, when the number of participants and their interest in the project exceed a critical mass and the initial specification of the project expands, project leaders continue to coordinate the development efforts or hand over their role to one of the active participants. They are driven by reputation, recognition from the Open Source community members and software firms, the ability to signal future trends in the ICT market or by opportunities to recruit genuine programmers to their commercial activities (Raymond, 1999; Lerner and Tirole, 2002).

One aspect of the decision of the firm to embrace Open Source involves the expectation that by disclosing the software technology to the public domain, other complementary activities offered by the firm can commercially be exploited and expand the diffusion of the proposed technology. Further, a firm that discloses its source code expects that its product would gain a dominant position in the market, enjoying both technical superiority over proprietary products, as Open Source applications are usually nourished by communities of skilled users.

Hence, the release of source code for free use is perceived by firms as a method to foster adoption of their technologies and to turn them into market standards. Small and medium firms, which cannot compete with market leaders, may apply Open Source strategies to improve their position in the market and to facilitate extensive implementation of their products. Red Hat Linux is an example of a successful business model that is fully based on Open Source applications. Red Hat acquires the source code at no cost, tests and improves the software, and then sells it in the market. The company distributes Open Source applications that can also be downloaded for free from the Internet, but it generates its revenues from provision of full guarantee and technical support to customers who purchase the products. Although Red Hat Linux may be installed and used for free (both are permissible by Linux licensing terms), most of its customers prefer to buy an original copy of the software, as an "insurance premium" to receive the firm's guarantee and additional services (Young, 1999).

Examining the success of Red Hat, one should cautiously conclude about the possibilities of other firms to profit by adoption of a similar model for their business activities. Indeed, Open Source software is available to distributors at no cost and in many cases offers consumers superior solutions than "closed applications".[19] Further, the implementation of a purchased copy reduces the implementer's risk. However, the formation of communal cooperation in the development of advanced applications and their use by computer experts, and recently by home users, questions the need for extensive frameworks of intellectual property rights for software technologies and suggests that legal protection of software by patents and copyrights should be reduced.[20] Under this type of business strategy, or this rationale of creating some Open Source, a firm must be able to create both open and proprietary software. To maintain the second class, there are two possible strategies: to deploy property rights, or to enforce trade secrecy. If the second option combined with network externalities is a possibility (and this seems quite feasible in software technologies) then traditional IPR policies will be inappropriate for the software market, being unnecessary to create incentives to innovate. More interestingly, they are inappropriate in the context of Open Source, as they do not provide the structure that Open Source needs to thrive (in fact they hamper it). If the Open Source production mode continues to have the technological successes that it enjoyed in the past, it would provide a strong argument against the current trends in software IPRs.

## 4.7 Conclusions

Patents and copyrights are well-known methods to guard technological advances and creative arts. However, these regimes are traditional in the sense that both were articulated when technological advances in physical goods were the norm.

[19] Users are able to copy parts of open source systems and implement them in other systems, modify them according to their needs or distribute them to others at no cost.

[20] Software producers hardly rely on IPR regimes to prevent unauthorized duplication and most of them rarely implement technical means for this purpose (Stolpe, 2000).

Since the 1960s we see the emergence of a new technological paradigm, namely knowledge–based economies, which are often called the *weightless economies*. Knowledge–based goods are based in their large part on intangible modes of distribution and use rather than on physical elements. In recent years, the growth of patent applications in those new industries shows a growing attempt by innovators to strengthen the legal rights over their ideas.

The development of the personal computer and the Internet, common representatives of knowledge–based technologies, as well as other new technologies that evolved during this period, have not only opened new scientific and technological avenues, but also initiated a debate around the contribution of patents, copyrights and licensing strategies to innovation. Although the technical contents of each regime differ, some arguments in the debate on the nature of IPR protection are similar.

First, the success in preserving the balance between monopoly and disclosure of technical know–how is under doubt. On the one hand, the possibilities of unauthorized duplication, distribution and use of information goods imply that legal provisions are, to some extent, under–protective. On the other hand, network effects lead to the emergence of a single technology as a market standard and create monopoly over technology that is empowered by legal regimes.

Second, as information goods have become accessible worldwide, mainly by the Internet as an infrastructure for global communications and retrieval of contents, information providers (such as software publishers, database producers and news agencies) have confronted vast scales of copyright violations.

Third, opposite effects that emerge from the development of technological means that restrict accessibility to information, compounded with the effects of strengthened protection by recently formed regimes (for example the US doctrine of software patenting and the EU Database Directive), have been argued to put scientific and technological advance at stake by monopolizing the content.

Fourth, and most importantly, policy makers around the globe attempt to resolve those issues by applying old legislative frameworks of IPRs to new technologies. Misapplication of current IPR regimes to evolving technologies may be the result. Moreover, policy changes that aim at providing adequate protection to technologies are often approved a decade or so after radical changes in technology have taken place, whereas in the meantime technology continues to evolve, presenting further puzzles.

As stated in the beginning of the chapter, regulations against software piracy are found to be far from watertight. The nature of software goods, as well as other intangible goods, confronts policy makers with evolving needs of the software industry not only to explore new methods for enforcement, but mostly to adapt the current regimes to the dynamics of technologies.

At the same time that highly protective legal intellectual property regimes for software have been criticized as destroying the balance between incentives to invent and the diffusion and use of technological knowledge, alternative models of intellectual property use, based on the tradition of Free or Open Source in which openly available software is used as the basis of a profit–making venture, have developed.[21] Recent research in economics has attempted to explain the rationale of participants, both firms and individuals, taking part in Open Source projects. A development method, originally started with the Free Software Foundation to foster endogenous growth of innovation in software technologies (Stallman, 1999), has become a profitable business model in which reliance on intellectual property regimes is (almost) prohibited.

The Open Source model indeed demonstrates a creativity paradox. Inventors of software technologies could take advantage of incentives provided by intellectual property rights, based on traditional IPR regimes, by obtaining monopoly rights and thus an advantageous market position. Nonetheless, new developments succeed technologically and commercially where those incentives are ignored, IPRs are not implemented and software is freely disseminated.

The Open Source development mode not only seems to be a paragon for software production, but also dramatically weakens the argument that strong property rights are necessary to create incentives for inventors in software technologies to innovate. Open Source communities demonstrate how technological advances and progressive communication platforms can efficiently foster innovative efforts in a way not taken into account in traditional models of innovation and property rights. The Open Source movement, at the same time producing rapid innovation of good technologies and avoiding application of traditional IPR regimes, strongly suggests that software IPRs is a case of the *tragedy of the anti–commons*: Software is "a

[21]In contrast to many opinions in the field (for those mainstream views see Reichman, 1994; Samuelson et al., 1994; Schumm, 1996), Cohen (1999) argues for a stronger IPR regime. The idea is that if property rights were stronger, dominant standards of core technologies would emerge more quickly. By reducing resources expended on competing technologies, more resources would be available for rapid development of applications.

resource [that] is prone to underuse ... when multiple owners each have a right to exclude others from a scarce resource and no one has an effective privilege of use" (Heller and Eisenberg, 1998).[22]

Finally, although the echoes of former debates in software economics have not yet dissolved, technological developments in the field and progressive communication platforms may confront us, due to their evolving abilities and functionality, with new levels of complexities, far from the traditional economic and legal models as currently known.

[22]Other known "tragedies" that arise from the extension of traditional IPR regimes to include knowledge-based technologies in their scope of protection are genetic expressed sequence-tags patenting (Heller and Eisenberg, 1998) and the EC Directive for the Legal Protection of Databases (David, 2000).

# 5

# Benefiting from Intellectual Property and Free Disclosure

## 5.1 Introduction

Since the beginning of the 1990s, we have seen a significant increase in the development of computer programs as Open Source applications, publicly offered with a free–use and distribution license. Open Source applications cover a wide variety of fields from operating systems and communications to desktop publication programs and Enterprise Resource Planning packages (prominent and widely implemented examples are Linux, Apache, Open Office and Sendmail).[1]

Part of the success of the Open Source movement is explained by the rapid growth of the Internet as a communication network between users and developers. The design and programming of new applications progresses online. Users continuously download updated versions, test them and indicate faults in their operation or propose additional features to develop (Raymond, 1999; Jeppesen and Molin, 2003). The architecture of the Internet and the connectivity of vast numbers of users enable communities of software developers to coordinate widely distributed programming efforts and skills online. Those skills are turned into a continuous improvement of computer programs and solid technical support at virtually no cost (Lakhani and von Hippel, 2003).

While the early modern history of computer software involved considerable Open Source development, mostly in the academic milieu, in recent decades (par-

[1]Listed Open Source initiatives and active projects in a variety of fields can be found in http://sourceforge.net/.

ticularly since the rise of the personal computer) commercial programs dominate the major share of software markets and Open Source has moved to the fringe of the industry. However, in the past few years, major firms have decided to integrate Open Source methodologies in part of their projects. Cowan and Jonard (2003) explain Netscape's decision to disclose the source code of its browser, arguing that "[W]hat the Internet may have done is to create a large enough community of collaborators to make the gains from collaboration outweigh the costs perceived in loss of proprietary control (which may, of course, include loss of market power, technological secrets, trade secrets and so on)." A recent example is the release of the source code of IBM's Eclipse project, a new software platform on which information systems are built, in November 2001. Before its release as an Open Source application, it was a proprietary software that was developed at the cost of 40 million dollars (as reported by the *Industrial Computing Magazine* in November 2001).

Despite an extensive legal framework that enables software developers to generate revenues from their programs and inventions,[2] many developers prefer to offer their creative output at a zero price tag. Firms that provide Open Source as a part of their business model expect to raise their profits and their market share by disclosing their core asset for free use, modification and re–sale by removing any intellectual property claims from it. Other firms disclose their source code and technologies via industrial consortia that prevent competitors from "hijacking" substantial market shares with their own proprietary standards (Rice, 2003). Firms, in particular small and medium enterprises, apply Open Source to gain a competitive advantage by fostering the diffusion of their technologies and by expanding the installed base of their users. Bonaccorsi and Rossi (2003) argue that although Microsoft succeeded in establishing a dominant position in the desktop market and disrupting wide diffusion competing Open Source applications, Open Source software obtained a stronghold in the web servers market. Alternatively, the decision of firms to embrace Open Source involves the expectation that by disclosing the technology to the public, complementary services (for example implementation and technical support) can expand through the rapid diffusion of freely–offered contents.

[2] Increasing numbers of software patents submitted and approved by the United States Patent and Trademark Office (USPTO) and the rising number of lawsuits over patent disputes in information technologies reflect the wide adoption of IPRs as strategic means by software companies (Granstrand, 2000; Cowan and Harison, 2001).

Red Hat Linux is a prevalent example of a successful business model that is fully based on Open Source software. The company distributes Open Source applications that can be downloaded for free from the Internet. However, Red Hat provides its customers full guarantee and technical support for its products if they are purchased by the user. This business model enables Red Hat to generate profits, as it acquires the source code at no cost, tests and improves it, and then sells it in the market. Although Red Hat Linux may be installed and used for free (both are permissible by Linux licensing terms), most of its customers prefer to buy an original copy of the software as an "insurance premium" and enjoy the guarantee of the firm (Young, 1999).

As the use of software applications expands, so do their "production externalities". Knowledge spillovers that foster technological advance increase with the level of openness of the source code, as skilled users integrate new features into the base code. Therefore, when the numbers of subroutines that are made public increase, the technical quality and the performance of the product are likely to rise too, as the scales of labour involved in design, programming new features and improving the code increase when external programmers can join the development process.[3] Further, by "outsourcing" other tasks of R&D to Open Source communities (for example documentation, quality control and bug fixing), software firms reduce their development costs.[4] However, the major drawback in the decision of firms to adopt Open Source methodologies is the removal of intellectual property claims from the disclosed features, as a precondition for involving external programmers in the development process. Consequently, the revenues from open versions may become lower than the revenues obtained from proprietary versions. Thereby, many software firms choose an alternative strategy and distribute their products as *hybrids*, in which part of the source code remains proprietary and the other is made open. Alternatively, firms customize the licensing terms of their products to make them "hybrid" (McKelvey, 2001). For example, the Sun Community Source Licensing (SCSL) for Sun's Java–based applications integrates both Open Source and proprietary policies according to the use of those products. Users

[3]Results of several benchmark studies comparing the main variables of performance and stability in Open Source vs. proprietary applications have shown superiority of the Open Source Linux over its proprietary rival, Windows 2000 (see for instance: Rothman and Buckman, 2001; *PC Magazine*, 2001, 2002).

[4]Software firms had long ago reduced their testing costs by introducing *beta versions* of computer applications to potential users before releasing the final products.

can download the Java developers' kits and use them at no cost, but licensing fees are charged when the standard environment is modified for their own purposes.[5]

Software development and distribution strategies closely affect the licensing terms. Those terms define whether parts of the code can be integrated into proprietary programs, modified or re–distributed, and whether the license is "viral" (that is, programs that apply part of the source code should be protected by the same type of license) or non–restricting (see Table 5.1). The licensing terms also determine the conditions and restrictions for developing and distributing future "generations" of the technology and its product versions. The dissemination and use of derivative and complementary applications in which parts of the code are embedded, are subject to the same license of the original program.

Reese and Stenberg (2001) argue that Copyleft licenses hinder cooperation between Open Source programmers due to their exclusive scope. Copyleft licenses (primarily the GPL license) require that every piece of source code that was made executable should be disclosed to the public and code–lines covered by Copyleft terms cannot be integrated into other programs if their licensing terms impose "further restrictions" or lesser degrees of disclosure. The extensive *scope of disclosure* restricts the subsequent use of Copyleft protected programs by firms, and presents "no notion of proportional fairness. The *quid pro quo* [i]s in reality a *quodque pro quo*".[6] Consequently, Copyleft protection discourages participation of commercial programmers in the development process (the authors argue that contributions of software developers employed by firms are the most active in Open Source projects). Lessig (2002) holds an opposite view on the benefits of Copyleft licenses to Open Source projects and innovation in software technologies, which is based on analysis of the structure of competition in the Open Source market. He argues that Copyleft licensing terms foster innovation by disclosure of improved versions and maintain incentives to initiate new Open Source projects. If changes in the source code of Open Source programs were left undisclosed, rivals could have obtained them for free, improve and redistribute them as low cost proprietary products that directly compete with the original applications. Smith (2002)

[5]The Open Source model shares similar concepts with other business models, such as shareware, in which products versions with partial or downgraded functionality are offered at no cost. However, the main difference is that Open Source requires disclosure of the source code and hence users are able to adapt the software to their own needs.

[6]Quid pro quo – something given in return for something else; Quodque pro quo – everything in return for something.

| License | Code can be used in non–OS programs | Modifications taken without disclosure | Software re–licensed by anyone | Privileges for the original copyright–holder over changes |
|---|---|---|---|---|
| GPL | | | | |
| LGPL | X | | | |
| BSD | X | X | | |
| NPL | X | X | | X |
| MPL | X | X | | |
| X–License | X | X | X | |

**Table 5.1.** Licensing terms of frequently–used Open Source licenses (Source: Perens, 1999).

proposes balancing measures between private and public interests, in which application of Copyleft terms is limited to software developed by public institutes for non–private use.

In the model that follows, we assume that Open Source programs are distributed under the permissive terms of "X–license" that enable free use, commercialisation, development of new features and "mixture" of free, open and proprietary software. By using the model as a baseline case, future research may assess the impact of other licenses that are present in the open and free software community (for example GPL and BSD) on the development of information technologies.[7]

A positive effect of free dissemination of software products, which even exists in software piracy, is the increasing number of users that choose to adopt them (that is, the *installed base* of computer programs). Firms may benefit from disseminating unprotected versions, since the demand and the propensity to pay higher revenues for legally–purchased copies increase with the total number of licensed *and* unlicensed users of their products (Conner and Rumelt, 1991; Shy and Thisse, 1999). However, this strategy would succeed only if the elasticity of substitution between paid and unpaid use is larger than 1, that is, the growth in profits from purchased copies exceeds the losses from illegal duplication. Yet, research on the economic effects of software piracy and unauthorized use examines software pro-

[7]In some cases, analytical modelling can be far more complicated than the general model presented here, considering the "viral" characteristics of licensing terms and the opposing views on the links between Copyleft licenses and their contribution or impediment to innovation.

grams mainly as final goods (that is, compiled software packages), overlooking the other type of benefits that source code disclosure involves. Whereas the success of proprietary software and its endurance to changes in the market are recognized by "locking–in" the majority of consumers to a single market standard, the success of Open Source projects is not measured by the same token. Instead, Open Source programs succeed by attracting many agents who implement them, provide technical support to other users and produce new and improved versions on a continuous basis.

On the supply side, various scholars suggest that developers that participate in Open Source projects and disclose their intellectual and professional output at "no cost" are driven by behavioural determinants, such as self satisfaction or "altruism", rather than by a more "traditional" economic rationale.[8] Others argue that new opportunities to "socialize" with members of online communities who share common interests and background and the reputation gained in professional circles are the main motives behind partaking in Open Source (Lerner and Tirole, 2002). However, whether one social factor is more dominant than the others, common observations mention that the development of open sources essentially remains unaffected by any changes in the market and, therefore, it can be represented in economic terms as a non–elastic supply of skills.[9]

In the following sections, we look at the underlying dynamics of software markets, where producers of software platforms and major applications (such as operating systems or Internet communication servers) are able to choose different degrees of disclosure, in terms of technical quality and profits. Our model analyzes how different degrees of source code disclosure influence the performance of software products and technologies and the profitability of producers. Section 5.2 describes a model of R&D in software firms, where a short–sighted firm applies a level of disclosure that optimizes single–period profits.

Section 5.3 expands the model and analyzes how disclosure affects long–term profits and social welfare and whether both measures correspond to each other. Section 5.4 expands the scope of the discussion by illuminating potential strategies

[8] Although it is reasonable to assume that professional programmers prefer developing commercial applications rather than free software in their spare time, in any Open Source community roughly half the developers are professional programmers (Hertel et al., 2003).

[9] The phenomenon of Open Source communities is more likely to be found in information technologies rather than in electronic engineering or biotechnology, since new entrants are not required to make high capital investments in hardware in order to participate in the production of new computer programs.

in several common market scenarios. Finally, we compare between markets of myopic and forward–looking firms, where similar degrees of disclosure generate different levels of profitability and future investments in R&D and draw conclusions on the links between software disclosure, technical quality and profits.

## 5.2 Intellectual Property vs. Disclosure: Description of the Model

Software products and technologies are composed of different *technological features*, various components that execute information processing and computational functions that are involved in the operation of computer programs. Software features are merged into a single and coherent application and usually do not overlap either in their functionality or tasks.[10]

The essence of the model is based on the decision of the firm to disclose part of its source code in order to enhance its profits. Since the disclosed features are freely disseminated and used, the firm must "compensate" for this disclosure by increasing its revenues from proprietary features. Open Source features become available to both users and rival firms, hence we can assume that revenues are not generated from them. If the software market has a monopolistic competition structure, profits are made through product differentiation. But thinking in Lancasterian terms, if two products share a feature, there is little ability for the two firms to differentiate their products using that feature. Thus, the ability to differentiate, which is central to the ability to earn profits, depends on having features that other products or firms do not have. This is captured in a very straightforward way by assuming that firms earn no revenues on anything developed as Open Source (since competitors can easily copy them) and their revenues must come from features that differentiate their products from rival applications.

This approach implies that software is hybrid in that parts of it are open and other parts are closed. Hybrid software may be relatively uncommon, but some important examples exist. The Macintosh operating system is based on a BSD Unix version (called Darwin), on top of which is a proprietary user interface. The LindowsOS is another example of an operating system that was built on the basis of Debian Linux. The system offers compatibility with Windows applications (which

[10]One of the main reasons to avoid such an overlap, which a key concept in the design of software, is the ease of maintaining the source code if changes in one of the features are required.

does not exist in Linux versions), graphic and user interfaces similar to Windows XP and other advanced features (for example anti–virus, anti–spam filters and WiFi detector).

At the same time, the model can be interpreted as representing the firm's portfolio of software. Some products are offered as Open Source, and others are proprietary. This avoids the issue of hybrid packages *per se*.

The model presents a stylized version of a real–world "software consumption" behaviour, in particular with regards to the demand side. Since the links between revenues and openness are in principle unclear, we look instead for bounds on revenue response, such that Open Source becomes a viable development mode. While this makes the model appear simplified and quite unrealistic in a way, it captures the basic motivations of firms to develop their products as open or as proprietary versions and avoids the difficulties involved in a fully–blown demand side interpretation.

## 5.3 A Myopic Firm Model

Nordhaus's model of technical change (1969, Ch. 2) describes how the quality and the performance of technology expand when new features are added, either by the firm's R&D or by its users. *Technical quality* signifies the performance of technology, which can be represented as a position on a "quality ladder" (Grossman and Helpman, 1991). Following this definition and Nordhaus's model, firms continuously improve the technical quality of their products by investing in R&D. The incremental change in the *technical quality* of software is denoted $R$ in our model.

Assume for simplicity that development of new features involves no risk. Therefore, the development of features by users fully substitutes the R&D of the firm if the code–lines of this feature are disclosed.

The model addresses the problem of a single firm. Given the costs of the two modes of development and the relationship between openness and revenue, the firm aims at maximizing its profits by choosing the degree of openness, $\alpha \in [0, 1]$ (the complementary share of the technology, $1 - \alpha$, remains proprietary and developed by the firm in–house).[11] Initially, we examine the case in which revenues do not

[11] At one extreme lies full protection by IPRs and consequently full ownership of the technology. At the other extreme technology is developed only by public communities

respond at all to openness, and then ask about the conditions on the relationship between revenue and openness that encourage or discourage firms to open their source.

The cost to the firm of developing a new feature is $\bar{c}$ if it is developed in-house and $c_1$ if accomplished through Open Source communities. Since Open Source programmers carry out major tasks without compensation from the firm, $c_1 < \bar{c}$. Consequently, the R&D expenditure of the firm includes the cost of developing proprietary features, $\bar{c} \cdot (1-\alpha) \cdot R$, and the cost of Open Source features, $c_1 \cdot \alpha \cdot R$.

The revenue of a single proprietary feature is a function of the level of disclosure, $\Psi(\alpha)$.[12] Revenues are generated only from features that are distributed as proprietary sources, $(1-\alpha)R$. One-period profits of the firm are achieved by subtracting its development costs on Open Source and proprietary features from its revenues.

The firm maximizes its one-period profits, $\pi$, by evaluating the trade-off between R&D expenditure on Open Source features vs. the expenditure on developing proprietary features and the revenues that it achieves:

$$\pi = (1-\alpha)\Psi(\alpha)R - [\bar{c}(1-\alpha)R + c_1\alpha R] = (1-\alpha)\Psi(\alpha)R - [\bar{c} - \alpha(\bar{c} - c_1)] \cdot R \quad (5.1)$$

Figure 5.1 illustrates the mechanism graphically, showing the consistency requirements among the variables. Given the change in the technical quality of software, $R$ (the horizontal axis in the north east quadrant), a firm chooses a degree of openness $\alpha_1$. $\alpha_1$ is the argument in the revenue equation, $\Psi(\alpha)$, and the revenue is determined in the south west quadrant. The revenue, $\Psi_1$, determines the profits in the following way. Revenue is generated only on closed software, and is defined as $\Psi_1 \cdot (1-\alpha_1)R$ (light grey plus medium grey). Total costs are the sum of open development costs (dark grey) plus closed costs (medium grey). Thus, profits are the difference between the profits on closed software and open development costs (light grey minus dark grey). Increasing $\alpha$ can increase the

and, hence, can freely be copied, disseminated and installed. However, in reality, full disclosure is more of a descriptive expression rather than an existing state, as part of the technical know-how always remains tacit within the domain of its inventors. The scenario of complete protection is also far from reality as firms disclose essential software components to developers of complementary applications. We assume that the technical know-how obtained from the share of proprietary software is only marginal.

[12] If a firm includes some proprietary and some Open Source features in its product, rivals can duplicate the non-proprietary features in their own product versions. Hence, ignoring the possibility that users are interested in "bundles" rather than in features, a firm can only extract revenues from its proprietary features.

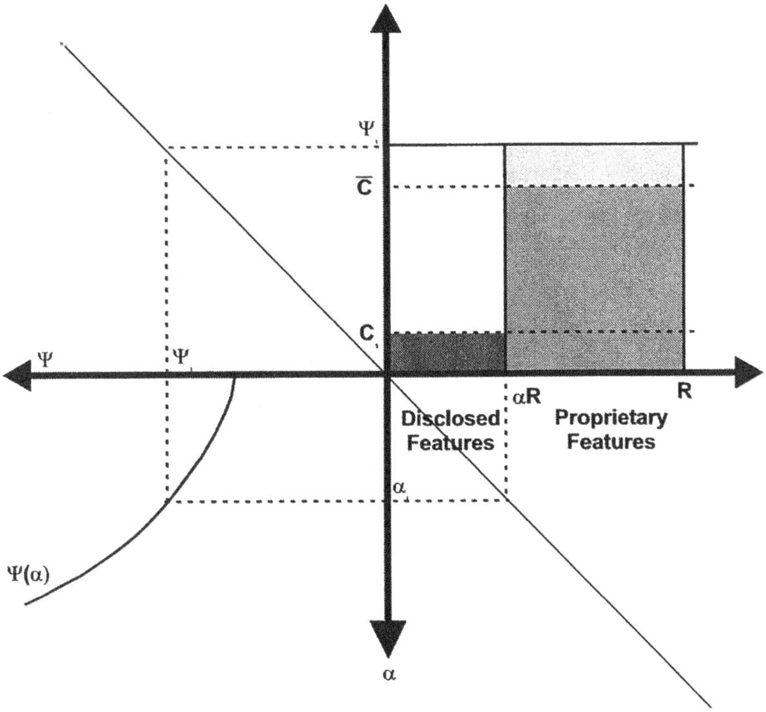


**Figure 5.1.** Illustration of the single period model.
For any given $R$, changes in $\alpha$ change both the proportion of $R$ on which the firm receives revenues and through $\Psi(\alpha)$ the revenue "per feature".

revenue per feature, but it decreases the quantity of software on which the firm earns revenues. This explanation captures the firm's basic trade–off.

A marginal increase in the degree of disclosure has three effects on the costs and gains of the firm:

(1) Revenues decrease by $\Psi(\alpha) \cdot R - (1-\alpha)\frac{d\Psi(\alpha)}{d\alpha} \cdot R$ as the firm expands the non–remunerative segment of the product,

(2) the total costs of Open Source development increase by $c_1 \cdot d\alpha \cdot R$, and

(3) the costs of in–house development decrease by $\bar{c} \cdot d\alpha \cdot R$.

The solution of the firm's problem depends heavily on revenue responsiveness to openness. First, we examine the extreme case in which revenue does not respond to openness.

Differentiate Equation 5.1 to find the cumulative effect on the profits of the firm:

$$\frac{d\pi}{d\alpha} = -\Psi(\alpha) \cdot R + (1-\alpha)\frac{d\Psi(\alpha)}{d\alpha} \cdot R + (\bar{c} - c_1) \cdot R \tag{5.2}$$

**Proposition 1** *When the revenue per module is fixed ($\Psi(\alpha) = \Psi$), the optimal strategy is to keep all software features proprietary.*

**Proof.** From Equation 5.2: $\frac{d\pi}{d\alpha} < 0$ when $\frac{d\Psi(\alpha)}{d\alpha} = 0$, so $\alpha^* = 0$. ■

If revenues do not respond to openness, the firm would prefer to keep its features undisclosed. However, an observation in today's software market is that firms are changing (notably, increasing) the degree of openness in their software development. In the extreme, they can extract no revenues from Open Source software. Thus, a change in the degree of openness must be accompanied by a change in revenues of proprietary features to maintain the level of firm's profits. Following Equation 5.2, we identify the conditions on revenue responsiveness for which (partial) openness is applied by the firm.

**Proposition 2** *If $\frac{\partial \Psi}{\partial \alpha} > \left[\frac{1}{1-\alpha} \cdot (\Psi(\alpha) - (\bar{c} - c_1))\right]$ at $\alpha = 0$ and $\Psi(1) > (\bar{c} - c_1)$ then $0 < \alpha^* < 1$.*

**Proof.** Find the terms in Equation 5.2 for which $\frac{d\pi}{d\alpha} > 0$ for $\alpha \to 0$ and for $\alpha = 1$. ■

An interesting benchmark then is the relationship between $\alpha$ and $\pi$ such that profits do not change as $\alpha$ changes.

Differentiate Equation 5.1 and set to zero. Re–arranging:

$$\Psi(\alpha)\Big|_{\alpha=\alpha_1} = (1-\alpha)\frac{d\Psi(\alpha)}{d\alpha}\Big|_{\alpha=\alpha_1} + (\bar{c} - c_1) \tag{5.3}$$

Or:

$$\frac{d\Psi(\alpha)}{\Psi(\alpha) + (\bar{c} - c_1)}\Big|_{\alpha=\alpha_1} = \frac{d\alpha}{1-\alpha}\Big|_{\alpha=\alpha_1} \tag{5.4}$$

By integrating the terms in Equation 5.4, we obtain a revenue function for stable profits:

$$\Psi^*(\alpha) = (\bar{c} - c_1) + \frac{\Psi_0}{1-\alpha}, \tag{5.5}$$

where $\Psi_0$ is constant. By substituting Equation 5.5 into Equation 5.1 we can generate the non–negative profits constraint: $\Psi_0 > c_1$.

Following this line of discussion we can state

**Proposition 3** *If $\Psi(\alpha)$ is continuous and $\Psi(\alpha^*) \gtrless (\bar{c} - c_1) + \frac{c_1}{1-\alpha^*}$ then a firm operating with $\alpha = \alpha^*$ will increase (decrease) its level of openness.*

**Proof.** As discussed above. ■

We can summarize these results briefly. If revenue is unresponsive to openness, software is only ever released as a proprietary product (Proposition 1). Further, if the revenue responds slowly to openness, the source code stays closed. However, if the revenue is highly responsive to openness, the firm would open its source code. But since no revenue on fully Open Source is generated, part of the features remain proprietary (Proposition 2). When there is an exogenous change in the relationship between revenue and openness, Proposition 3 describes the conditions on the change, such that a firm will increase or decrease its degree of openness.

## 5.4 Forward–Looking Firms

We extend the model to include intertemporal dynamics, keeping the basic terms and definitions of the previous model unchanged.[13] Define $R(t)$ as the increment of quality of software in period $t$ from the addition of new features, either by the users or by the firm. The firm decides *ex ante* what share of features, $\alpha \in [0, 1]$, is developed as Open Source. The revenue received from a single proprietary feature changes with the degree of disclosure. In this dynamic setting of the model, we re–interpret $\Psi(\alpha)$ as the present discounted value of the gross revenue from a closed–source feature. Thus, $\Psi(\alpha(t)) \cdot R(t)(1 - \alpha(t))$ is the present discounted value (PDV) of the revenue from technical advance in period $t$:

$$RV(t) = (1 - \alpha)\Psi(\alpha)R(t) \tag{5.6}$$

The total expenditure of the firm on R&D in period $t$ is allocated between development of open and closed sources:

$$RD(t) = \alpha R(t) \cdot c_1 + (1 - \alpha)R(t) \cdot \bar{c} = [\bar{c} - \alpha(\bar{c} - c_1)]R(t). \tag{5.7}$$

[13] The dynamics of the two models represent the behaviours of myopic and non–myopic firms, as the forward–looking firm captures a multi–period problem in which the firm re–invests its profits in R&D. Following this rationale, one can also interpret the costs and the revenues in the basic version of the model as present values of cash flow.

Assume that a constant share of firm's profits in each period, $\rho \in (0,1)$, is invested in R&D in the following period.[14] Therefore, the total investments in R&D are determined by the profits of the firm in the preceding period, $\pi(t-1)$, so $RD(t)$ is:

$$RD(t) \equiv \rho \cdot \pi(t-1) \tag{5.8}$$

Subtract the costs of R&D from the revenues of the firm (Equation 5.6) to obtain the PDV of features introduced in period $t$:

$$\pi(t) = (1-\alpha)\Psi(\alpha)R(t) - [\bar{c} - \alpha(\bar{c} - c_1)]R(t) = (1-\alpha)\Psi(\alpha)R(t) - \rho\pi(t-1) \tag{5.9}$$

Substitute Equation 5.7 into Equation 5.8 to obtain $R(t)$ as a function of the degree of openness, $\alpha$, and firm expenditure on R&D in period $t$:

$$R(t) = \frac{RD(t)}{\bar{c} - \alpha(\bar{c} - c_1)} = \frac{\rho\pi(t-1)}{\bar{c} - \alpha(\bar{c} - c_1)} \tag{5.10}$$

Substitute $R(t)$ into Equation 5.9 to obtain an intertemporal link between the firm's profits in successive periods:

$$\pi(t) = [\frac{(1-\alpha)\Psi(\alpha)\rho}{\bar{c} - \alpha(\bar{c} - c_1)} - \rho]\pi(t-1) \tag{5.11}$$

The firm's goal is to maximize the present value of its stream of profits. If $\delta$ is the discount factor, its objective function is

$$\Pi = \sum_{t=0}^{\infty} \delta^t \pi(t) \tag{5.12}$$

Equations 5.11 and 5.12 show that we can use a simple induction argument to find optimal levels of $\alpha$. In each period the firm's problem is identical to that of the previous period. The profits of last period, $\pi(t-1)$, serve only as a scaling factor in the optimization problem of period $t$. On the assumption that the system converges to a steady state, a simple induction argument shows that $\alpha^*$ is constant.

Differentiating $\pi(t)$ with respect to $\alpha$:

$$\frac{\partial \pi}{\partial \alpha} = \frac{-\Psi(\alpha)c_1}{[\alpha c_1 + (1-\alpha)\bar{c}]^2} + \frac{(1-\alpha)\frac{\partial \Psi}{\partial \alpha}}{[\alpha c_1 + (1-\alpha)\bar{c}]} \tag{5.13}$$

Following Equation 5.13 we can state

[14] Empirical evidence supports the assumption that R&D is a fixed proportion of profits. The intensity of R&D in the French software and information sector is estimated to be 14 per cent of their sales and it remains relatively stable over time (Abi–Saad et al., 2001).

**Proposition 4** *If $\Psi(\alpha)$ is constant then $\alpha^* = 0$.*

**Proof.** If revenues are fixed with respect to $\alpha$ ($\Psi(\alpha) = const.$), then from Equation 5.13 we see that $\frac{\partial \pi}{\partial \alpha} < 0$ and it is optimal for a firm to keep all of its software proprietary ($\alpha^* = 0$). ∎

This proposition contains the apparent result that firms do not open their source in the short run, in order to make rapid advances, and then reap benefits in the future by closing their source. This is explained by the fact that firms never generate revenues on modules that were developed in the open paradigm. Any feature developed as Open Source is available to all competitors. Hence, if there are potential revenues from that feature, all competitors will offer it, thus eliminating it as a source of product differentiation, and so eliminating revenues. Only features developed as closed source contain potential revenues. In this model, rapid advances today do not result in higher revenues tomorrow. For this sort of investment to be possible, the model would have to include some secondary effects of rapid advance. Perhaps working through network externalities and sufficiently rapid increase in the installed base can capture the market share effects.[15]

If the change in revenue per feature compensates for the change in the total income of the firm from modifying its open/closed mix (that is, changing $\alpha$), then it is possible that it may be optimal for the firm to open its source code. From Equation 5.13 follows:

**Proposition 5** *(a) If $\Psi(0) \geq \left[\frac{\partial \Psi(0)}{\partial \alpha} \cdot \frac{\bar{c}}{c_1}\right]$ at $\alpha = 0$ then $\alpha^* = 0$.*

(b) If $\Psi(0) \geq \left[\frac{\partial \Psi(0)}{\partial \alpha} \cdot \frac{\bar{c}}{c_1}\right]$ at $\alpha = 0$ and $\Psi'(1) \leq 0$ at $\alpha = 1$ then $0 < \alpha^* < 1$.

**Proof.** See Appendix A. ∎

Finally, in parallel with the analysis of the myopic firm, setting $\partial \pi / \partial \alpha = 0$ in Equation 5.13 and solving for $\Psi(\alpha)$ gives

$$\Psi^*(\alpha) = \left[\bar{c} + c_1 \frac{\alpha}{1-\alpha}\right] \cdot \Psi_0. \tag{5.14}$$

If Equation 5.14 holds, then $\alpha^* \varepsilon (0,1)$. This gives us directly the following proposition.

[15] On this issue see, for example, Givon et al. (1995) and Laffont et al. (1998).

**Proposition 6** *If $\Psi(\alpha)$ is continuous and $\Psi(\alpha_1) \gtrless \left[\bar{c} + c_1 \frac{\alpha_1}{1-\alpha_1}\right] \cdot \Psi_0$ at $\alpha = \alpha_1$, $\alpha_1 \varepsilon (0, 1)$, then the firm will increase (decrease) its level of openness.*

**Proof.** See Appendix A. ∎

Propositions 2 and 5 and Propositions 3 and 6 give different results for optimal amounts of openness and the critical openness–revenue relationship. These differences are driven by the fact that in the myopic case (Propositions 2 and 3) the degree of technical advance is fixed in each period and the R&D expenditure varies, whereas in the non–myopic case, since R&D expenditures are determined by the last period's profits, the reverse is true.

Notice that if revenues are fixed with respect to openness, technical advance is at a minimum ($\frac{\partial \pi}{\partial \alpha} < 0$ in Equation 5.13; and technical advance each period, $R(t)$, is determined by profits the previous period: $R(t) = \rho\pi(t-1)$). However, if the goal is to maximize technical advance, the optimal development mode is entirely Open Source, which is approached if revenues increase rapidly with openness. It is almost certainly the case, though, that maximizing technical advance is sub–optimal due to its effects on accelerating depreciation. From a policy maker's perspective (driven by the view that some intermediate rate of technical advance will maximize social welfare), generating an interior amount of openness is desirable and has to be supported by a complementary pricing mechanism whereby the effective revenue to a firm from advance in its software's technical quality increases with openness, but only to a point. This is likely to be a non–trivial policy problem.

In the model developed above, it was not possible for a firm to capture revenues from anything developed in the Open Source mode. It could be, though, that due to reputation effects or packaging effects, a firm may be able to generate revenues from these features. This can be captured in the model by introducing the parameter $\Psi_1$. It is reasonable to assume that while $\bar{c} > c_1$ similarly $\overline{\Psi} > \Psi_1$. Clearly, if $\overline{\Psi} - \bar{c} < \Psi_1 - c_1$ then the optimal strategy for any firm is to embrace Open Source for all of its development. The more interesting case is when $\overline{\Psi} - \bar{c} > \Psi_1 - c_1$. In this case, the analysis follows in a straightforward way, re–writing the revenue definition in Equation 5.6 as $RV(t) = [\alpha\Psi_1(\alpha) + (1 - \alpha)\Psi_2(\alpha)] \cdot R(t)$. Still, however, no interior solution exists when revenues do not change with the degree of openness.

## 5.5 The Dynamics of Prices of Proprietary Sources

The decision on the level of disclosure is largely affected by the pricing policy of the firm. In former sections of this chapter, we discovered that the firm's profits are closely correlated with the marginal price to disclosure ratio. Hence, the firm's pricing policy has a major effect on both the firm's strategy and on its profits. The price–disclosure curve for forward–looking firms (Equation 5.14) is illustrated in Figure 5.2. For most values of $\alpha$, the marginal price of proprietary features increases very moderately. As $\alpha$ approaches 1 (full disclosure), the price increases very steeply. Further, the minimal price of proprietary features changes with the cost of in–house and Open Source R&D. When the cost of developing software within the firm increases in comparison to the cost of Open Source projects, it would be harder for the firm to recover its expenses and it would choose to distribute larger proportion of its features as proprietary software. When the cost of developing Open Source features is closer to the cost of in–house R&D (that is, the ratio $\frac{\bar{c}}{c_1}$ decreases), the the prices of proprietary features increases very rapidly for smaller values of $\alpha$ and the firms would choose to disclose larger parts of its source code.

As concluded in Section 5.2 and 5.3 above, when the degree of disclosure increases, the price for proprietary features increases too (for both myopic and far–sighted firms). From the social welfare perspective, this is a conflicting situation. On the one hand, policy makers attempt to foster the diffusion of advanced technologies to increase the level of social welfare (in terms of *technical quality* of the technology in use). Software developers are willing to offer larger shares of their products as Open Source in return for charging higher prices for a smaller share of proprietary features. However, higher prices will reduce the demand for advanced proprietary features and will hinder the adoption of the technology by many users, who will favour partial functionality and less expensive products. On the other hand, policy makers perceive disclosure as a positive effect on innovation and technical change, as individual knowledge is shared among other users and firms. Further, Open Source communities can carry out trivial tasks and enable firms to utilize their resources by allocating more personnel to R&D. Provision of a price subsidy for proprietary features can increase both the diffusion of the technology and knowledge spillovers from Open Source products. The level of the subsidy as a share of the price of proprietary features, $s(\alpha)$, can be determined as

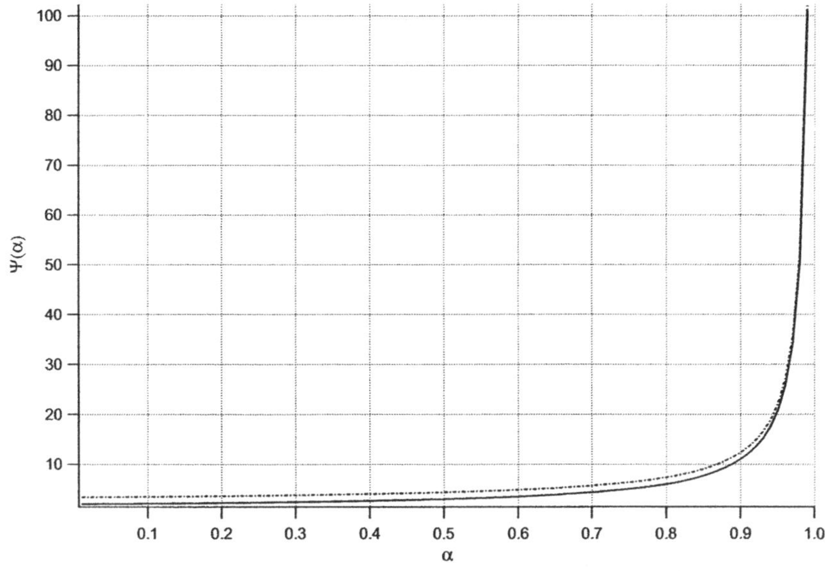


**Figure 5.2.** Minimal price of a proprietary feature as a function of the degree of disclosure for different ratios of development costs: $\bar{c}/c_1 = 2$ (continuous line) and $\bar{c}/c_1 = 3.33$ (broken line).

follows:

$$s(\alpha) = \frac{\Psi(\alpha)}{\Psi(\alpha = 0)} - 1 \tag{5.15}$$

When the price of proprietary features increases, so does the subsidy $s(\alpha)$ for any value of disclosure. The subsidy curve shifts to the left as $c_1$ increases towards $\bar{c}$, and *vice versa*, suggesting that the subsidy will be higher when firms choose to develop more features in–house. Alternatively, this subsidy can deploy public support to Open Source communities to develop free–use alternatives.

The analysis of the links between disclosure, price and single–period profits in Section 5.2 reveals negative correlation between disclosure and profit when fixed prices are chosen (see also Figure 5.4a). However, when the price of proprietary features is selected as a function of $\alpha$, the result is a non–linear profit function, $\pi$. The complex behaviour of the profit function enhances the difficulty to derive generic "rules of thumb" that will help policy makers in steering the strategies

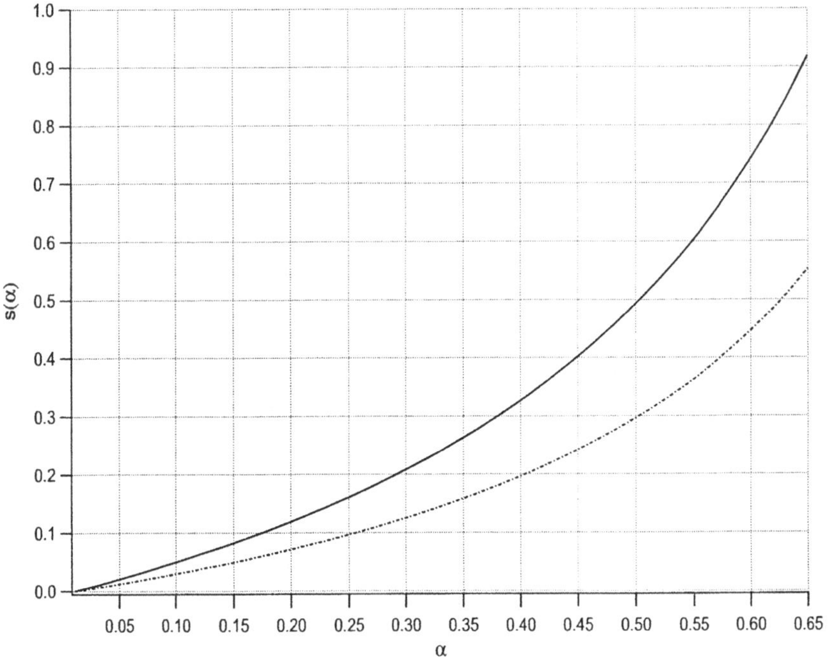


**Figure 5.3.** The level of subsidy as a function of the degree of disclosure for different ratios of development costs: $\frac{\bar{c}}{c_1} = 2$ (continuous line) and $\frac{\bar{c}}{c_1} = 3.33$ (broken line). $s(\alpha)$=the increase in the price of proprietary feature.

of software firms, as non–linearity exists even in simple scenarios where the price $\Psi(\alpha)$ is a linear function of $\alpha$ (Figures 5.4b and 5.4c). In some cases, as stated in Proposition 5(b) and exemplified by Figure 5.4b, an intermediate level of disclosure (that is, a software "hybrid") provides maximum profits, whereas full protection or complete openness are less profitable.

## 5.6 Discussion

We have seen the following strong result: The negative relationship between the degree of openness and profits implies that a profit maximizing firm will keep all its code proprietary. Yet, application of Open Source methodology gains popularity among commercial firms, which publicly release the source code of their products.

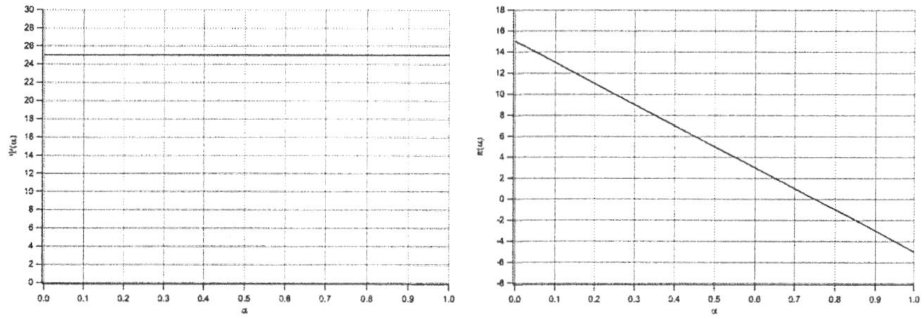


(Fig. 5.4a)

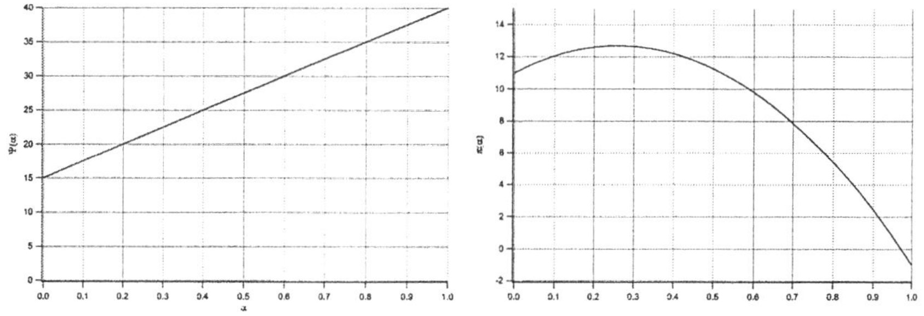


(Fig. 5.4b)

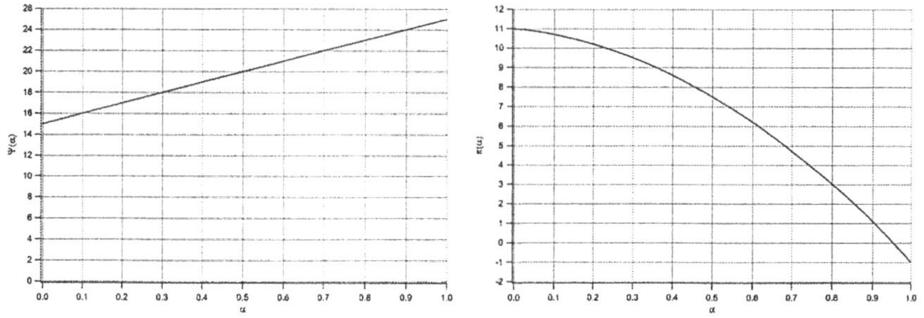


(Fig. 5.4c)

**Figure 5.4.** Myopic firm's one–period profits ($\pi$) in various pricing strategies of proprietary features ($\Psi(\alpha)$): (a) fixed price; (b) price increases with disclosure; (c) Price increases with disclosure (different set of parameters).

What is their motivation?

In the model, the increment of technical quality, $R(t)$, is determined simply by the R&D expenditure and the degree of openness, since Open Source and proprietary software have different costs. If Open Source has an independent effect on quality (for example it is more reliable, as some suggest), then this would support an increase in revenue as openness increases.

A second explanation has to do with quantities. Implicitly, $\Psi(\alpha)$ is the revenue attributed to the current increment of technical quality. If larger openness increases sales, then $\Psi(\alpha)$ increases with $\alpha$. This is made stronger by the observation that for software goods marginal cost is essentially zero, so average costs fall with output. The motivation for a firm to open its source code (apart from potential threats from the Justice Department), can be to increase its sales. In a larger model, in which network externalities would play a role in competition for a market share, firms are more motivated to choose Open Source strategies, as an increasing market share can have the positive effect of locking a competitor out of the market and providing a monopoly in the future.

This chapter has presented a lower bound on the responsiveness of revenues to the degree of openness for software firms that choose strategic application of Open Source for their products. Critical in this bound is the difference in the costs of developing a module as open versus closed source for the firm. It is important to remember here that Open Source development is not free, even though a significant proportion of the inputs are.

We obtain a knife–edged result such that if the revenue increases rapidly enough with openness, the optimal strategy changes from entirely proprietary to a strictly positive degree of openness. Like most knife–edge results, this one is extreme, but it does suggest that following certain environment changes in which it becomes possible to capture more revenues from Open Source or reduction in the costs of Open Source development, we would expect to see firms that historically developed only proprietary software moving aggressively towards Open Source.[16] We have seen this strong move from proprietary software to Open Source with IBM's Eclipse, Netscape's Mozilla project and Sun's move from Star Office to create Open Office, among others. Using this idea as a basis for further analysis, it is possible to pursue the investigation of Open Source as a firm strategy. Understanding why firms engage in this strategy then devolves to understanding the

[16] Note that incentives of firms to invest in R&D are not endogenized in this model.

mechanisms by which this strategy increases revenues or how the responsiveness of revenues rises above the threshold.

## 5.7 Conclusions

IPR regimes for software technologies have evolved since the mid 1980s, aiming to resolve issues of piracy and unauthorized use by expanding the guidelines of traditional legislation, that is, patents and copyrights, and by including information technologies in their scope of protection. However, along the same period, alternative models of intellectual property use, based on the tradition of Free or Open Source, in which a rapid diffusion of unprotected software is used as a basis for profit–making ventures, have developed.

The existing body of literature explores positive externalities in software piracy and infringements of intellectual property in computer programs. For example, emergence of network effects generates higher utility for users and expands the diffusion of software products among legal users and their propensity to pay for the product. However, this faculty of thought treats computer programs in a form of final products (that is, compiled software packages) and does not evaluate the role of knowledge spillovers in advancing the technology, had the source code of computer programs been made accessible to skilled users.

Our model includes "production externalities", contributions of users to the technical quality and to the functionality of software, positively correlated with the degree of openness. The model analyzes the relations between software protection, its price and firms' profits in markets of myopic and forward–looking firms. The first part of the model presents new insights on the links between openness and firms' profits. When a fixed–price policy is applied for proprietary features, the correlation between disclosure and profits is negative. Firms would prefer to migrate from in–house development to Open Source methodologies if higher profitability is guaranteed. The model supports the rationale that firms prefer to apply the "*bazaar model*" of Open Source on the traditional modes of software development only if they expect higher rewards than the gains from proprietary products. Hence, our model approves the strategic rationale beyond the decision of firms to disclose their main asset, the source code, in particular conditions. Further, when the price of proprietary features does not change with the degree of openness, complete protection is favourable in terms of firms' profits and technological performance. However, price dynamics depend on the difference between the costs of developing software as Open Source or in–house, among other attributes of the firm's strategy. The closer those costs become, the higher the price of proprietary features is at any degree of disclosure. Those results emphasize the complexity of the behaviour in markets of software technologies. Policies that aim at fostering technology by modifying pricing, R&D costs and disclosure may divert the technological trajectory to different directions than meant. Hence, innovation and technical change in ICT require implementation of a diverse and implausible approach towards software openness, rather than application of a general and somewhat sophistic framework. Another important lesson is associated with the use of fiscal tools to foster higher degrees of innovation and technical quality in software products. As the firm is impelled to maximize its profits in the short and in the long run, higher degrees of technical quality of software are achieved at the cost of lower openness of the source code. However, policy makers may maintain the pace of technological development by implementing subsidy schemes that elevate the demand of users for the non–disclosed share of the technology. By reducing the prices of proprietary features, for example by directly subsidizing the price of proprietary features, endowing firms' R&D in return for source code disclosure or establishing free–software consortia, technology would progress more rapidly, as skilled users would devote their skills and efforts to promote technical performance and quality of software technologies.

## 5.8 Chapter Appendix: Symbols Used in this Chapter

**Parameters:**

| | |
|---|---|
| $\bar{c}$ | Cost of developing a new feature in–house by the firm. |
| $c_1$ | Cost of developing a new feature via Open Source communities. |
| $\rho$ | Share of revenues invested in R&D. |
| $\delta$ | Discount factor. |

**Variables:**

| | |
|---|---|
| $\alpha$ | Degree of software openness. |
| $\alpha^*$ | Optimal degree of software openness. |
| $R$ | Incremental change in the technical quality of software. |
| $\Psi(\alpha)$ | Revenue of a proprietary feature. |
| $\pi$ | Firm's profits. |
| $R(t)$ | Incremental change in the technical quality of software in period $t$. |
| $RV(t)$ | Present discounted value of the revenue in period $t$. |
| $RD(t)$ | R&D expenditure in period $t$. |
| $\Pi$ | Present value of firm's stream of profits. |
| $s(\alpha)$ | Subsidy for an Open Source feature. |

# 6

# Designed for Innovation: The Structure of IPR Regimes and the Evolution of Information Technologies

## 6.1 Introduction

Innovation in software and information technologies is characterized by an ongoing process that produces a variety of goods that differ in quality and performance. Most information technologies develop in a cumulative manner, as recent technical knowledge gradually builds upon prior know–how and is continuously applied in new products and contexts, whereas scientific and technological breakthroughs rarely occur (Scotchmer, 1991).[1] Empirical evidence describes the development of most technologies as an evolutionary rather than a revolutionary process (Freeman and Soete, 1997). *Technological breakthroughs* seem to be rare exceptions rather than the norm in the majority of technological fields.

The impact of innovation extends beyond new product versions and largely affects incumbent technologies. Introduction of products with advanced features, higher quality and improved performance removes older versions from the market. In many technologies, including ICT, innovation is described as a process

[1]The process of innovation in other industrial sectors, such as consumer electronics (Wade, 1995), telecommunications (Maloney and McCormick, 1995) and automobiles (Kim, 1998) is similar to technological advance in information technologies. However, innovation in other industries, such as glass fabrication, is characterized by larger numbers of *technological discontinuities* (that is, more significant and less frequent improvements of the technology) (Anderson and Tushman, 1990).

of *creative destruction*, in which new technologies evolve on the ruins of their technological predecessors (Schumpeter, 1975; pp. 82–85).

Software developers continuously release improved software versions during short and fixed periods. Major shares of users, in turn, upgrade their installed versions when improved applications are introduced or replace the installed software with rival programs.[2]

The effects of sequential innovation and creative destruction on social welfare are somewhat ambiguous from the social planner's standpoint. On the one hand, continuous diffusion and implementation of improved products enhance economic efficiencies by providing better technical prospects, quality and performance. On the other hand, adoption of new technologies and disposal of older products entail significant social costs.

The influence of creative destruction on the market is emphasized or restrained by the application of different IPR regimes. Theories of technological diffusion and economic growth show the significance of IPRs in stimulating innovation through disclosure of technical know–how and knowledge spillovers between firms (for example Mansfield, 1986; Dosi, 1988). The positive impact of the legal regime on innovation and technical change is encapsulated in fostering disclosure of novel technical knowledge through patenting.

Those desirable effects of the patent system on innovation and technological learning of innovators are offset by provision of long period monopoly rights. Firms, other than the patent–holder, are prohibited from exploiting protected know–how or even from introducing improved product versions, unless they significantly differ from patent–protected technologies. Consequently, firms that are engaged in R&D activities enter *patent races* against rival developers, in which the first to innovate dominates the technology (and potential markets) for the patent lifetime. Other firms can enter similar technological markets with competing products without infringing the patent–holders' rights if they succeed in "inventing around" patent–protected inventions or develop distinguished product features that lie beyond the scope of existing patents. Alternatively, similar products can be released by rivals after patents expire, or by licensing protected inventions.

The case of software patents is of a particular interest. The inclusion of software and algorithms within the scope of patents by the USPTO propelled a con-

[2] In many cases, users must upgrade the software in use to maintain technical support.

tinuous debate on the contribution of patents to innovation and economic growth. The effects of the frequent changes in the patent policy were linked also to other sectors of the knowledge–based economy, where computer programs are extensively used and may have major impact on recent technological developments, for example multimedia (Mansell and Steinmueller, 2000; Ch. 7), electronic commerce (Kuester and Thompson, 2001) and bioinformatics (Schonfeld and Restaino, 2002).

Further, intellectual property rights in software and information technologies have developed in reactive rather than in pro–active ways. Legislation was adapted to single precedents and often lagged by more than a decade after technological advances (Cowan and Harison, 2001). As the "old" patent system has incrementally been modified in an attempt to fit to the characteristics of emerging technologies, historical effects created a regime partially mal–suited to the needs of new products and technologies (David, 1993). Yet, the main issue of whether IPRs may elevate or impede technological diffusion and innovation in software remains unresolved.

In the large body of legal literature on IPRs, contradictory arguments over the contribution of IPRs to innovation persist. On the one hand, empirical evidence indicates high rates of software piracy worldwide, which result in lower levels of revenues and R&D expenditure. On the other hand, imitation and reverse–engineering entails the advantages of acquiring broader knowledge over a large number of product features.[3] Moreover, patent protection over software technologies contributes to the emergence of concentrated market structures. If firms cannot develop new features that exceed the patent–protected level of the technology, they are not allowed to release their products to the market. Firms that patent early inventions can preempt rivals from entering the market by suing them for infringing their patent rights, even though those firms have never exploited any of their patented inventions. Legal and economic scholars often argue that the development of information technologies is offset by the long patent duration and by lack of novelty in many software patents issued by the USPTO. The value of patents is largely influenced by the ability of firms to gain exclusive rights over a variety of technologies and to control the access rights of competitors to them, and not necessarily by their innovative or technical merits. Consequently, patent–holders are granted monopoly rights over a wide range of applications of their

[3] See discussion in Chapter 3.

invention. Further, minor changes in the structure of software patent claims can become a major vehicle for raising the value of patents, as "by understanding the claim styles ... the practitioner can spend a few extra dollars and a few additional hours when initially drafting and prosecuting a software patent application to derive millions more dollars in value from an issued software patent." (Witek, 1996)

Proposals for alternative regimes aimed at balancing incentives for innovators against knowledge disclosure, overcoming major shortcomings in the design of the present legislation by offering voluntary dismissal of intellectual property claims (for example the Open Source movement) or by modifying the existing Law. Samuelson et al. (1994) propose enactment of *sui–generis* regimes, specially formed to provide software technologies and products with adequate legal protection. Merges (1999) applies a different approach and suggests reforming the administrative organization of the patent system and the examination process of patent applications in the USPTO with minute alterations of the present legislation, in order to enhance the quality of software patents and to reduce the "error rate" of issuing invalid patents.

This chapter aims at developing a coherent view of market dynamics and innovation by constructing a dynamic model of the market. The model simulates the interactions between software producers and users and their choices, while developing and adopting new products. First, we review the methodology and provide formal presentation of the model. Then, we present the results of the model and assess the impact of different legal regimes on the pace of innovation, on the market structure and on the emergence of a dominant technology. Finally, we draw conclusions and policy implications regarding the suitability of different IPR regimes to promote innovation in software and information technologies.

## 6.2 Methodology

We apply a multi–period model to identify the links between the design of the patent regime and the evolution of software technologies and the market dynamics. Those attributes are projected and analyzed under different structures of the market and alternative designs of the legal regime.

In contrast to much of the literature on intellectual property rights and technology diffusion, this study emphasizes the heterogeneity of software users and explicitly incorporates the technical performance of the technology into the decisions of both users and software producers with different levels of R&D expenditure and know–how. The model also represents releases of new products and technologies that create waves of creative destruction, as consumers prefer purchasing updated product versions over older generations of the technology (Aghion and Howitt, 1992).

On the supply side, firms introduce their own product versions by developing them in–house or by legally imitating rival products (that is, without infringing valid patents of their competitors). Firms also patent their inventions if they achieve sufficient degree of technical novelty.

The design of the patent regime is defined by patent length (the duration of exclusive rights over inventions) and height (the minimal degree of technical advance required for granting new patents). The functionality and performance of software products are represented through the level of their *technical quality.*

The model builds upon insights from several literatures. First, software innovation is highly evolutionary in that it tends to come in versions or generations, each being a modification of its predecessor. Consequently, early computer programs are substituted by advanced applications, and new products often dominate the whole market (Evans et al., 2002). The technical quality of product features is described by a *quality ladder*, a continuum on which products are represented and can be compared according to technological merit. Similar representation of products on a quality ladder appears in O'Donoghue et al. (1998), where higher R&D expenditure shortens the time between inventions. However, our model is loyal to the characteristics of the software development process and differs from O'Donoghue et al.'s model in several aspects: Inventions and product improvements (albeit minor) are continuously generated and released, whereas in O'Donoghue et al. the time between inventions depends on the investment of the firm in R&D.

In our model the firm's investments in R&D are taken as a share of the firm's revenues and the size of technical progress increases with R&D expenditure. Consequently, decreasing revenues are followed by lower degrees of R&D expenditure. This can result in lower innovative output of the firm in the short term. In the long term, lower levels of R&D investments induce slower development of innovation and advanced technologies. Hence, the intensity of competition and the market share of the firm may largely affect its revenues and R&D investments and the technological advances that the firm achieves.[4]

Our model captures the essence of the product variety and complexity of software technologies by defining a product as a set of multiple features. Every feature is positioned on a separate quality ladder. To compare, O'Donoghue et al.'s model represents each product as a point on a single quality ladder. Products may have a relative advantage in some features, while other features may be technically inferior to those of other products.

Innovation and the firm's learning are of a continuous and cumulative nature. Knowledge is acquired by firms, cached, and serves as a basis for generating new technological competences and advanced product features. The evolution of the technology is described in the model as an incremental process, in which technology endogenously develops through diffusion of improved product versions.[5]

Patents have a major impact on the firm's strategic and competitive behaviour. Its ability to compete with new product versions is more or less restricted due to the design of the patent regime. Technical achievements and advanced product features can be produced as long as no patents are infringed.

Economists usually emphasize the role of patents in providing incentives to innovate in return for knowledge disclosure (see, for example, David, 1993). However, Green and Scotchmer (1995) suggest that a somewhat different approach should be taken while examining the effects of the patent regime on technologies characterized by cumulative and sequential innovation. In those technologies, the profits of second-generation producers, who improve upon existing goods, generate higher profits than the inventors of those products. In many cases, second-generation producers directly compete with the inventors with advantageous product versions. Hence, the patent system functions as a profit-sharing mechanism that ensures that inventors are able to recoup their costs from second-generation producers who benefit from their know-how. Thereupon, "[W]hen innovation is cumulative, an important incentive problem is to ensure that each innovator is rewarded enough to take account of the benefits conferred on future innovators ... Intellectual property law has a rich set of policy levers, both for providing profit

[4]Conner and Rumelt (1991) base their analysis of software piracy on a similar perception of the market.

[5]A similar model was developed by Silverberg and Verspagen (1994) to assess how innovation and learning affect economic growth. Bessen and Maskin (2000) assess the influence of stronger and weaker patent regimes on the development of software in markets with two symmetric firms.

and for governing the division of it" (Scotchmer, 2005; pp. 170–171). Following this argument, the dimensions of the patent regime can be interpreted as follows: The minimal inventive step of patents[6] provides the first inventors with the right to block competitors who build upon their inventions and enables them to recoup their R&D investments, while patent length determines the period in which they are able to deter rivals from using and improving upon them. Despite recognizing cumulative innovation as a long–term process that varies and significantly changes the technological landscape over time, most studies, including those of Green and Scotchmer (1995), O'Donoghue et al. (1998) and Denicoló and Zanchettin (2002) examine the innovative process via equilibrium–based models with homogeneous agents and two stages ("periods").

A large literature in industrial organization is used as a basis to represent the effects of IPR protection on different aspects of competition. Models of the patent regime provide a conceptual framework through which use of IPRs to manipulate market position can be observed. Gilbert and Newbery (1982) explore the relations between the structure of patent rights, the use of preemptive patenting to block new entrants, the level of R&D expenditure and the resulting technical progress within a static frame–of–analysis. Reinganum (1983) furthers Gilbert and Newbery's basic model and compares R&D investments of an incumbent monopolist (whose market position is empowered by patents or by other means) with those of a potential entrant ("challenger") in a game theoretic model with a stochastic inventive process. She concludes that incumbents are likely to invest in R&D less than new entrants, due to their dominant position in the market. Hence, provision of broad patent rights to incumbent firms would lower their propensity to develop new products and would preempt other firms from competing in the market and from furthering technology. Klemperer (1990) and Gilbert and Shapiro (1990) present neo–classical models with a tradeoff between patent length and breadth and discover the optimal patent design for different degrees of monopoly revenues (that is, the innovator's expected "reward"). Green and Scotchmer (1995) assess the potential effects of the patent design (in terms of length and breadth) on the structure of the market and argue that broader scope enables first–inventors to proceed to developing the next stage of innovation without fearing fierce competition, as rivals are deterred from producing improved product versions that infringe existing patents. Further, Merges and Nelson (1994) conclude that "there

[6] Scotchmer (2005) uses the term *leading breadth* to describe the same parameter.

[is no] reason to believe that more narrowly drawn patents would have damped the incentives of the pioneers and other early comers to the field. In cumulative systems technologies, superior design, production, and marketing rather than strong patent protection, are the principal source of profit" (Merges and Nelson, 1994; p. 21).

Our study develops a different approach that incorporates the essence of innovation in software technologies as a long–term and cumulative process with the strategies of firms that operate within technological, IP–protected environment. Therefore, the effects of legislation on innovation and market dynamics are investigated over long periods. The model is based on a dynamic framework that includes heterogeneous users and firms. Products include a set of features and represented through a set of quality ladders, which ensures variation of products, consumers' preferences and firms' choices. Innovation is represented as a long–term and continuous process, in which technology gradually evolves over multiple periods, hence capturing events that are beyond the timeline of other models. Finally, the model explores how various structures of the patent regime and the market (defined by the number of firms) affect the evolution of information technologies.

The model provides a test–bed to explore the impact of different IPR regimes on the development of technology within a large variety of market terms and to assess how the evolution of information technologies is affected by the structure of the market and by the legal regime. The model entertains the possibility that regulators can change the dimensions of patents to enhance the degree of technological progress. It can also be employed to produce benchmark analyses of various designs of the patent regime under different degrees of competition.

## 6.3 The Model

### 6.3.1 Description

The model represents economy with several firms. Each firm continuously develops a single product that competes in quality and price. Technology is represented as a set of technical features and products are described by the technical quality of their features.

Demand arises from a large population of heterogeneous consumers with diverse preferences for the various product features. Preferences of users are represented by a vector of *perceived qualities*, the value given to product features by users.[7] Users maximize utility by repeatedly choosing between upgrading the product in use and purchasing another product. They decide which software to use by comparing the prices of products and the technical properties with their own preferences.[8] The utility of consumers increases when the "distance" between the quality and their own preferences is lower, or when the price decreases.[9]

Every period firms improve one feature, which is selected by a rule of thumb based on an *address model*: Each firm calculates the average preferences of users and compares them to the quality its own product. Then, it chooses the least advanced feature in comparison to the average preference. Firms can improve the technical quality of features through internal R&D, imitation, or application of patented know–how whose protection has expired. The amount dedicated to R&D is taken as a fixed share of the revenues in the last period. Quality improvements are positively correlated with the amount of R&D. Every period firms distribute installation versions and product upgrades and determine different prices for them.

Firms patent their inventions if they are sufficiently novel. We assume that the costs of patenting are marginal. Products with improved features are released when they do not infringe patents of other firms or when they are sufficiently novel (and then they are also patented). Otherwise, firms are prohibited from disseminating products with improved features and must keep them as part of their internal know–how.

The following section provides a formal presentation of the model.

### 6.3.2 The Market

The model consists of $M$ firms. Each firm produces and distributes one product with $J$ technological features. $Q_{ij}(t)$ denotes the technical quality of feature $j$ of firm $i$'s product that is released to the market in period $t$. $q_{ij}(t)$ measures technical know–how that remains in–house and is not embedded in its product. Hence, the total know–how of the firm is $\overline{Q_{ij}}(t) = Q_{ij}(t) + q_{ij}(t)$.

Firms determine two price levels for their products: $\overline{p_i}(t)$ for installation ver-

[7]For example, some users would prefer purchasing a product with detailed graphic interfaces, while others find those feature less importantly than advanced communication protocols.

[8]In some cases, network externalities are important for choosing technology. However, in this model they are ignored for the sake of simplicity.

[9]The *distance* is determined by summing up the difference between users' preferences and the technical quality of features.

sion and $\underline{p_i}(t)$ for the upgrade. $\overline{p_i}(t)$ is bigger than or equal to $\underline{p_i}(t)$, as the firm decides. Formally:

$$p_i(t) = \begin{cases} \overline{p_i}(t) & \text{, if } I_n(t) \neq I_n(t-1) \quad \text{(user changes the product in use)} \\ \underline{p_i}(t) & \text{, if } I_n(t) = I_n(t-1) \quad \text{(user upgrades the product in use)} \end{cases} \tag{6.1}$$

where $I_n(t)$ is the product used by consumer $n$ in period $t$.

On the demand side, $N$ consumers with heterogeneous preferences repeatedly choose one of the products. Every period users may change the product in use or upgrade it. Each consumer's preferences are defined by vector $\vec{V_n} = (V_{n_1}, V_{n_2}, ..., V_{n_J})$. Heterogeneity enters here as different consumers have different preferences, formalized by set of $\vec{V_n}$ and distributed as $J$–variate normal.

The decision which product to adopt is taken on the basis of quality and price. Users measure the distance $d_{in}(t)$ between their preferences and the quality of products or alternatively, the extent to which their "desires" are not satisfied:

$$d_{in}(t) = \sum_{j=1}^{J} [V_{nj} - Q_{ij}(t)], \qquad \forall V_{nj} > Q_{ij}(t) \tag{6.2}$$

The utility that consumer $n$ derives from product $i$ is based on the distance between her preferences and the quality of the product (Equation 6.2) and on the price (Equation 6.1):

$$U_{ni}(t) = \sum_{j=1}^{J} V_{nj} - d_{in}(t) - p_i(t), \qquad \forall n \in N \tag{6.3}$$

Consumer $n$ chooses product $I_n(t)$ that maximizes her utility. Therefore:

$$I_n(t) = \arg\max[U_{ni}(t)], \qquad \forall i \in I, n \in N \tag{6.4}$$

The revenues of firms are determined by the purchasing decisions of users (Equation 6.4):

$$R_i(t) = \sum_{n=1}^{N} [p_i(t) \cdot \omega_n(t)] \tag{6.5}$$

Where:

$$[\omega_n(t), p_i(t)] = \begin{cases} [1, \overline{p_i}(t)] & \text{, if } I_n(t) = i \text{ and } I_n(t) \neq I_n(t-1) \quad \text{(change)} \\ [1, \underline{p_i}(t)] & \text{, if } I_n(t) = I_n(t-1) = i \quad \text{(upgrade)} \\ (0, 0) & \text{, if } I_n(t) \neq i \quad \text{(otherwise)} \end{cases} \tag{6.6}$$

### 6.3.3 Firms and Technical Change

Technology continuously evolves by building upon prior inventions. Firms develop new competencies that result in new features that are added to recent product versions or kept as proprietary know–how within the organization.

Every period firm $i$ improves the least advanced feature, $j_i^*$, by comparing product quality to the average preferences of users, $\overline{V_j}$:

$$j_i^*(t) = \arg\max[\overline{V_j} - Q_{ij}(t-1)], \qquad \forall \overline{V_j} > Q_{ij}(t-1) \tag{6.7}$$

Where:

$$\overline{V_j} = \sum_{n=1}^{N} [V_{nj}/N], \qquad \forall j \in J \tag{6.8}$$

The firm can further the quality of its product in one of the following ways:

(i) carrying out independent research and development (see section 6.3.4),
(ii) legal imitation of rival products (see section 6.3.5), or
(iii) acquisition of knowledge from expired patents (see section 6.3.5).

Firms compare the expected quality improvements that can be achieved in each way and choose the optimal method to acquire knowledge. Denote the maximal expected improvement $E\Delta Q_{ij}(t+1)$.

The pricing mechanism is based on the expected improvement in the firm's product and in the products of its rivals. First, the firm predicts the expected quality of its product in the following period by summing up the present quality level and the expected improvement in quality. Second, it assesses the quality improvements of its rivals, taking into account their expected investments in R&D (a fixed share of their revenues), their ability to imitate rival products or to learn from patents. Third, it calculates the utility of the "average user" from purchasing other firms' products. Finally, the firm determines a competitive price, for which the utility from purchasing its product surpasses the maximal expected utility gained from using other products. Each firm repeats this process for users of its product ("loyal customers") and for users of rival products ("potential customers").

Formally, the price of a new product is determined as follows:

$$\begin{aligned} p_i(t+1) &= \sum_{j=1}^{J} \overline{V_j} - \overline{d_i}(t+1) - \max_{k \neq i} EU_k(t+1) \\ &= \sum_{j=1}^{J} Q_{ij}(t) + E\Delta Q_{ij}(t+1) - \max_{k \neq i} EU_k(t+1) \end{aligned} \tag{6.9}$$

We assume that the costs of production and distribution per product unit are equal to zero. R&D expenditure is taken as a fixed share of the revenues, $\rho < 1$.

From Equation 6.5, the expenditure of firm $i$ on acquisition of know–how is

$$RD_i(t) = \rho \cdot R_i(t-1) = \rho \cdot \sum_{n=1}^{N} I_n(t) \cdot p_i(t) \tag{6.10}$$

and its profits are

$$\pi_i(t) = (1-\rho) \cdot R_i(t) = (1-\rho) \cdot \sum_{n=1}^{N} I_n(t) \cdot p_i(t) \tag{6.11}$$

### 6.3.4 Innovation via Independent R&D

Technological progress is positively correlated with R&D expenditure (Klette and Griliches, 1998) and the one–period progress rate is normally distributed (Arora et al., 2003):[10]

$$\xi_{ij_i^*}(t) \sim N[f_a(RD_i{}^{\beta}), \zeta)], \qquad \forall i, j \tag{6.12}$$

where $\beta$ is the elasticity of innovation with respect to R&D.

New inventions increase firm $i$'s internal know–how by $\xi_{ij_i^*}(t)$:

$$q_{ij_i^*}(t) = q_{ij_i^*}(t-1) + \xi_{ij_i^*}(t), \qquad \forall i, j_i^* \in J \tag{6.13}$$

Product quality improves when advanced features are produced on the basis of in–house knowledge and released without infringing patents:

$$Q_{ij}(t) = Q_{ij}(t-1) + q_{ij}(t) \tag{6.14}$$

The firm then begins in augmenting new know–how, therefore $q_{ij}(t) = 0$.

### 6.3.5 Patents, Imitation and Release of New Products

The model simulates a market with firms that operate under different patent regimes. Firms protect new inventions by patents when their technical quality exceeds the minimal inventive step over the most advanced technology. Products are released to the market when they do not infringe living patents (that is, when

[10] The simulation runs are based on $\beta = 0.65$, estimated for computers and office equipment by Arora et al. (2003).

other firms' patents have expired, when the firm was granted patents over the features or when they are sufficiently novel). Otherwise, technical know-how is augmented and remains proprietary within the firm. Firms can improve their products by developing them in-house, by imitating unproteced features of their rivals or by implementing knowledge disclosed in patents that have expired.

Both the patent duration, $L$, and the minimal inventive step, $s$, are exogenous parameters that are determined by regulators. Simulations cover a range of designs of the legal regime with $L = 0...L_{max}$ periods and $s = 0...s_{max}$ quality units. We then compare the resulting patterns of quality, $Q_{ij}|_{(L^*,s^*)}$, under different patent regimes.

A feature can be protected by several patents, each patent being granted over and protecting a particular part of the technology, $[Q_{P_{min}}, Q_{P_{max}}]$, for $L$ periods.[11]

Patenting is possible if inventions are sufficiently novel, that is, when the technical quality exceeds the inventive step over the patented quality level, either when former patents are still valid or have already expired. Formally, firms can patent technical advances when $Q_{ij}(t-1) + q_{ij}(t) \geq Q_{jp_{max}} + s$. When a patent is granted, the firm can embed it in its product and release an improved version to the market.

A firm can release a product with minor improvements when that firm improves upon product features that it protected before (that is, $Q_{jp_{max}} < Q_{ij}(t) + q_{ij}(t) < Q_{jp_{max}} + s | i = I_p$) or when patents held by rivals have expired (that is, $Q_{jp_{max}} < Q_{ij}(t) + q_{ij}(t) < Q_{jp_{max}} + s | t > T_p + L, i \neq I_p$). When an improved version of product $i$ is released, the quality of feature $j$ increases. Formally: $Q_{ij}(t) = Q_{ij}(t-1) + q_{ij}(t)$. Otherwise, the technical quality remains unchanged.

Figure 6.1 illustrates the possibilities for firms to protect their inventions by patents and to use them in new product versions. Assume that a patent over a feature was granted to Firm A in period $t = 0$. The quality segment protected by the patent is $[Q_{P_{min}}, Q_{P_{max}}]$ (dark bar). Firm B develops a competing product that improves Firm A's good by $q_B$ units (grey bar).

We consider three possible scenarios that involve Firm A's patent and Firm B's product:

In the first scenario, Firm B invents within the period of patent protection

[11] A patent is represented in the model by the vector $\vec{\Psi_j} = \{T_p, I_p, Q_{jp_{min}}, Q_{jp_{max}}\}$ that includes the following variables: the patent grant date ($T_p$), the index of the inventing firm ($I_p$) and the protected technological parcel ($Q_{jp_{min}}, Q_{jp_{max}}$). We assume no difference between the grant date, $T_p$, and the application date.

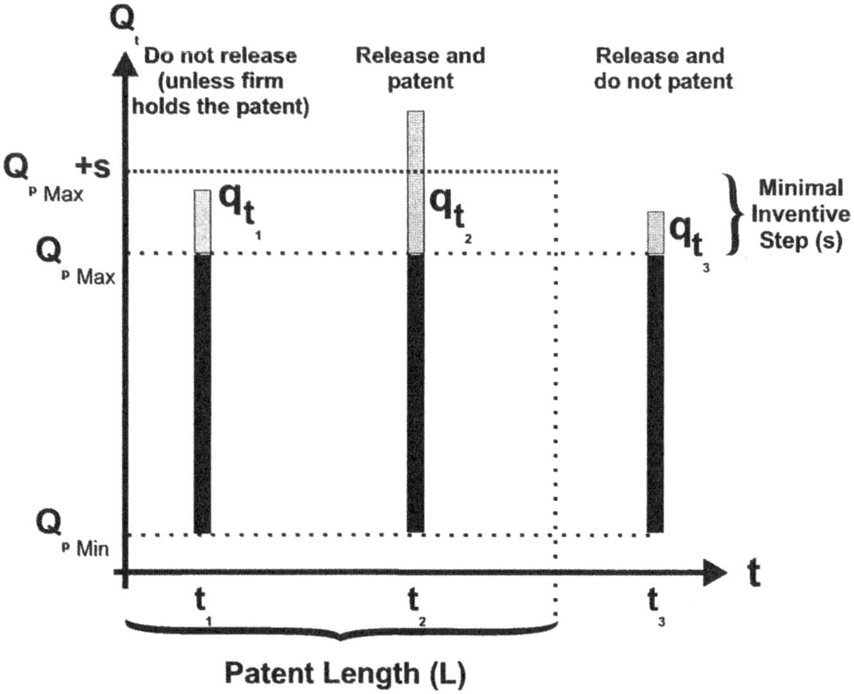


**Figure 6.1.** Possibilities of patenting and releasing new features.

(for example in period $t_1 < L$) and its invention fails to present sufficient degree of novelty, that is, $Q_B(t_1) + q_B(t_1) < Q_{p_{max}} + s$. Firm B can neither release an improved product without infringing Firm A's patent, nor can it protect its invention.

In the second case, Firm B produces a sufficiently novel invention with a quality level that exceeds the minimal inventive step, $Q_B(t_2)+q_B(t_2) \geq Q_{p_{max}}+s$, before Firm A's patent expires (for example in period $t_2 < L$). Firm B will receive a new patent that protects the segment $[Q_{p_{max}} + s, Q_B(t_2) + q_B(t_2)]$ for the period $[t_2, t_2 + L]$. Firm A will be prohibited from introducing a product with quality level $(Q_{p_{max}} + s, Q_B(t_2) + q_B(t_2) + s]$ as long as Firm B's patent is valid.

In the third case, Firm B invents after Firm A's patent has expired (for example in period $t_3 \geq L$). An improved version of Firm B's product can be released, but it cannot be patented if its quality does not exceed the minimal degree of novelty, $s$.

## 6.4 The Simulation

The set of results describes the evolution of technologies and the innovative output of firms under various structures of the patent regime and the market. The results of the model were obtained for 1000 consumers with normally–distributed, heterogenous preferences. The series of simulation runs were accomplished with five, ten and twenty firms to explore how the links between the patent regime and the level of technical quality vary under different scales of competition. Each firm produces a product with 15 technical features. Following the statistics on R&D expenditure in French software firms (Abi–Saad et al., 2001), we set the share of revenues dedicated to R&D, $\rho$, equal to 15 per cent.

The results were recorded for different patent durations that vary from 0 to 30 periods and for inventive step that varies from 1 to 50 quality units. Since quality improvements are normally distributed, they produce some degree of a *Gaussian noise*. We apply nonparametric kernel regression as a statistical smoothing technique that reduces the noise–to–wave ratio. The kernel regression implemented a bivariate box–smoothing filter with an optimal bandwidth to guarantee high degrees of accuracy of the data transformations.[12]

## 6.5 Results

Figures 6.2–6.4 describe the results of the simulation model on three axes. The independent variables (inventive step and length) are represented by the (x,y) axes. The dependent variables (average quality, quality variance and the share of developing firms) are described by the grey scale.

Analyses of the average quality of product features reveal strong links between the different dimensions of the patent regime and the evolution of technology under various market structures. Figure 6.2 illustrates the average quality in markets with five, ten and twenty firms. The effects of different structures of the patent regime on technology are more significant in competitive markets than in less competitive economies. Comparing Figure 6.2c with Figure 6.2a and 6.2b, we can state:

**Proposition 7** *Quality rises with the number of competing firms.*

[12] A detailed description of the method is found in Bowman and Azzalini (1997; Ch. 3).

The impact of differences in the design of patents on technical quality is found to be insignificant in markets with a small number of firms (Figure 6.2a). Innovation is influenced, to some extent, by different structures of the legal regime in markets with intermediate levels of competition (Figure 6.2b). However, the structure of patents has prominent effects on innovation and technological development in competitive markets (Figure 6.2c), which are described and analyzed in the course of the discussion. In this respect, Figure 6.2b illustrates an intermediate situation between markets with minor degrees of competition, where patents have a small impact on firms, and competitive markets, where the impact of the regime is stronger.

Following the comparison between the average quality levels obtained under different structures of the patent regime, we observe that

**Proposition 8** *a) Quality increases when patent duration decreases, ceteris paribus.*

*b) Quality increases with minimal inventive step, ceteris paribus.*

Proposition 8 stands in contrast to the widely–accepted rationale of the patent system offered by *reward theory.* Reward theory suggests that R&D investments of firms increase with patent duration and, consequently, the technical quality improves. The results of the model indicate that patents with shorter duration are better suited to support technological development. The highest scales of technical quality of products are achieved when short patent durations (one to three periods) are applied for any degree of the inventive step. *Reward theory* suggests that extended patent term increases the incentives of firms to engage in R&D activities, as inventors generate monopoly revenues over longer periods, are able to recoup their prior investments in R&D (see Nordhaus, 1969, 1972; Scherer, 1972). The results of our study illustrate how the negative effects of elongated monopoly over technologies overturn and exceed the benefits of long–term revenues and protection. Using Nordhaus's terminology to describe the impact of the legal regime on innovation, extended patent duration narrows down the invention possibility function of firms rather than expands it as Nordhaus suggested. Further, one may recall the debate between Klemperer (1990) and Gilbert and Shapiro (1990) over the desirability of infinitely–living patents. From the results of our analysis we conclude that long, or even intermediate patent durations would hamper innovation; the highest degree of technical quality is achieved when short–term patents are applied.

Patentability of small improvements (that is, patents with a small inventive step) impedes the pace of innovation, as firms are deterred from exploiting their own technological advances for long periods. Consequently, firms that operate under this structure of the patent regime are poor performers in terms of achieving high levels of technical quality, in comparison to other markets. Hence, legislation that enables patenting of small technological advances harms innovation in the long run, rather than contributes to it.

**Proposition 9** *When patent length increases, the minimal inventive step should increase to maintain the level quality.*

And similarly:

**Proposition 10** *When the minimal inventive step decreases, patent duration should be shortened to maintain the level of quality.*

Figure 6.2c provides an interesting result by revealing close links between the length and the minimal inventive step of patents. Intermediate levels of technical quality are achieved when short–term protection with a small inventive step is applied. Those degrees of quality remain unchanged if the minimal inventive step increases when the duration is extended. Those findings highlights a trade–off between patent length and inventive step. Klemperer (1990) and Gilbert and Shapiro (1990) suggest that narrower patent scope substitutes for longer patent duration, and *vice versa*, to maintain the amount of incentives (and revenues). However, their analyses refer to the breadth of patent claims and to possible extension of patent protection to neighbouring technologies and applications, rather than to patenting large or minor technological advances. Van Dijk (1996) discusses another trade–off between patent breadth and inventive step ("height") and possible designs of patent regime that yield optimal degrees of innovation. Therefore, the findings of the model, stated in Propositions 9 and 10, affirm the presence of another trade–off between patent length and inventive step, overlooked by other studies.

The variance of technical quality serves as a measure for the degree of competition between firms and for their ability to "catch–up" with rival technologies. Figure 6.3 illustrates how the quality variance in each market differs under various patent regimes (dark regions represent high scales of quality variance). Following the results of the analysis, we can state:

**Proposition 11** *Technical quality decreases and its variance increases as markets become less competitive under long–term patents with a small inventive step.*

Merges and Nelson (1990) argue that higher levels of competition are necessary to produce technological progress. Rivalry between firms maintains the diversity of products and techniques and fosters the creation of new goods, upon which advanced features can be furthered or devised. Their views are supported by empirical evidence from the early days of the radio and the aviation industries. Therefore, they advocate the enactment of a patent regime that does not impede entry of firms and assures ongoing competition with incumbent firms. The authors arrive at the same conclusion as Proposition 11, despite the differences between software and physical products in the nature of goods, frequency of new releases and product life cycle.

As Proposition 11 indicates, high levels of variance in the quality of products appear when long–living patents are granted to minor advances (upper–left corner of Figure 6.3). This result persists for any number of firms that operate in the market, but it is stronger as the number of firms increases.

The differences between products are influenced by the design of the patent regime and do not result from diverse strategies of product differentiation that firms apply (firms use the same average consumer profile and rules to determine which product features should be improved). Longer patent terms and smaller inventive steps foster introduction of more diverse products. However, Figure 6.2 reveals that the scales of technical quality under this patent regime are significantly lower than under different patent designs. The graphs indicate the emergence of non–competitive market structures, assisted by strong IPR regimes, as firms are able to monopolize larger fragments of the technology for longer periods. Patents with a long duration and with a small inventive step impede the efforts of firms to follow technological leaders and to introduce their own advances. Over time, these forms of protection produce negative externalities for innovation.

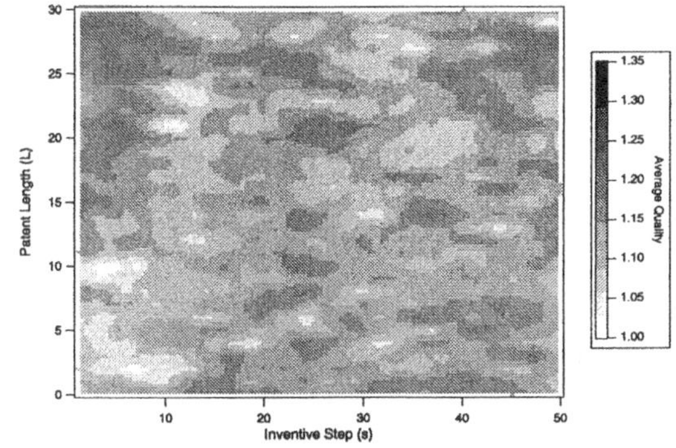


(5 firms)

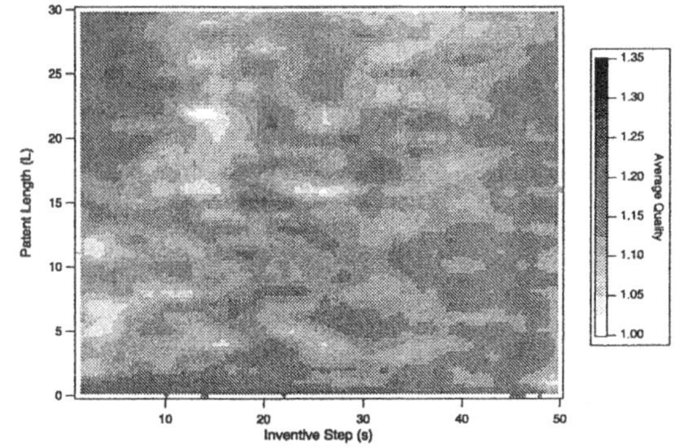


(10 firms)

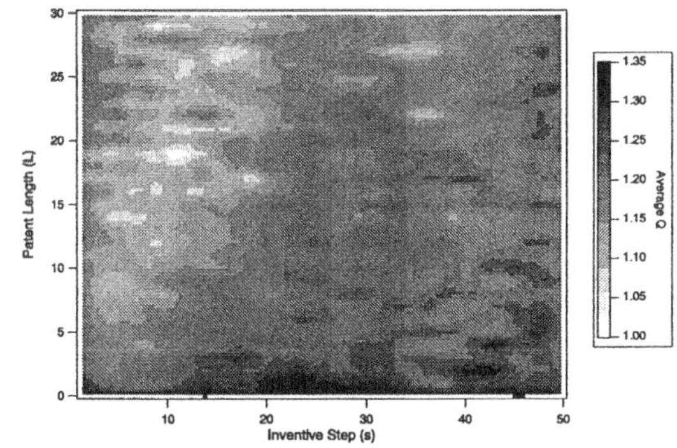


(20 firms)

**Figure 6.2.** Normalized average technical quality under different IPR regimes after 50 periods.

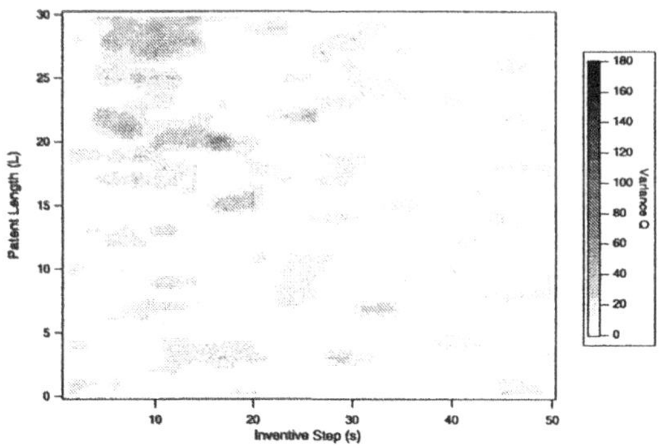


(5 firms)

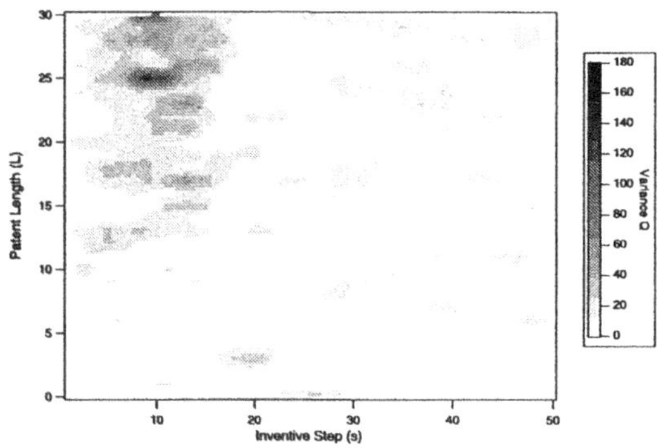


(10 firms)

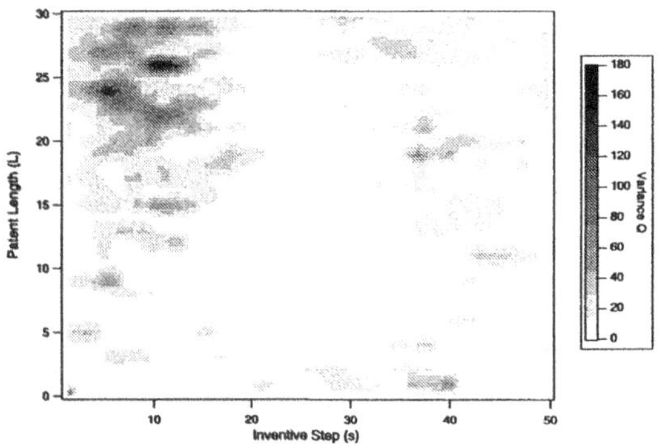


(20 firms)

**Figure 6.3.** Variance of the technical quality under different IPR regimes after 50 periods.

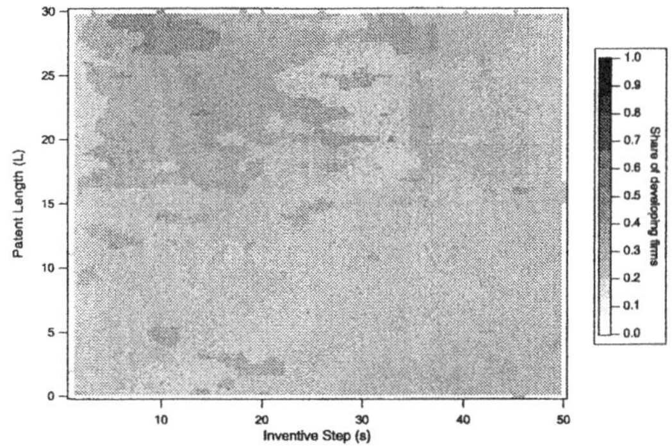


(5 firms)

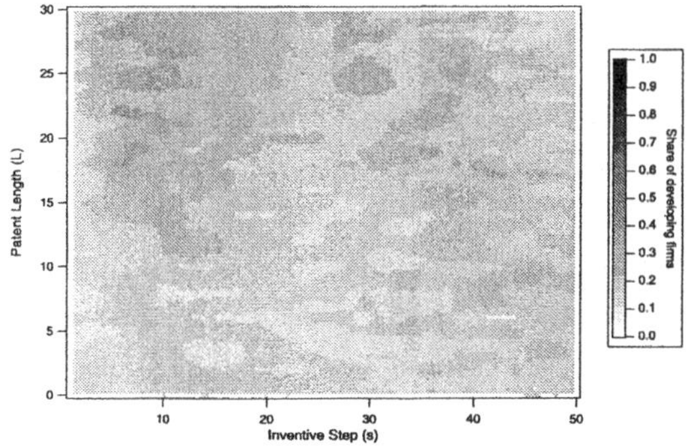


(10 firms)

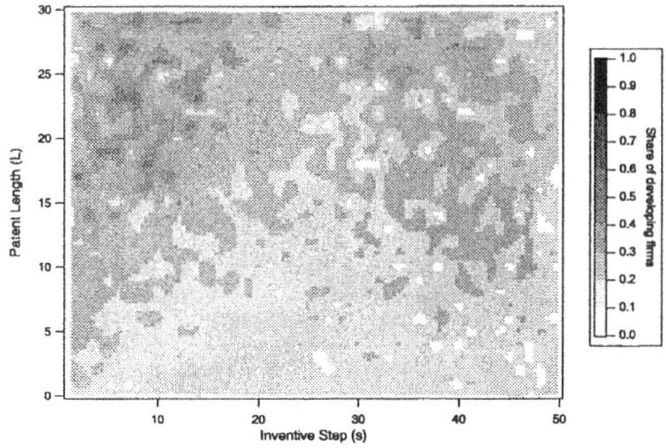


(20 firms)

**Figure 6.4.** The share of developing firms over time ($t = 1...50$).

Following the behaviour of firms under different structures of the regime (Figure 6.4), we conclude:

**Proposition 12** *a) The propensity of firms to imitate (to innovate) increases (decreases) with the minimal inventive step.*

*b) The propensity of firms to imitate (to innovate) decreases (increases) with patent lifetime.*

When the duration of patents is shortened and/or the inventive step increases, that is, patenting becomes more difficult and patents protect inventors for shorter periods, the number of developers goes down and more firms would prefer imitating rival products over investing in developing their own technologies (Figure 6.4).

Further, following Figure 6.4, when small improvements are protected by patents for long periods (that is, $L$ is high and $s$ is relatively small), internal R&D is favoured over imitation. The propensity of firms to patent increases when the inventive step decreases, even though rival firms are able to exceed a smaller inventive step to overcome valid patents and to be granted patents for their own advances. In this case, the previous patent–holder can continue to compete efficiently with the new patentee as the "second–best" (since the differences in technology between the two firms can be relatively minor, considering the small inventive step), while preempting technological laggards from acquiring dominated market shares.

## 6.6 Conclusions

The chapter evaluates how alternative structures of the patent regime affect innovation in information technologies by using simulation of the market and the patent regime. On the one hand, lack of protection fosters knowledge spillovers and development of superior technologies by rivals. However, high scales of imitation remove part of the firm's revenues and lower its propensity to invest in R&D. On the other hand, stronger patents provide higher incentives to innovate, but restrict the access to recent developments.

Following the results of the model, we conclude that firms operating under less protective regimes are more innovative and produce higher quality products, despite imitation by the majority of firms. At the extreme, if patents are granted to minor improvements and protect them for long periods, rival firms would be preempted from introducing advanced product versions and from furthering the technology. This regime is clearly overprotective, as it provides excessive monopoly rights over inventions and results in inferior technological performance of firms in comparison to less protected markets.

Interpretation of the results of the model leads to the inevitable conclusion that "real world" patents, whose duration is 20 years (both in Europe and in the US) most probably hamper the development of technologies at any degree of the inventive step. The inclusion of software within the scope of protection of patents during the 1980s has slowed down the pace of development in information technologies. However, complete abolition of patent protection for software technologies ($L = 0, s = 0$) is not desirable and may yield non–optimal degrees of innovation. The results suggest that the performance of firms under the Open Source mode of development is superior to the present regime, but it is less efficient than under short–term patents. Finally, patent protection granted to minor technological advances for long periods retards the evolution of technologies in the long run, even though more firms prefer developing their own technologies in–house on imitating rival products.

The desirable design of the IPR regime consists of a short patent lifetime and an intermediate to high level of the minimal inventive step. Under those conditions, inventors enjoy protection of significant technological advances rather than limited protection of rare breakthroughs. Moreover, exclusion of minor improvements from the scope of patents and a shortened duration of patents enable firms to access and to implement novel know–how. Consequently, both competition and technological progress are enhanced in the long run.

The results also suggest that the incentives of firms to innovate are positively correlated with the degree of protection provided by the legal regime. Imitation is the least preferred method under a strong regime (that is, long patent duration and small inventive step), as imitators are limited in their possibilities to acquire recent developments and to leapfrog over technological leaders by first *legally* imitating them. When firms operate under weaker IPR protection, their propensity to distinguish their products by in–house development decreases and imitation is more often chosen. Hence, R&D producing firms can achieve better competitive positions in the market than can imitators under a strong patent regime.

When the market contains a large population of firms, each firm confronts fierce competition and, in order to survive, it has to distinguish itself by continuously "re–inventing" its own product. Policy makers can then provide incentives to innovate by creating stronger protection schemes. Those means should be carefully applied when the competition intensifies, for example when many firms join the market, as stronger patents may decrease the level of technical quality.

The results of the model support the application of weak patent regimes in early stages of the technology, when large numbers of firms pursue new technological opportunities and compete mainly by releasing advanced product versions. At this stage, application of strong IPRs may create a sequence of monopolies over inventions. Firms with broad patent portfolios gradually exclude other firms from the market. As the level of competition decreases, the remaining firms would increasingly turn from imitation to R&D. In latter stages of the technology, when a small number of firms remains in the market, strong IPRs would provide major incentives to accomplish continuous development by the remaining firms by ensuring a stable stream of revenues over time. This regime is favourable for increasing the pace of innovation and technical change, despite steadily growing market concentration and higher barriers for entry.

The links between competition and innovation are particularly interesting in light of Schumpeter's observation that large and monopolistic firms are well–suited to produce innovation. Their profits that are generated by practicing dominant position can finance costly R&D activities. However, the results of the model are in contrast to Schumpeter's arguments and suggest that monopoly over technology accommodated by strong patent rights is likely to impede the pace of innovation. Those results call for further investigation of the contribution of IPRs to the development of new technologies in less competitive markets.

The model includes several assumptions that assist in identifying the major effects of the patent regime on innovation in a system that is already very complex. However, those assumptions can be relaxed or modified in advanced versions of this model. First, we assume that R&D expenditure is taken as a fixed share of firms' revenues. In practice, firms may adopt different strategies to determine their R&D investments. Second, the pricing mechanism is based on the distance between the technical quality of products and on the average preferences of users. However, firms apply price discrimination strategies to attract different users (for example offering "student packages" with a lower price tag), rather than base their pricing on the preferences of the "average user". Third, we assume that the technical quality and the prices of products have equal importance in purchasing decisions of different consumers. In reality, some users are more sensitive to the product price than others (compare, for example, the purchasing decisions of private users and corporations).

## 6.7 Chapter Appendix: Symbols Used in this Chapter

**Parameters:**

| | |
|---|---|
| $M$ | Number of firms (products). |
| $J$ | Number of product features. |
| $N$ | Number of consumers (users). |
| $i$ | Firm's index. |
| $j$ | Feature's index. |
| $n$ | Consumer's index. |
| $\rho$ | Share of the revenues invested in R&D. |
| $L$ | Patent length. |
| $s$ | Minimal inventive step. |

**Variables:**

| | |
|---|---|
| $Q_{ij}(t)$ | Technical quality of feature $j$ of product $i$, released to the market in period $t$. |
| $q_{ij}(t)$ | Technical know-how associated with feature $j$ and remains undisclosed within firm $i$'s domain. |
| $\overline{p_i}(t)$ | Price of an installation version of product $i$ in period $t$. |
| $\underline{p_i}(t)$ | Price of an upgraded version of product $i$ in period $t$. |
| $V_{nj}$ | Consumer $n$'s preference (value) of feature $j$. |
| $\overline{V_j}$ | Average consumers' preferences. |
| $U_{ni}(t)$ | Consumer $n$'s utility from using product $i$ in period $t$. |
| $d_{in}(t)$ | The distance between consumer $n$'s preferences and product $i$'s quality in period $t$. |
| $\omega_n(t)$ | Consumer $n$'s buying decision in period $t$. |
| $I_n(t)$ | Product used by consumer $n$ in period $t$. |
| $R_i(t)$ | Firm $i$'s revenues in period $t$. |
| $\pi_i(t)$ | Firm $i$'s profits in period $t$. |
| $RD_i(t)$ | Firm $i$'s R&D expenditure in period $t$. |
| $j_i^*(t)$ | Feature selected by firm $i$ for improvement in period $t$. |
| $\xi_{ij_i^*}(t)$ | Technical progress of feature $j_i^*$ in period $t$. |
| $\beta$ | Elasticity of innovation w.r.t. R&D. |
| $[Q_{p_{min}}, Q_{p_{max}}]_j$ | Patent-protected segment of feature $j$. |
| $T_p$ | Patent grant date. |

# 7

# Owning Technology: The Structure of Intellectual Property Ownership in Software Technologies

## 7.1 Introduction

### 7.1.1 Background

This chapter aims at exploring how the structure of the ownership of patent rights in software technologies has changed over time in comparison to other technologies. We analyze how the changes in the US patenting policy have affected the structure of patent ownership and reveal similarities and differences between patents over *generic* inventions and over specific applications. Finally, we analyze the relations between Open Source and proprietary software by comparing the development of public domain projects with patent records in the relevant classes.

Intellectual property is the main source of value and profits in software firms. Software products, information goods and the source code of programs generate major shares of revenues in information technologies. Users' installed base, licensing agreements and technical support are among the other assets of software producers. Yet, valuations of firms' assets often overlook the real value of their intellectual property or reflect only a small fraction of it, as value estimates of intangible goods are notoriously difficult to accomplish.[1] Similarly, the scales of

[1]Aboody and Lev (1998) discuss the conflicts between different estimates of value of computer programs, software development projects and information systems, determined by a variety of existing accounting standards. OECD (1998b, c) and Vosselman (1998)

lost revenues as a result of unauthorized reproduction and use of computer programs and software packages ("software piracy") are difficult to assess. Piracy rates, that is, the share of users of illegal copies of commercial software, serve as a simple indicator to evaluate the scales of unauthorized use of computer programs. They can be easily obtained through users' surveys and questionnaires or by validating their unique electronic signatures when they are connected to the producers' servers. Piracy rates are often used by software producers in order to demonstrate loss of potential income as a result of illegal reproduction and use of software packages. Statistics showing significant levels of piracy supports the pleas of the software industry in favour of stronger IPR regimes. For example, piracy figures, published by the software industry, indicate that over 90 per cent of copies of commercial applications used in some developing economies, 35 per cent in Europe and 25 per cent in the US are illegally reproduced. The estimated loss of revenues of software producers is approximately 1.2 billion dollars (SIIA, 2001; SPA, 2002). In reality, the loss of potential revenues is significantly lower than those figures. Had Copyright Law been fully enforced, part of the users of unauthorized copies would have chosen to implement alternative and less costly applications instead of the products in use. In economic terms, the elasticity of substitution between legal and illegal copies is lower than 1, and depends on the price of legal copies.[2]

Elements of computer programs are also vulnerable to imitation and reproduction, mainly by competitors. Fragments of source code, algorithms, interfaces and operational features can inexpensively be copied or reverse–engineered to produce *software clones* with similar functions and a lower price tag. However, technically imitation and reverse–engineering of software elements is more complex than reproduction of additional copies of the final product. Consequently, it is far more difficult to observe and to prove violation of IPRs over *original* elements of computer programs than infringement of software copyrights (see Chapter 8). Nevertheless, IPRs fulfil a major role in the appropriation strategies of software firms.

Since the changes in IPR legislation in the US and the expansion of the scope

---

highlight the challenges involved in measuring and comparing investments in intangible goods in industrialized nations and attempt to solve the problems by presenting a new frame of analysis with harmonized definitions.

[2]Indeed, in developing countries, where the prices of software are above the income level of many users, piracy rates are significantly high.

of patents and copyrights to protect software–based inventions were implemented, firms can safeguard their main sources of income (that is, the source code, the final products and elements embodied in programs) more easily by applying legal means. Moreover, patents are used as important strategic means by IT firms, not only to protect their intellectual property but also to preserve market shares and revenues. Those phenomena are largely observed by the increasing numbers of patent applications and grants for software and computer–based inventions and by the rapid growth of patent portfolios held by software firms.

Changes in legislation have influenced the dynamics of the market. By re–shaping the environment in which firms operate, IPR legislation has also affected their decisions and business practices. A prominent effect of frequent changes in the IPR regime and the growing numbers of litigation cases in which software firms were involved was to increase the degree of uncertainty, which in turn influenced firms' operations (including their R&D investments, licensing policies and entry into new markets). Similarly, the propensity of firms to protect their inventions by patents, which involves disclosure of novel know–how, has varied not only due to the legal allowances to protect elements of software as intellectual property, but also according to the nature of the competition in the market and the phase of technological development. In early stages of the technology, firms prefer to protect technical advances by patents, in order to gain dominance over broad shares of the market and over a variety of downstream applications that are expected to appear as development proceeds. However, when technology reaches maturity, firms apply different strategies that are based on lead–time and on learning curves of competitors to protect their inventions (see Chapter 3 for overview of appropriation methods).

The strategic behaviour of firms can be explored by following the development of their patent portfolios. A firm's decision to protect its technology by patents or by trade secrecy, or even through disclosure of its source code, is influenced by changes in the market and by the decisions of its rivals. Consequently, the ways in which ownership of intellectual property evolves are closely linked to competition, emergence and decline of technologies, business models and to changes in regulation. Therefore, the structure of ownership of intellectual property can be used to analyze the responses of firms to historical changes in the market, such as shifts in the legal, technological and economic paradigms.

### 7.1.2 What Do Patents Reveal?

Patent data serve as a rich source of information on the innovative activities of firms. Patent records provide a variety of quantitative indicators and a contemporary and historical outlook on research and development activities in firms, the technological fields in which they operate, their innovative output and whether they have succeeded in achieving substantial technological advances. Patent data provide information on innovation and on the evolution of technologies in the micro–, meso– and macro–economic levels. We can assess *ex post* the pace of innovation and technological discoveries, the extent to which innovation is cumulative and relations formed between technically close or adjacent technologies. It is important to acknowledge that patent records do not provide perfect indicators on the innovative activities of firms. Firms may prefer using strategies that are based on product lead–time and learning curves of competitors over patenting. Nonetheless, we can use patents to analyze the innovative output of firms and the structure of patent ownership.

Patent records include the application date, in which the request for a patent was submitted by the assignee. The application date is often taken as a proxy for the discovery date of inventions.[3] Applications are approved if the degree of novelty is sufficient (that is, if significant advance over the state–of–the–art of technology has been achieved). The grant date follows the application date and signifies the date in which the Patent Office approved the application and granted exclusive rights over the invention.

Patent records disclose the identity of inventors and assignees (that is, holders of patent rights) and their geographic locations. Those data provide wealth of information on knowledge spillovers from public research institutes to firms and among firms, between technological fields (Jaffe and Trajtenberg, 2002) and between geographical regions (Verspagen and Caniëls, 2001). Patent data can be coupled with other sources, such as financial data and inventors' surveys (Jaffe et al., 1993) to reveal links between innovation and other dimensions of firms' activities and performance.

Patent records classify inventions by technological fields and provide a detailed description of the technology, its utility and applications. Since innovation is by essence cumulative and inventors "stand on the shoulders of giants" seeking aspi-

[3]Most firms submit their patent applications close to the discovery date to gain priority over competitors and to win the *patent race*.

ration and solutions in prior discoveries (Scotchmer, 1991), patent records include references to *prior art* – scientific and technical articles and preceding patents through which inventors have revealed their own discoveries. Patents cite previous patents ("backward citations") to define their scope and to avoid "trespassing" into other patents' domains. We can assess the importance of inventions and their degree of novelty by identifying which patents are more cited than others ("forward citations"). Patent citations also reveal how different genres of knowledge are used to produce new innovations and how particular know–how diffuses into new fields.

## 7.2 Aims of the Chapter

The main purpose of this chapter is to portray the structure of ownership of software patents. A second aim of this chapter is to reveal how firms adapt to changes in the legal environment and the extent to which their strategic choices to protect their software inventions by patents were affected by the frequent changes in the legislative framework.

The research evaluates whether firms are consistent in their patenting behaviour over time and along different classes of the technology, particularly while they protect multi–use (generic) technologies vs. targeted applications. We evaluate the inventive value and the "quality" of software patents and how changes in the patenting policy have affected them. Finally, we explore possible links between Open Source and proprietary software by comparing the pace of development of selected Open Source projects with the structure of intellectual property ownership in related fields.

## 7.3 Methodology

### 7.3.1 Definitions

Different studies on patenting software and computer–implemented inventions, algorithms and business methods use diverse definitions of "software patents" and thereby include different patent classes in their analyses. Studies that build upon wider definitions of software patents apply bibliometric searches with related keywords to identify relevant patent records. However, those searches include also computational components that are applied in physical machinery. Wider criteria encompass any patent with the term "software" in the description and the claims (for example OECD, 2002; Ch. 3). However, those studies include patents granted for programmable elements within different apparatus, such as electronic kitchenware, which should only doubtfully be regarded as software patents.[4]

Allison and Lemley (2000) include "pure" software patents in their study on patent litigation on the basis of the USPTO definitions of software, "electrical" and "computer related" patents.[5] Bessen and Hunt (2007) apply wide criteria that do not rely on the USPTO definitions for classifying software patents. Instead, the population of software patents in their study was identified by searching for software–related keywords and terms within patent records. The resulting research population is much broader than in other studies and includes patents that refer to any form of software components and algorithms that were recognized patentable by the USPTO guidelines and the ruling of *Diamond v. Diehr.*[6] However, the scope of this definition of software patents is far too broad and may include, for example, inventions that perform a series of steps, as many process patents describe, and may be associated in one way or another with the operation of digital processors. Yet, the production of those inventions does not resemble any form of software development and programming and, therefore, it is weakly associated with any of the conflicts or the challenges related to software patents.

Graham and Mowery (2002) use a somewhat different method for the classification of software patents to assess their commercial value and to measure the propensity of software firms to protect their inventions by patents. Patents from eleven International Patent Classes (IPC) linked to software inventions were included.[7] However, their research population is limited to 358 patents that were granted to 100 major US firms between 1987 and 1997. Therefore, the results do not reflect the changes in patent legislation and in the USPTO's policy (in particular those of 1996) and major trends in software and information technology markets.

---

[4]Whether many of those patents are indeed "software patents" and hence should be included in empirical studies is open to different interpretations.

[5]The authors do not disclose the list of the classes included in their analysis.

[6]The ruling stated that the "concept of software patent involves a logic algorithm for processing data that is implemented via stored instructions; that is, the logic is not hard–wired. These instructions could reside on a disk or other storage medium or they could be stored in firmware, that is, a read–only memory, as is typical of embedded software" (p. 8).

[7]The classes are: G06F/3 5 7–9–11–12–13–15; G06K/9–15; H04L/9.

Our study includes virtually all US software patents in ten technological classes that are essentially associated with software, computer programs and algorithms and were granted between 1980 and 2003. We are cautious in applying a conservative definition of software patents in our analysis that includes only "pure" software patents. It refers to methods of developing and operating computer programs and to information processing techniques. The population of this study encompasses patent records that are explicitly associated with software technologies and novel algorithms. We exclude patents that describe operation and control of physical apparatus. In most cases, those patents barely resemble any form of software or computational processes, even though many of them use some digital components. Otherwise, those patents would have been (re)classified by the Patent Office in one of the categories that are included in this study.[8] The number of patents surveyed in this research is smaller than the research population of some other studies. The use of those definitions exhibits a higher degree of conformity to the classification of inventions that are part of the production of advanced software applications. The distribution of patent records in the USPTO classes that are included in our survey is described in Table 7.1. As each patent can be classified under more than one class, the total number of patent classifications presented in Table 7.1 is higher than the number of patent records.[9]

### 7.3.2 Data

The chapter analyzes the changes in the structure of ownership of intellectual property in software technologies by using US patent records that were granted between 1980 and 2003. We compare the structure of ownership in software to two other technologies: cryptography and image analysis. Those fields were selected as they are knowledge–intensive technologies, and in the beginning of the 1970s, early applications of cryptographic and image analysis techniques appeared in the same period when the use of commercial software packages significantly increased. By contrast, though, patented inventions that are classified under cryptography and image analysis are usually embedded in tangible media or in machinery.

[8]Patents can be attributed to one or several technological fields, due to the technologies that are included in the invention. For example, US patent no. 6,807,492 is classified Class 703 (Data processing: structural design, modelling, simulation and emulation) and under Class 435 (Chemistry: molecular biology and microbiology).

[9]For example, a patent record that is classified under classes 703 and 705 is counted twice.

| *Patent Class* | USPTO Classification | No. of Patents |
|---|---|---|
| 703 | Data processing: structural design, modelling, simulation, and emulation | 5,270 |
| 704 | Data processing: speech signal processing, linguistics, language translation, and audio compression/decompression | 14,584 |
| 705 | Data processing: financial, business practice, management, or cost/price determination | 13,484 |
| 706 | Data processing: artificial intelligence | 6,459 |
| 707 | Data processing: database and file management or data structures | 23,303 |
| 709 | Electrical computers and digital processing systems: multicomputer data transferring or plural processor synchronization | 26,657 |
| 710 | Electrical computers and digital data processing systems: input/output | 26,426 |
| 715 | Data processing: presentation processing of document | 6,941 |
| 717 | Data processing: software development, installation, and management | 7,114 |
| 718 | Electrical computers and digital processing systems: virtual machine task or process management or task management/control | 3,446 |
| Total | | 133,684 |

**Table 7.1.** The distribution of patent classifications.

Lists of patents in each technological class and detailed patent records were obtained from the USPTO database. Complementary information on assignees, such as private/corporate ownership of patents, was obtained from Derwent Innovation Index. Finally, patent records were sorted their by assignees.[10]

The research population includes:

- 62,000 software patents in ten patent classes granted to 20,400 assignees.
- 4,000 cryptography patents (Class 380) granted to 2,000 assignees.

[10]Note that some of our analyses in this chapter distinguish between patents that are held by firms and those that are held by individuals.

- 5,000 image analysis patents (Class 382) granted to 2,900 assignees.

(Distribution of the number of patents by year and class is found in Appendix B).

By analyzing the patterns of the patenting behaviour of firms and comparing them with the other two technologies, we discover how firms' behaviour was affected by the frequent changes in the software patenting doctrine and how firms adapted their strategies to the changing legal environment. Moreover, while prior studies combine the variety of software patents into a single proxy (and therefore assume uniformity among technological classes), our study distinguishes between patents in different classes and analyzes how the patenting behaviour differs in separate areas.

## 7.4 Findings

### 7.4.1 The Structure of Patent Ownership: A Comparative Analysis

Since the mid–1990s, the number of software patents has continuously and exponentially increased. Not only has the total number of software patents constantly grown since the 1980s, but also the scale of patents per annum has increased from dozens of patents in 1980 to over 18000 patents in 2003. Those figures are indeed striking when compared to other technologies, as "pure" software patents (patents included in the classes that were surveyed in this study) account for 3.2 per cent of the US patents that were granted in 2003 (USPTO, 2004). To compare, the number of patents in cryptography and image analysis grew from similar scales, that is, dozens of patents in 1980 to hundreds of patents per annum in the mid–1990s and their share in the total number of patents is marginal. However, the significant increase in the number of software patents since the beginning of the 1990s has not affected the patenting behaviour of firms in other technological areas. Figure 7.1 demonstrates a moderate growth in the number of patents in image analysis and cryptography in comparison to software.[11]

This substantial growth in software patents since the mid 1990s has various origins, which have altered the long run dynamics of the market. Those phenomena

[11]Rapid growth in patenting is also observed in other emerging areas of knowledge–based economy, such as biotechnology (Jaffe, 2000).

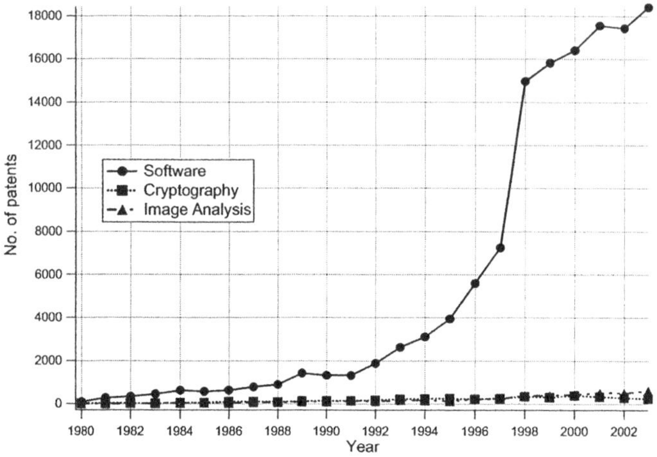


**Figure 7.1.** Number of patents per annum, 1980–2003.

are associated with changes in the strategic behaviour of software producers and other firms and the increasing value of intellectual property in software technologies, as much as they are linked to the rising expectations for profit-making in ICT (later referred to as the "bursting bubble" of the Internet). The modifications in the legislative framework and Court's verdicts in major litigation cases have gradually expanded the opportunities to protect software inventions and algorithms by patents[12] and have been followed by changes in the structure of ownership of patent rights.

Since the mid 1980s, firms have continuously adapted their strategies and appropriation methods to the evolving legislation and to contemporary jurisdiction. Whether changes in the structure of ownership of intellectual property were influenced by a single factor of the legislation or by all of it is doubted. The patenting behaviour of each firm is largely affected also by other attributes, such as size, dominance in the market and technological competences. Yet, legislation has reshaped the legal environment of firms and has formed a new set of conditions that has steered their strategies and patenting behaviour. Those legislative changes have also affected competition, as firms had to modify their market behaviour according to new possibilities of protecting their intellectual assets or responded to actions of rivals.

[12]See review in Chapter 4.

The changing legislation and the growth in the volume of software patents could have affected the emergence of one out of four possible market structures: First, incumbent firms could react to the changes in their business environment by expanding their patenting activities and by increasing the number of patent applications. Second, firms that rely on different appropriation mechanisms could engage in patenting activity more than before. Third, the new guidelines enabled the protection of new inventions by patents and consequently have increased the volume of R&D investments. As a result, more discoveries were made and were granted patents. Fourth, the patenting activity in software–related fields has grown by increasing the R&D efforts and by matching them with patent–oriented strategies.

We compare the structure of patent ownership in software technologies, cryptography and image analysis for the complete population of US patents granted between 1980 and 2003. We assess the general effects of the legislative changes on software patenting in general (patents owned by both individuals and firms) and in particular on the behaviour of firms (patents held by firms).

The Lorenz curve presented in Figure 7.2 reveals a highly concentrated structure of ownership of software patents: 6 per cent of the firms and individual assignees hold 70 per cent of software patents. The structure of patent ownership in the other two technologies is more fragmented: 21 per cent of the assignees hold 70 per cent of the cryptography patents, and 30 per cent of the assignees hold the same share of image analysis patents. Yet, cryptography and image analysis patents are not evenly distributed between assignees.

Figure 7.3 provides analysis of patents whose rights are held only by firms and indicates an even more polarized structure of IP ownership. The majority of software patents were granted to a small number of large firms, and only a small share of them was obtained by SMEs (6 per cent of firm assignees, or 522 firms, hold 80 per cent of the software patents). To compare, 27 per cent of firm assignees (323 firms) hold 80 per cent of the cryptography patents. The same share of image analysis patents is held by 33 per cent of the firm assignees (511 firms). Further, the top ten assignees of software patents include the *Majors* of the ICT industries, with IBM as the largest software patent–holder.[13] Those ten firms hold one third

[13]Since 1980, IBM sustains its share of software patents at around 10 per cent of the patents granted per annum. Since the late 1960s, software patents play an important role in IBM's appropriation strategies, in particular as "hardware producers in the US, with

| *Assignee* | % of firm–owned patents | % of all patents |
|---|---|---|
| IBM Corporation | 12.9 | 10.6 |
| Hitachi | 2.9 | 2.4 |
| Microsoft Corporation | 2.5 | 2.0 |
| Intel Corporation | 2.4 | 2.0 |
| Fujitsu | 2.3 | 1.9 |
| NEC Corporation | 2.0 | 1.7 |
| AT&T Bell Labs | 2.0 | 1.7 |
| Sun Microsystems | 2.0 | 1.7 |
| Hewlett–Packard | 1.9 | 1.6 |
| Toshiba | 1.5 | 1.3 |

0.5cm

**Table 7.2.** Major assignees in software patents, 1980–2003.

of the firm–owned software patents, or 27 per cent of all the patents (Table 7.2).

The Gini Coefficient is used for measuring the degree of concentration of patent rights held by various assignees and collapses the Lorenz curve to a single number. The Disordered Gini Coefficient is calculated as follows:

$$G_1 = \frac{2}{n^2\overline{x}} \cdot \sum_{i=1}^{n} \left[ (i - \frac{n+1}{2}) \cdot x_i \right], \qquad 0 \leq G_1 \leq 1 \qquad (7.1)$$

where $n$ is the number of assignees, $x_i$ is the number of patents granted to assignee $i$ and $\overline{x} = \frac{1}{n}\sum_{i=1}^{n} x_i$.[14] The Gini Coefficient for patents owned by individuals and firms is significantly higher in software patents ($G_s = 0.72$) than in cryptography ($G_c = 0.59$) and image analysis ($G_{ia} = 0.53$).

The effects of the changes in the legal environment of software firms on their R&D and appropriation strategies can be revealed by following the direction in which the structure of ownership of software patents has evolved over time. The Gini Coefficient for the share of patents held by different assignees is calculated per grant year. Figure 7.4 presents the values of the Gini Coefficient for software, cryptography and image analysis patents that were granted between 1980 and 2003.

---

the notable exception of IBM, have received a diminishing share of their revenues from software production" (Steinmueller, 1996).

[14] Alternatively, we can use the Ordered Gini Coefficient, $G_2 = \frac{2}{n^2\overline{x}} \cdot \sum_{i=1}^{n} (i \cdot x_i) - \frac{n+1}{n}$, if the data are sorted by the decreasing number of patents per assignee.

The results suggest that the structure of intellectual property ownership in software is highly concentrated in comparison to the two other technologies. In software technologies, smaller numbers of assignees were granted broader exclusive rights over software inventions than in other knowledge–intensive fields. The structure of patent ownership in those three technologies became increasingly concentrated between 1980 and 1998.

Since 1999, the structure of ownership of software patents has significantly changed and has become more fragmented (as shown by decreasing values of the Gini Coefficient). Despite the potential effects of the legislative changes in the patenting policy on cryptography and image analysis patents, those technologies have not been affected as software patents. The level of concentration of patent ownership in both technological fields has continued to grow during this period, with some transient fluctuations.

Patents granted since 1999 exhibit a significant change in the structure of ownership of software patents. During the last five years, the concentration of ownership of software patents has steadily decreased, and by the end of 2003 the value of the Gini Coefficient has returned to the same level of 1988. Those figures indicate a more even distribution of patent rights between assignees. This result can be associated with the new legislation and its effects on markets of software and information technologies. New firms enter the market and increase the degree of competition. Other effects of the legislation are associated with the growing numbers of firms that apply patent–based appropriation methods to protect their R&D investments and innovative output.

### 7.4.2 Assessing the Quality of Software Patents

The quality of patents is usually evaluated on the basis of their forward citations, that is, by identifying which succeeding patents ("patent children") cite preceding patent records ("parent patents") as prior art. Patents are cited for two major reasons: First, citations indicate that the invention has built upon prior technical advances and it should be granted a patent, having proved its utility and novelty (patent applications cite scientific and technical publications for the same reason). Second, prior patents are cited to distinguish the invention from them. Inventors draw borderlines between their own discoveries and *prior art* to assure that no equivalence claims will be submitted by other patent–holders. Yet, the number of citations can be affected by the "density" of patents in neighbouring domains of

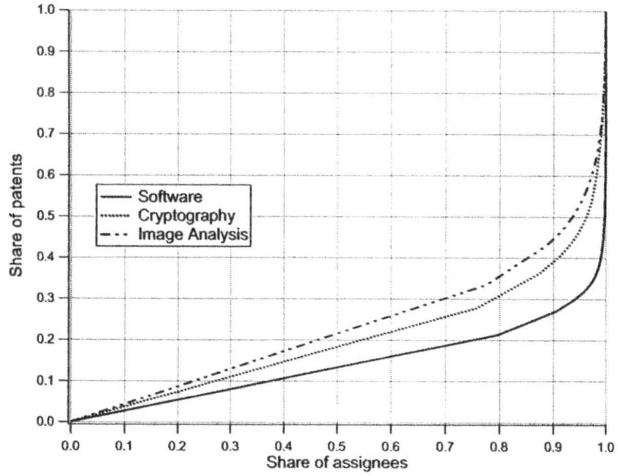


**Figure 7.2.** Ownership of patents by individuals and firms, 1980–2003.

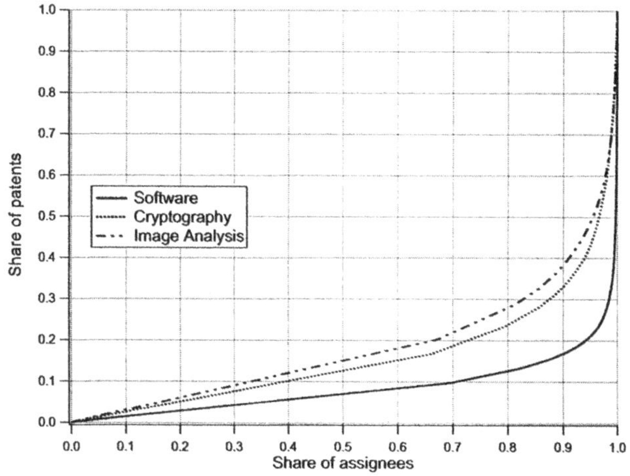


**Figure 7.3.** Ownership of patents by firms, 1980–2003.

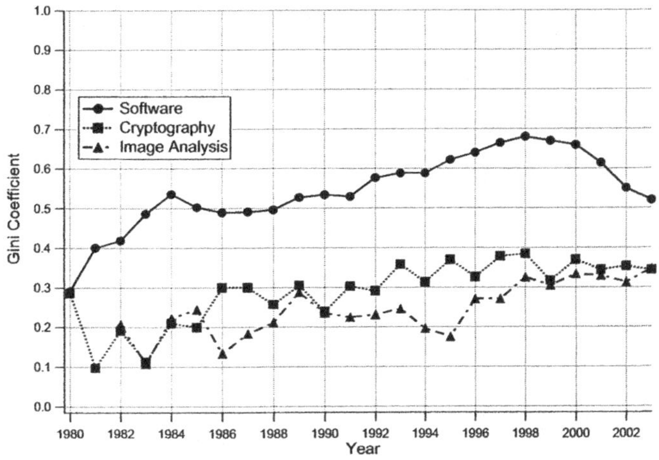


**Figure 7.4.** The structure of patent ownership over time.

the invention, by the *crowding–in* effect of firms determined to win property rights over emerging technologies or by construction of as–wide–as–possible patent portfolios that serve as tradable currency in cross–licensing agreements (Jaffe, 2000; Hall and Ziedonis, 2001). Therefore, forward citations can produce a variety of indicators that combine forward citations with other data within patent records. For example, those data can be employed to assess the innovative value of a particular invention by counting its forward citations, or to measure knowledge spillovers from a technology, represented by a set of related patents, by comparing their citations by patents from the same technical class and from other classes (see for example, Hall et al., 2001; Jaffe and Trajtenberg, 2002).

The quality of patents that were issued in different periods can substantially vary due to differences in patenting policies, in the examination guidelines (for example different utility and novelty criteria) or in the examination process (for example as a result of different training programmes of the patent examiners). In what follows, we use the number of forward citations within five years from the grant date to evaluate how the quality of software patents has changed over time. Further, we use indicators that are based on forward citations of software, cryptography and image analysis patents that were issued at the same time to compare their quality and innovative value.

Figure 7.5 presents the average number of forward citations of software, cryptography and image analysis patents by the grant year of "parent patents". The average number of citations of software patents has steadily grown since 1981, which might appear to indicate that the quality of software patents has also improved over time. However, this result can be explained by the exponential growth in software patents, which increased the likelihood that a growing number of citations is made by the succeeding patents. Therefore, this measure has to be corrected by taking into account the number of patents granted in the same year as the "parent patent" (and could be cited too within five years). Hence, the probability of patents to be cited within five years, $P_c$, is calculated as follows:

$$P_c = \frac{CPP}{N_G \cdot N_A} \qquad (7.2)$$

where $CPP$ is the number of citations of the "parent patent" within five years from grant date, $N_G$ is the number of patents that were approved during the grant year of the "parent patent" and $N_A$ denotes the total number of patent applications within five years.

Figure 7.6 presents the probability of patents to be cited within five years from the grant date.[15] During the whole period the probability of software patents to be cited was significantly lower than the probability of cryptography and image analysis patents. This result implies that the quality of software patents is lower in comparison to the other technological fields. However, the probability of software patents to be cited, which continuously decreased until 1996, has steadily increased since 1997. The other two technologies present similar results with some exceptions, as the values of probability were fluctuating during the early 1980s and patents granted for cryptographic inventions in 2000 are slightly less likely to be cited than patents that were granted a year before.

Two other measures illustrate the recent increase in the quality of software patents. The *spotting age* of patents defines the time between the grant date of "parent patents" (that is, the date of disclosure of patented know–how) and the application date of "child patents" (that is, approximately the time of succeeding inventions). The average spotting age is used to assess whether recently–granted patents are more valuable than older patents. If indeed younger "parent patents" are more often cited, their innovative value surpasses the quality of patents that were granted earlier.

[15] The number of patent grants and applications for 2004 was estimated on the basis of 2000–2003.

The other measure is the *reference year* of patents. It signifies the year in which the most valuable patents were granted, that is, the period in which the most cited "parent patents" were issued. The reference year is calculated by subtracting the average spotting age from the application year of "child patents". If the reference year increases with the application year (that is, recent inventions refer to more recent patents), the quality of patents has been sustained, as recent patents refer to newly patented inventions. However, if patent applications that were submitted in subsequent years continuously refer to patents from the same reference year, the value of patents is decreasing over time, as more recent patents are less frequently cited.

Until 1996 the spotting age of software patents has steadily increased, indicating that on average older patents held greater inventive value (or better quality) than recent patents (Figure 7.7). However, patent applications that were submitted after 1996 have cited significantly younger "parents".

The changes over time in the reference year of citing patents provide complementary outlook on the quality of patents (Figure 7.8). From 1998 onwards, software patents depart from cryptography and image analysis patents and refer to increasingly newer patents.[16] The decrease in the reference year of software patents, followed by an increase starting in 1999, clearly indicates significant improvement in their quality since 1996, as citing patents refer more often to those records.

The figures also suggest major improvements in the value and quality of patents which were submitted after 1996. The occurrence of a structural change in the quality of patents is affirmed by the results of the Chow Test for structural change (Table 7.3), which examines the extent to which variations in the spotting age of patent applications from different periods are significant. Patent applications that were submitted after 1998 mostly cite patents that were granted close to or after 1996 and less frequently refer to older patent records.[17]

---

[16] Cryptography and image analysis patents seem to "catch up" with software patents, as their reference years notably increase between 2000 and 2001.

[17] Table 7.3 also shows a structural change in the spotting age of cryptography patents in 1999. However, the origins of this development remain unclear, as no policy changes concerning cryptography patents or significant technological developments were reported.

| Application year | | Software reference year | Cryptography reference year | Image analysis reference year |
|---|---|---|---|---|
| 1985 | $Pr > F$ | 0.3924 | | |
| | $F$ | 1.06 | | |
| 1986 | $Pr > F$ | 0.3835 | 0.1563 | |
| | $F$ | 1.09 | 2.05 | |
| 1987 | $Pr > F$ | 0.6378 | 0.3242 | 0.3280 |
| | $F$ | 0.58 | 1.27 | 1.27 |
| 1988 | $Pr > F$ | 0.6130 | 0.4633 | 0.3472 |
| | $F$ | 0.62 | 0.91 | 1.21 |
| 1989 | $Pr > F$ | 0.7914 | 0.5527 | 0.3233 |
| | $F$ | 0.35 | 0.73 | 1.29 |
| 1990 | $Pr > F$ | 0.8269 | 0.5937 | 0.1279 |
| | $F$ | 0.30 | 0.66 | 2.31 |
| 1991 | $Pr > F$ | 0.8420 | 0.5886 | 0.1695 |
| | $F$ | 0.28 | 0.66 | 1.99 |
| 1992 | $Pr > F$ | 0.8289 | 0.5714 | 0.3849 |
| | $F$ | 0.29 | 0.69 | 1.11 |
| 1993 | $Pr > F$ | 0.7999 | 0.5750 | 0.5347 |
| | $F$ | 0.34 | 0.69 | 0.77 |
| 1994 | $Pr > F$ | 0.7460 | 0.6148 | 0.7719 |
| | $F$ | 0.41 | 0.62 | 0.38 |
| 1995 | $Pr > F$ | 0.8519 | 0.5999 | 0.7704 |
| | $F$ | 0.26 | 0.64 | 0.38 |
| 1996 | $Pr > F$ | 0.8344 | 0.5491 | 0.4744 |
| | $F$ | 0.29 | 0.74 | 0.89 |
| 1997 | $Pr > F$ | 0.4619 | 0.7265 | 0.7396 |
| | $F$ | 0.90 | 0.44 | 0.42 |
| 1998 | $Pr > F$ | 0.0380* | 0.9992 | 0.5795 |
| | $F$ | 3.56 | 0.01 | 0.68 |
| 1999 | $Pr > F$ | 0.1882 | 0.0099** | 0.1430 |
| | $F$ | 1.80 | 5.76 | 2.18 |
| 2000 | $Pr > F$ | 0.1089 | | |
| | $F$ | 2.37 | | |
| 2001 | $Pr > F$ | 0.1194 | | |
| | $F$ | 2.27 | | |
| Total R–Square | | 92.1% | 86.0% | 97.0% |

**Table 7.3.** Chow test for structural changes in the reference year of patents (* $P \leq 0.05$, ** $P \leq 0.01$).

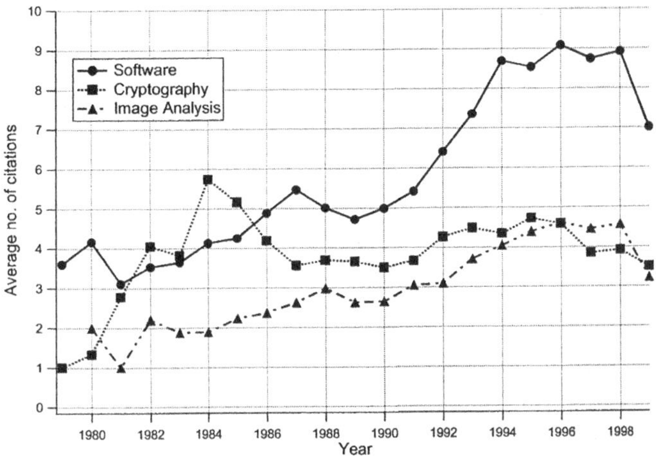


**Figure 7.5.** The average number of citations within five years from grant date.

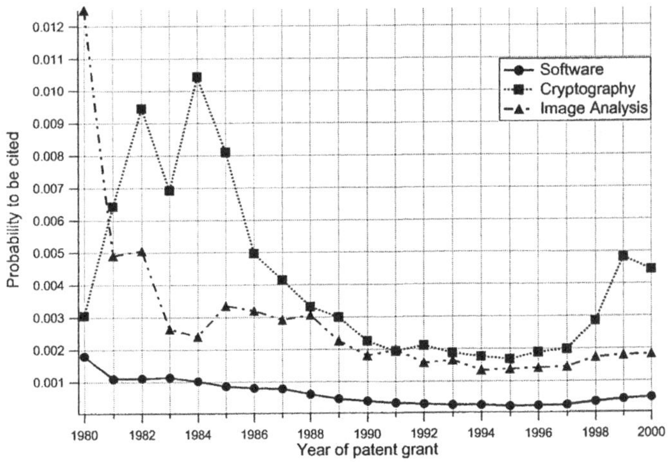


**Figure 7.6.** The probability of patents to be cited within five years.

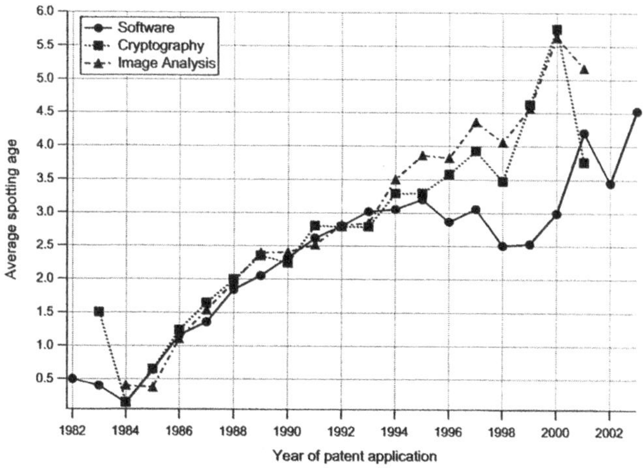


**Figure 7.7.** The spotting age of patents.

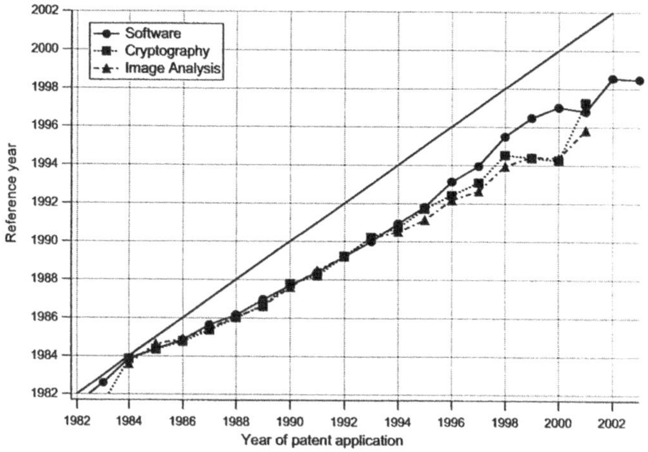


**Figure 7.8.** The reference year of patents.

### 7.4.3 Generic vs. Specific–Use Patents

Ownership rights over software technologies may grant assignees with excessive rights if those patents protect core inventions with a wide range of applications in other fields. For example, encryption algorithms are generic inventions and can broadly be implemented in a variety of fields, including secure communications, payment systems and computer networks. The patentees of encryption algorithms, such as the IDEA and the RC5, can license them or preempt any party from using them.

Analysis of software patents by class reveals major dissimilarities in the patenting behaviour of firms that operate in different, though close, technological areas. We aim at exploring whether patenting activity has increased in all areas, in generic classes or particularly where inventions are targeted toward specific uses. For example, substantial growth in the number of patents in generic technologies would indicate that the holders of patents over core inventions can dominate a wide spectrum of their applications. This scenario may easily turn to the "tragedy of anti–commons" in software technologies, in which a small group of assignees are "fencing out" core inventions by obtaining patents over them and forbidding their use by competitors in new contexts and applications (Heller and Eisenberg, 1998). The risks of excluding large numbers of inventors from the market by ownership of property rights over wide technological areas are tangible in software and information technologies due to interoperability and compatibility effects between different components of computer programs (David and Greenstein, 1990) and due to strong technological interrelatedness among software applications (Antonelli, 1993). However, if most of the patents were issued for inventions with specific uses, the possibility that a small number of patents would form excessive monopoly rights over a large variety of technologies is comparatively small. In this case, assignees can exercise their monopoly power over a limited range of vertical markets and applications.

The number of citations of software patents by other software–related classes is used as an indicator to explore the nature of patents in different areas of software technologies (Table 7.4). However, cross–citations are largely influenced by the number of patents in the citing and cited classes. Therefore, we use a corrected ratio of cross–citations to patents, $CC_p$, which is defined as follows:

$$CC_{p_i} = \frac{CC_i}{N_i \cdot N_c}, \qquad \forall i \in I \tag{7.3}$$

| *Citing/ Cited* | 703 | 704 | 705 | 706 | 707 | 709 | 710 | 715 | 717 | 718 | Total |
|---|---|---|---|---|---|---|---|---|---|---|---|
| 703 | – | 113 | 432 | 300 | 1215 | 1592 | 1842 | 396 | 1178 | 432 | 7,500 |
| 704 | 89 | – | 654 | 458 | 1832 | 1162 | 476 | 1193 | 311 | 99 | 6,274 |
| 705 | 294 | 663 | – | 542 | 3924 | 5178 | 1082 | 1174 | 791 | 579 | 14,227 |
| 706 | 429 | 550 | 716 | – | 1625 | 1088 | 389 | 535 | 513 | 277 | 6,122 |
| 707 | 400 | 876 | 2032 | 688 | – | 7180 | 2152 | 2195 | 2187 | 1153 | 18,863 |
| 709 | 409 | 550 | 2027 | 415 | 5097 | – | 5490 | 1463 | 1953 | 1293 | 18,697 |
| 710 | 417 | 275 | 809 | 136 | 2816 | 6984 | – | 586 | 1398 | 1694 | 15,115 |
| 715 | 172 | 991 | 1334 | 489 | 3461 | 3020 | 828 | – | 723 | 326 | 11,344 |
| 717 | 297 | 156 | 536 | 235 | 2250 | 2290 | 1113 | 553 | – | 621 | 8,051 |
| 718 | 169 | 87 | 353 | 109 | 1595 | 2280 | 1633 | 310 | 917 | – | 7,453 |

**Table 7.4.** Cross–citations by citing and cited classes.

| *Citing/ Cited* | 703 | 704 | 705 | 706 | 707 | 709 | 710 | 715 | 717 | 718 | $CC_p$ |
|---|---|---|---|---|---|---|---|---|---|---|---|
| **703** | – | 0.02 | 0.08 | 0.06 | 0.23 | 0.30 | 0.35 | 0.08 | 0.22 | 0.08 | **1.42** |
| 704 | 0.01 | – | 0.04 | 0.03 | 0.13 | 0.08 | 0.03 | 0.08 | 0.02 | 0.01 | 0.43 |
| **705** | 0.02 | 0.05 | – | 0.04 | 0.29 | 0.38 | 0.08 | 0.09 | 0.06 | 0.04 | **1.06** |
| 706 | 0.07 | 0.09 | 0.11 | – | 0.25 | 0.17 | 0.06 | 0.08 | 0.08 | 0.04 | 0.95 |
| 707 | 0.02 | 0.04 | 0.09 | 0.03 | – | 0.31 | 0.09 | 0.09 | 0.09 | 0.05 | 0.81 |
| 709 | 0.02 | 0.02 | 0.08 | 0.02 | 0.19 | – | 0.21 | 0.05 | 0.07 | 0.05 | 0.70 |
| 710 | 0.02 | 0.01 | 0.03 | 0.01 | 0.11 | 0.26 | – | 0.02 | 0.05 | 0.06 | 0.57 |
| **715** | 0.02 | 0.14 | 0.19 | 0.07 | 0.50 | 0.44 | 0.12 | – | 0.10 | 0.05 | **1.63** |
| **717** | 0.04 | 0.02 | 0.08 | 0.03 | 0.32 | 0.32 | 0.16 | 0.08 | – | 0.09 | **1.13** |
| **718** | 0.05 | 0.03 | 0.10 | 0.03 | 0.46 | 0.66 | 0.47 | 0.09 | 0.27 | – | **2.16** |

**Table 7.5.** The ratio of cross–citations to patents by citing and cited classes (generic classes emphasized).

Where $CC_i$ is the number of cross citations by non–class $i$ patents, $N_i$ is the number of patents in class $i$ and $N_c$ is the number of patents that could potentially be cited. $I$ denotes the group of classes that are included in the survey.

We define classes in which the average number of cross–citations is larger than 1 as *generic* classes and other classes are defined as *specific–use* technologies. Following this definition, classes 703, 705, 715, 717 and 718 are defined as generic, whereas other classes are targeted toward specific uses of the technology (the generic classes are presented in bold typeface in Table 7.5).

Figure 7.9 presents the growth in the number of patents by class. Most of the classes that are included in Figure 7.9 show steep and continuous patterns of growth in the patenting activity. Some of the technological classes (703 – modelling and simulation; 717 – software development, installation, and management) present more moderate growth in the number of patents in comparison to the majority of patent classes.

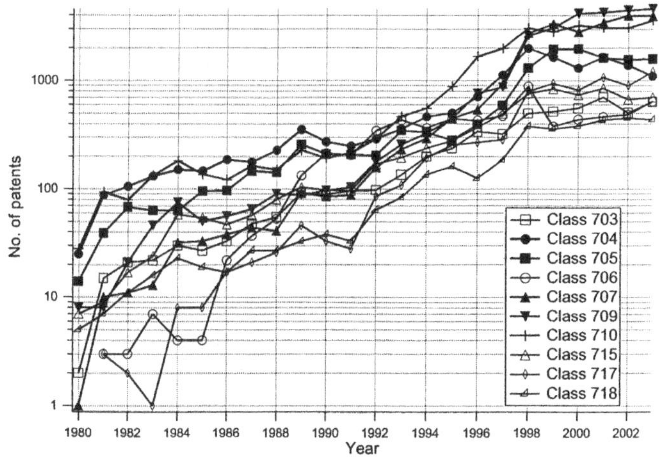


**Figure 7.9.** Technological classes with significant increase in the number of patents, 1980–2003.

Until 1995, the patterns of growth in software patents were similar among different classes. From 1996 onwards, the growth patterns of software patents significantly vary among different classes. The results brought in Table 7.5 and Figure 7.9 reveal that the prominent growth in the volume of patents has occurred mainly in the specific–use classes and in the generic class 705. The increase in the patenting activity has been moderate in generic classes and the annual number of patents is lower than in specific–use classes.[18]

Those findings indicate that acquiring patent rights over specific inventions and applications is more important than obtaining exclusive rights over a broad spectrum of technologies and uses. Since 1996, most software firms patent their inventions to protect them from exploitation in specific markets. Firms are less motivated to expand their stronghold position to other markets or to block others from entering them by extensive development and patent protection of larger amounts of generic technologies.

[18]Recently, patenting activity has even decreased in class 704 and in class 705.

### 7.4.4 The Evolution of Open Source and Software Patenting

In this section, our analysis aims at identifying the dynamics of innovation and the links between proprietary and Open Source software, and whether the rise of Open Source has preceded or has followed technological developments in proprietary technologies. Had massive development of Open Source projects preceded the rise in the patent activity, it would imply that the Open Source mode of programming is more successful in generating innovation than firms' R&D. However, had the opposite phenomenon been identified, Open Source projects would typically follow and be influenced by the development of proprietary software within firms. In this case, Open Source projects would succeed in attracting developers *after* introduction of new technologies in proprietary forms.

The pattern of innovation in proprietary software is measured by the number of patent grants by their application year and class. The evolution of Open Source projects is measured via the number of new modules, added files and lines of code (LOC) per annum. The data on the development of various Open Source projects were obtained from the Libre Software Engineering website.[19] Four different Open Source projects were selected for analysis on the basis of data availability and popularity in use:[20]

- EMACS (Editor MACroS) – A text editor.
- OpenBSD – An operating system derived from the BSD version of the UNIX system, originally developed at the University of California, Berkeley.
- KDE – A graphical desktop environment for Linux and Unix workstations.
- GNOME – A desktop environment and a development platform for building applications that integrate into the user's desktop.

(Detailed descriptions of the projects and links to online communities of their developers and users can be found at www.sourceforge.net).

A group of six software scientists and engineers classified the projects according to the USPTO classes (the same process is carried out by the Patent Office

[19]The time series were read from the graphs in the Libre Software Engineering website by using graphic tools (with an estimated precision level of 99.5 per cent), after the Libre Software Engineering refused our requests to receive the data.

[20]See Ghosh et al.'s (2002) survey of software applications used by Open Source developers.

examiners when new patents are filed). The choice of classes to which each project was compared was based on the majority's opinion. We use the taxonomy of Open Source projects by class to compare the evolution of the projects with the emergence of patenting activity in the corresponding classes.

Figures 7.10–7.13 present the development of the projects in terms of LOC, modules and files. The results show that substantial growth in the volume of Open Source projects typically *follows* the emergence of innovative output in proprietary software (taken by the application date) by a period of over two years.

Innovation and the development of proprietary software seem to precede the technological trajectory of equivalent Open Source applications. Ghosh et al. (2002) report that half of the programmers in Open Source projects are employed in developing proprietary software. Active participants in Open Source projects seem to follow a "double part–time concept", spending half of their working time programming Open Source applications and the other half developing proprietary software. Therefore, proprietary know–how, developed within firms, may largely affect the development of Open Source applications by generating knowledge spillovers from programmers that are employed in software firms to Open Source communities in which they participate.

## 7.5 Conclusions

The chapter identifies a shift in the patenting behaviour of firms and consequent changes in the structure of ownership of software patents. Those changes largely result from the establishment of a new legislative framework of software IPRs by the USPTO in 1996.[21] Before 1996, jurisdiction had frequently been modified and typically built upon particular rulings that were interpreted and extended by Court to resolve new conflicts, often in unexpected ways (see Chapter 4). Consequently, inventors faced a high degree of uncertainty from relatively unstable legal environment, while entering new markets with competing products or investing in software R&D. For example, the likelihood of engaging in legal disputes with rivals over software inventions and the expected form of resolution could hardly be predicted on the basis of the existing jurisdiction.

[21] The changes have mainly affected patents that were granted after 1998, considering that 85 per cent of the patents that were granted since 1996 were submitted after 1996 and their examination period was over two years (USPTO, 2003).

The publication of the *Examination Guidelines for Computer-Related Inventions* (USPTO, 1996) formed a set of clear definitions and policy outlines to provide a coherent framework for the legal protection of software and algorithms by patents and copyrights and a doctrinal basis to resolve conflicts over ownership rights of software technologies and applications. Although the *Guidelines* are often criticized as overprotective,[22] the new legal framework has reduced the degree of uncertainty in the software industry and the risk of engaging in expensive legal disputes over development and use of software inventions. Since the implementation of the *Guidelines*, and in spite of their shortcomings, patents were granted to more assignees than before. Hence, the new legislative framework has strengthened the potential of new entrants to compete with their inventions against incumbent firms, to use them as "bargaining chips" in cross–licensing agreements to obtain access rights to protected technologies or to generate revenues by licensing them.

The volume of software patents has exponentially increased since 1980. However, until 1995, increasing numbers of patents were granted to a relatively small group of assignees. Since 1996, the total number of assignees and the share of holders of small patent portfolios are continuously increasing. The propensity of those patent–holders (mostly SMEs and individuals) to protect their software inventions by patents is higher than it was during the early– and mid–1990s. Hence, the structure of ownership of software patents has become less concentrated since the establishment of the USPTO's *Guidelines*. Yet, despite those fundamental changes and increasing concentration of ownership of cryptography and image analysis patents, software patents are less evenly dispensed than in those technologies.

The quality and the innovative value of software patents appears to have deteriorated until 1996. Multiple indices, based on forward citations, show continuous improvement in their quality and innovative value since 1996. Software patents that were granted after 1996 are cited more often than before. Patent applications rarely refer to older patents as prior art.

Until 1995 the number of software patents in different technological classes had grown evenly. Later, the growth of software patents has significantly varied by the type of the technology: the volume of patents increased in specific–use inventions, whereas the increase in the number of patents in generic classes was relatively moderate. Patents were more frequently used in protecting specific

[22] See, for example, Bessen and Maskin (2000).

applications than in appropriating a broad range of technologies. Those changes in the patenting behaviour of firms may be associated with the establishment of a new legislative framework in 1996 and with the re-organization of the patent examination process by the USPTO.

Finally, our analysis illustrates how innovation and technical know-how in software technologies are largely driven by development of proprietary technologies within firms. Open Source projects begin later, when large shares of the technology have already been patented, and they typically follow the evolutionary patterns of commercial software.

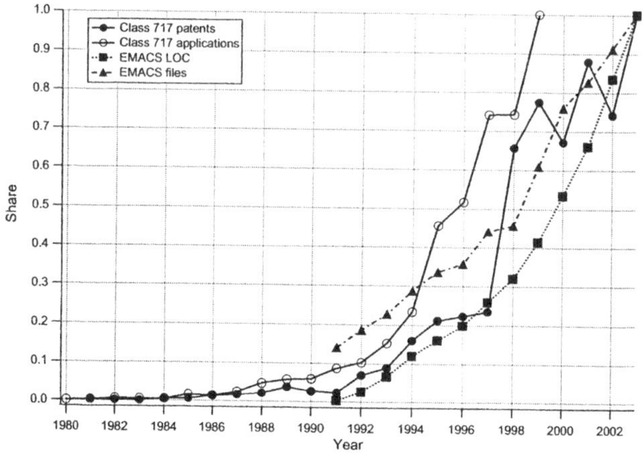


**Figure 7.10.** The evolution of the Open Source EMACS project and patenting in corresponding classes

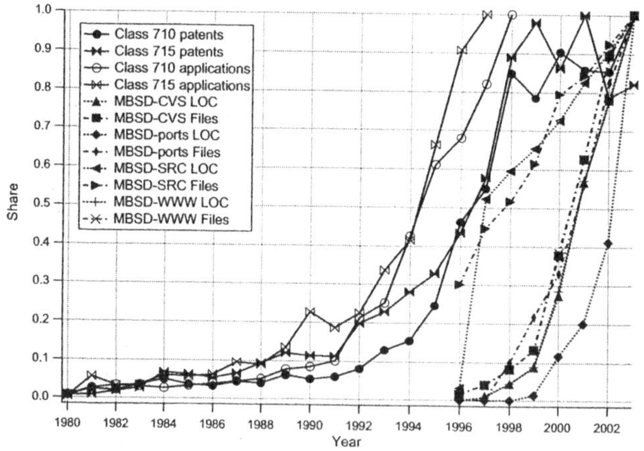


**Figure 7.11.** The evolution of the Open Source OpenBSD project and patenting in corresponding classes

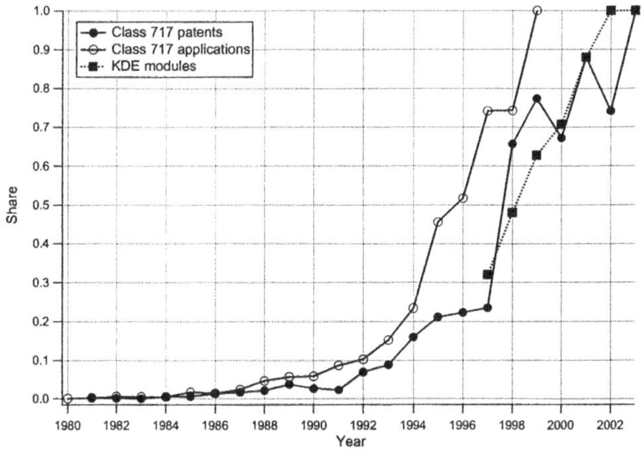


**Figure 7.12.** The evolution of the Open Source KDE project and patenting in corresponding classes

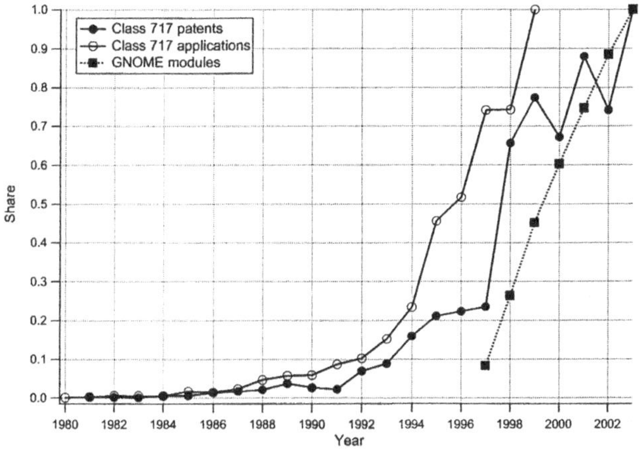


**Figure 7.13.** The evolution of the Open Source GNOME project and patenting in corresponding classes

# 8

# Proposed Framework for Analyzing IPRs in the Knowledge-Based Economy

## 8.1 In Need of a New Framework of Software IPRs

The debate on software IPRs highlights fundamental gaps in the representation of computer programs as economic goods and the appropriate legal schemes that should be provided to protect them. Further, various interpretations of software propose only limited perspectives through which particular elements of computer programs can economically and legally be assessed.

The following aspects of the legal and economic representation of software technologies and products also impose the main challenges in the public debate on their protection. Moreover, they can significantly affect the legal framework chosen to address them:

- The exact nature of software and computational processes and the ways in which they can be properly represented as economic goods.
- The similarities and differences between software applications and machines that perform similar tasks (and can be easily patented if their technological novelty is proven).
- Should computer programs enjoy IPR protection like their physical equivalents?

- The desirable design of the legal regime that can provide the maximal degree of social benefits while satisfying private and public interests.

The attempts to resolve those issues by forming legal definitions in Court have extended beyond the economic analyses that were initiated at the same period. As a result, rulings often resulted in incoherent definitions that only partially address the various aspects of software and in turn serve as a basis for future rulings, hence emphasizing the departure from the complementary economic rationale. Thereby, a more coherent approach that integrates the economic, legal and technical stanpoints regarding software IPRs is necessary to restore the a clear and market–oriented doctrine.

A possible resolution for those issues can emerge by pointing out the attributes that are common in software technologies and machinery, as well as by comparing the properties that distinguish them as economic goods. By following this method, we can recognize some of the sources of the controversy that surrounds software patenting and the reasons why physical inventions are patented without doubt and the protection of software technologies and products is continuously questioned. In addition, historical review of the evolution of information technologies and software and their development over time can be useful for analyzing the essential dimensions of those technologies, particularly for distinguishing the multifaceted entities of computer programs (namely computational "instructions", "texts" and "machines"). Throughout the discussion in this chapter, particular references to the *idea/expression* doctrine and to the difficulties in drawing parallels between software and physical equivalents are made to highlight the importance of forming a coherent juridical basis and legal policy of software IPRs.

The following section reviews the dissimilarities in the economic nature and in the market behaviour of ideas and expressions. The ways in which ideas and expressions are embedded in computer programs, stimulate innovation and contribute to their technological landscape are compared to those of tangible goods and assist in elucidating the sources of the conflict between public and private interests and intellectual property ownership over information technologies.

## 8.2 The Properties of Markets for Goods and Ideas

IPR doctrines distinguish between ideas and expressions, both in their legal definitions and in the ways in which they are treated as intellectual property. In the case of software, algorithms and techniques embedded in and carried out by computer programs are classified as "ideas" and protected by patents. The source code, interfaces and internal structure, sequence and organization of procedures and subroutines and the compilations,[1] are protected by copyrights as "expressions".[2]

Copyrights have become increasingly important particularly in protecting graphic user interfaces, program designs and the internal organization of computer programs and the sequence of computational operations that they perform. Although it seems that software patents outweigh copyrights both in importance and in inflaming the debate over them, copyrights remain a pivotal mechanism in safeguarding the different elements of computer programs. Nonetheless, copyright legislation is not necessarily simple and the rulings in recent copyright disputes demonstrate increasing juridical complexities and challenges.

Court's ruling in *Whelan v. Jaslow* (1986) significantly extended the scope of copyright protection for computer programs in the US and later steered the enactment of the legal doctrine of the USPTO on the patentability of computer programs and algorithms. The legal dispute began with copyright infringement of dental laboratory management software, *Dentlab*, originally programmed and distributed by Jaslow Dental Laboratory. Its procedures and functionalities were later re–written (in another computer language) and sold as a competitive application by Whelan Associates. In this precedent, Court held the opinion that "copyright protection of computer programs may extend beyond the programs' literal code to their *structure, sequence, and organization*" (*Whelan v. Jaslow*, 797 F.2d 1222, 1986; emphases added) and does not include only the final program or its code–lines. This doctrine, commonly known as the *SSO principle*, expanded the scope of copyright protection of software far beyond the measures that regulators had accepted (before Whelan, copyrights were granted only to published code–lines).

Traditionally, Patent Law protects ideas, technical and engineering solutions including significant components of computer programs, such as algorithms. Yet, the extension of the scope of copyrights by Court provides additional protection

[1]Compilation is the executable form of a computer program. It is produced by transforming the source code from a high–level, human–like language (such as Pascal or C++) into the binary form of machine language. It is also the format in which the final products are distributed to users.

[2]Chapter 4 provides a historical timeline and detailed analysis of the evolution of software IPRs.

to the internal organization and processes of computer programs, albeit those components are technical in essence and remain undisclosed.

The overlap between patents and copyrights in protecting intellectual property is peculiar to software. Similar doctrinal guidelines were not established for other technologies. Concerns over the joint protection by both copyrights and patents were raised during the hearings on the draft proposal of the USPTO *Guidelines*. When the final version of the *Guidelines* was finally accepted in 1996, it also became a main subject for legal criticism. In this respect, the role of the extended doctrine of copyrights in fostering innovation should also be thoroughly analyzed, in addition to other issues that were raised in this debate.

Reichman (1994) and Mackaay (1994) criticize Court's interpretation that extended that scope of protection to both copyrights and patents. They also advise against entrenching the rationale of Court's opinion while forming regulative guidelines of software IPRs and against granting copyright protection to other elements of computer programs, such as their interfaces and design, in addition to the source code.[3]

The possibilities of firms to learn from other companies by applying reverse engineering techniques are restricted, to a large extent, by both patents and copyrights. In software technologies, in particular, those possibilities are far more limited than in any other technological fields, as developers have to follow the orders of both Patent Law and the Copyright Act as well as numerous interpretations by Court. The developers of other technologies only avoid infringing the patented inventions in their field.[4] Reverse–engineering is permitted both by Copyright Law and by the Digital Millennium Copyright Act (DMCA) for the purpose of testing the interoperability between the product and other applications. However, special restrictions on the reverse engineering of content encryption methods are made by the DMCA.[5] Therefore, in various situations reverse engineering of rival programs or even application of them during interoperability tests is risky for software developers, as it may infringe the copyrights of other firms simply by *fixation* of the operated programs in the computer's memory. The result may have a hampering

[3] Finally, the USPTO decided to adopt Court's opinion and integrated the rationale of the Whelan ruling into its *Guidelines*.

[4] The case of *Bowers v. Baystate Technologies* (2003; 64 USPQ2d 1065, CA FC 2002) prohibits reverse engineering of software products albeit licensing thems.

[5] Samuelson (1999) indicates that the DMCA may hamper the development of those technologies, due to the restrictions on reverse engineering.

effect on innovation in information technologies, as interoperability between different software platforms, applications and product versions is essential to guarantee the successful operation of new programs before releasing them to the market.

Software patents present different challenges for the development of software. Innovation in software and information technologies is an incremental process that is largely based on re–programming existing components and integrating them in new ways (Cohen and Lemley, 2001). However, Patent Law does not include any privileges for re–use of reverse–engineered components, as the Copyright Act does. In most cases, their use is recognized as unlawful, since the functionality and the methods of operation of a protected invention are patented as well. Software inventions and algorithms can be patented without revealing their source code. Yet, it is possible to include in software patent applications "abstract" claims over wide technological areas. Consequently, the opportunities of software developers to offer advanced and improved software products are increasingly restrained by water–tight legislation. Further, the ability of firms to learn from existing inventions becomes more limited in the case of software technologies, as the degree of knowledge disclosure is lower in comparison to other technological fields.

The critique surrounding software IPRs also refers to the application of the *doctrine of equivalents.*[6] The application of the doctrine in Court in cases of software patent disputes may hamper the efforts of second–comers to enter the market by inventing around living patents due to with the relatively broad scope of legal coverage and due to the long duration of patents in comparison to the short life cycle of software products.

Opponents of the extended doctrine of patent and copyright protection ove software inventions anticipated that this legal framework would be used by firms as strategic means to preempt other companies from entering the market. The case of *Sony Computer Entertainment v. Connectix Corp.* (203 F.3d 596; 9th Circuit, 2000) demonstrates the strategic uses of software patents and copyrights and how those concerns were affirmed.

*Sony* sued *Connectix* for infringing its copyrights by reverse engineering the interfaces of the PlayStation console for and developing emulation of the product that can be used on personal computers. The company stopped the legal pro-

[6]The doctrine of equivalents allows infringement to be proved even when the claims are not literally infringed, when one introduces minor changes to existing patent claims to achieve the same function in substantially similar ways.

ceedings after its claims were rejected by Court. Attempting a different strategy against Connectix, Sony filed another lawsuit on patent infringement over the same technology.[7]

The complexity of IPR regimes, their advantages and shortcomings in terms of nourishing and developing technologies were discussed in the past and elaborated through various prisms. However, the main body of economic literature on IPRs treats different technologies in similar ways despite the dissimilarities in their technical attributes and market behaviour. Although legal and economic scholars, software developers, consumer organizations and interest groups devote substantial efforts to propose a coherent legal framework for software IPRs, the debate on the best scheme of protection is still ongoing. Policy makers continue to look for clear insights to follow while forming legislation for future information technologies.

## 8.3 Describing Software Applications as Economic Goods

### 8.3.1 The Various Dimensions of Software Products and Technologies

Software products vary in their technological and economic properties according to the stage of their development and to ways in which they are distributed. By expanding the taxonomy of entities that are embedded in computer programs,[8] we can distinguish between the different elements of computer programs, as follows:

1) The "behavioural" aspects of a program include the set of technical and operational features, functionalities and tasks that the program operates. For example, the Customer Relations Management (CRM) system manages the complete set of marketing activities: identifying potential customers, managing meetings with them, sending them quotes and handling their requests for information and complaints. The program calculates particular measures regarding the marketing activities of the firm (for example the volume of quotes sent to customers, the

[7] Sony withdrew its succeeding lawsuit and suspended any legal procedures against Connectix after settling this case out of court. In the past Sony used a similar strategy against another producer of PlayStation emulators, Bleem, suing it at first for copyright violation (214 F.3d 1002; 9th Circuit, 2000; plaintiff's claims for violation of its copyrights were rejected by Court) and later for patent infringement. Those legal proceedings were probably among the main reasons for Bleem's demise.

[8] A more restricted version of the taxonomy appears in Samuelson et al. (1994).

average number of scheduled meetings per sales–person in a given period) and presents the results in graphic and textual formats.

2) The general aim and the output of the program – for example, report design applications (for example *Jasper Reports*) acquire as an input a list of fields of the system databases, sets of criteria and a format in which the report should be presented. The product is a report that processes the stored data due to the seleced criteria and presents them in the requested format.

3) Subcompilations are software elements within a software application that perform particular operations. Their functionality can be examined and re–programmed by others to produce functions, features, processes and algorithms that are similar to those that appear in the original software objects.

4) Algorithms are sequences of ordered steps that perform particular functions in programs.

5) Technical and operational features that are carried out by a set of sub–routines and procedures.

6) Source code – program statements that are usually written in a programming language.

7) The final product is the software package (or a compilation), which is the product of transforming the source code into machine language.

The impact of imitation on the developer's market can vary according to the reproduced software elements and the markets targeted by second–comers. Second comers can imitate any software component, behavioural or operational feature with relatively small efforts. Further, imitation can take place to reduce the R&D expenses of rival developers and to introduce competing products at lower prices.[9] In a competitive scenario, imitation can threaten the revenues of the inventor in various ways, from duplicating final products (that is, software piracy) to more complex modes of reproduction of functionality and advanced program elements.[10] Inventors confront the risk of failing to recoup their investments in R&D, when

---

[9]This perspective is similar to the rationale of *Reward Theory* and to Nordhaus's (1969) analysis of the patent system, in which imitation produces perfect substitutes without technological improvements that compete with the inventor's product.

[10]Assessment of equivalence between features of applications is a key element in settling patent and copyright disputes. Nonetheless, in the case of software it is difficult to carry it out due to the abstract nature of the products. In comparison, the simple form of duplication, that is, software piracy, can be modelled with relative ease (several examples are presented by Conner and Rumelt, 1991; Givon et al., 1995; Stolpe, 2000). Chapter 6 demonstrates how those issues can be addressed by applying simulation methods.

| Market Proximity | Similar Market | Adjacent Markets | Remote Markets |
|---|---|---|---|
| Inventor | Action: Inventing and introducing new products to the market.<br><br>Mark: Main market for recouping R&D investments. | Action: Producing Derivatives applications.<br><br>Mark: Additional market for recouping R&D costs and generating future revenues. | Action: Development of applications for new contexts on the basis of existing know-how.<br><br>Mark: Inventor rarely recoups R&D costs in those markets. |
| Second-comer | Action: Cloning program functions.<br><br>Mark: Direct competition and lower prices remove shares of inventor's revenues.<br><br>Effect: Market destructive competition. | Decompilation, reverse-engineering and development of add-ons.<br><br>Mark: Competition with the inventor in related, derivative and future markets.<br><br>Effect: Partially destructive competition. | Software elements applied in new contexts.<br><br>Mark: Innovative use of existing applications in novel contexts.<br><br>Effect: No market destructing effects. |
| Regulative intervention | Blocking imitation for long periods. | Blocking imitation for short periods. | Lightly regulated, or not at all (re-use in remote contexts is allowed). |

**Table 8.1.** Potential hazards and factors of failure in various software markets (*Based on*: Samuelson et al., 1994).

imitation by competitors takes place. However, it is important to realize that imitation of less valuable elements of software or entry of second comers into remote market niches would typically generate insignificant effects on inventors. Therefore, economic losses that are caused by imitation should be evaluated in a wider perspective that includes not only the equivalence between products but also potential losses in present and future markets (see Table 8.1).

Software is usually vulnerable to imitation as applications reveal significant amounts of embedded knowledge and technicalities to programmers only by inspecting their external interfaces and operation. The internal structure of software technologies and products and the knowledge embedded in them can be revealed even when the source code remains undisclosed. Then, programmers can "clone" the applications and reproduce similar functionality and features with relative ease. In this respect, virtually every software component can be re-programmed and integrated into other applications and this sort of imitation is usually less costly than developing the same features (Mansfield et al., 1981). Thereby, users would prefer applying software "clones" that imitate other commercial applications due to their lower prices, better quality or favourable licensing terms.

Following the potential threats that imitation presents to inventors, legal protection should vary between long periods of exclusivity in markets that were originally targeted by the inventor (yet, this term should be shorter than the lifetime of patents and copyrights) to minor legal intervention when the applications of second comers are distant from the original uses of the inventions. However, one of the main challenges in applying this market–oriented policy is the ability to establish a new legislative framework and the degree of uncertainty that it will bring to the market. Hence, if the new policy fails to provide clear standards for evaluating *ex ante* whether new product versions are sufficiently "remote" from the original programs, it will probably create negative impact on the market.

### 8.3.2 The Textual Metaphor of Computer Programs

As programs are produced via a set of instructions in a human–like language (for example Pascal, C++ and Fortran), the obvious metaphor of software source code is text. Following this interpretation of computer programs, copyrights were originally used to protect their textual aspects. The legal status of the source code of programs has become similar to any printed material, such as books or magazines, which is automatically protected by copyrights.

Copyright protection applies to three elements of computer programs:

- The source code of the program.
- The structure, sequence and organization of the program.
- The final product (software package or compilation of the source code).

When likening the source code to published matter, as in the case of applying copyrights to protect computer programs, the functional and the technological essence of software is partially dismissed. The nature and the role of the source code should first be clarified in order to assess the appropriateness of the present IPR protection schemes. Although the source code is generated and represented as text lines, in practice it defines a sequence of instructions that are transformed into an executable machine code, which is carried out by computers. In this respect, the source code serves as intermediate means for producing products that carry out required functionality. Although the functionality of a program is reached through those textual means, software functions and the source code are legally and technically distinguished entities. Therefore, had copyrights granted protection only to the code–lines, they would have been restricted only to protection of the textual elements of programs. However, software can be reproduced without copying any segment of the original source code. Imitation mostly takes place by programming new versions of the source code that capture the very same "behaviour" of the original program without duplicating or even without inspecting its original source code. Put in a different way, programmers can follow a given application to produce a different version of the source code that imitates the functionality of the original program (for example by writing it in another computer language) without infringing the inventor's rights. In this respect, software can be described as a technological product whose means of production happens to be textual.

The second entity of software that is protected by copyrights is the *compilation* or the final software product. Like other copy–protected commodities (for example phonograms and photographs), software does not have to remain in its textual form to enjoy copyright protection, as copyrights prohibit unauthorized reproduction and distribution of the final product in a digital format. Therefore, unauthorized duplication of computer programs is recognized as wrongful by the Copyright Act (but it does not necessarily infringe the patent rights of the developers).

The third entity, the internal organization of the program, is perhaps the most challenging element in terms of constituting a legal policy with a well–stated economic rationale. Its scheme of protection should aim at preventing market destructive behaviour of competitors and at the same time has to avoid benefiting any private parties at the expense of public welfare. For instance, had the scope of protection covered only textual aspects of software, competitors could have imitated and cloned the functionality and "behaviour" of programs and easily compete with similar applications.

The ruling in the case of *Whelan v. Jaslaw* highlighted major issues surrounding the formation of a legal framework that protects the non–textual elements of computer programs through extension of the existing regime. While copyrights had been established to protect artistic and literary works, the ruling expanded the regime to cover operational and semi–functional elements. This case (which is elaborated in details in Chapter 4) exemplifies how the extended scope of a particular regime, in this case the scope of copyrights, may be in conflict with other legal schemes. As a result, the extended doctrine may go way beyond the aims of the regime and can produce further complexities and ambiguities.

Critique of the *Whelan* ruling relies on the analogy between computer programs and machines. The similarities between software and machinery suggest that the extension of the scope of copyrights beyond the source code and the final product can be compared to protecting the arrangement and design of machinery components by copyrights. Organization of a set of functional parts of a machine aims at achieving required "behaviour", that is desirable functionality and performance, either by physical or through intangible means. Similarly, software elements are incorporated into an application that can accomplish the same goals. Further, the Whelan ruling threatens to remove a substantial share of the semi-technical and operational features of computer programs from the public domain for very long periods. For example, the ways in which subroutines interact with other procedures according to given rules can become the property of developers for their lifetime plus 90 years.

The case of *SCO Group v. Autozone Inc.* demonstrates the potential threats to innovation from the expansion in the scope of copyrights. In March 2004 SCO, the owner of the copyrights and licensing rights of the UNIX V operating system, submitted a lawsuit against Daimler–Chrysler and Autozone (a retailer of car accessories) for non-permissible *use* of the Linux operating system. The plaintiff argued that Linux was "an operating system variant or clone of UNIX System V technology ... [Linux] is not just a clone, but is intended to displace UNIX System V" (*SCO Group v. Autozone Inc.*, 2004; § 13). Therefore, its implementation infringed the rights of the UNIX V owners, as Linux arguably imitates the *structure, sequence and organization* of the UNIX V system. SCO's case against Daimler–Chrysler was dismissed by agreement between the two parties. The case against Autozone still proceeds, but it is likely that SCO's arguments will be rejected, as the US District Court ruled in August 2007 that SCO does not own the rights over the Unix code.[11]

SCO has chosen to target Linux users in its lawsuit, as well as commercial distributors of the operating system, including Novell and IBM. It argued that the use of software "clones" (and not the unauthorized *reproduction* of its UNIX V system, as in other copyright disputes) infringes its copyrights. The strategy of SCO to sue users of competing operating systems has also been perceived as an attempt to expand the scope of copyrights beyond the SSO doctrine. Previously,

[11] *SCO Group Inc. v. Novell Inc.*, Civil Case No. 2:04CV139DAK.

software producers could be sued over copyright infringements on the basis of the SSO doctrine. Users would be sued only for non-permissible use of the plaintiff's products. However, SCO's strategy opened the way to other firms to sue also users of competing products that resemble their own goods. This legal practice can have engraving effects on the dynamics of software markets. Dominant firms would be able to strengthen their position in the market by threatening potential entrants from competing with them and by suing customers of competing products. SMEs, can be driven to prefer a particular application only to avoid legal disputes over the use of rival products, even when those products incur significant improvements and cost savings (as in the case of IBM's and Novell's versions of Linux).

### 8.3.3 Computer Programs as *Computational Machines*

The history of computer science suggests that our perspectives on software patents and their influence on the development of software technologies should go beyond the contemporary debate on the patentability of computer programs. Broader views that build upon the evolution of software provide a more coherent vision of the technical and economic properties of computer programs and the dynamics of innovation in this field.

Useful insights on computer programs as economic goods are obtained by likening software applications to *computational machines*. Computational machines were developed first as physical equipment and were employed in calculating single tasks, such as a particular mathematical function or an algorithm with a limited sequence of steps. Later, they evolved to *universal machines* that can perform multiple computational tasks and evolved to the digital computer. Historical evidence suggests that in numerous cases computational machines that were built to perform specific computational tasks increased productivity and innovative output and were granted patents without opposition.

Computational machines hold a large potential to utilize non-skilled labour and to deploy human resources in advanced tasks rather than to allocate them to trivial calculations, as the scarcity of professional and creative labour is similar to scarcity of other sorts of capital. This notion was highlighted by Nicholson (1892): "There are certain kinds of brain-capacity [that is, skills], the outcome of a conjunction of natural ability, education, experience and ... opportunity, which are comparatively rare, and like other rare things, command a scarcity value" (pp. 487–488). The scarcity of talented labour and its importance are particularly emphasized as "intellects of this sort also directly or indirectly save much labour, or increase the efficiency of labour, or more generally add to the wealth of society, and therefore ... deserve this scarcity value" (ibid.; pp. 488).

The efficient deployment of labour releases workers from trivial tasks to perform more sophisticated routines, as they can devote larger proportion of their time to discovery of new technological means and scientific methods. The historical case of the *human computers* exemplifies how the use of machinery replaced mathematicians in various tasks.[12] The automatization of arithmetic calculations was identified by Charles Babbage (1835) as a source for more efficient re–allocation of human resources and potential cost savings, naming it *the division of mental labour*. Babbage argued that the primary improvement associated with the use of automated calculations is to "avoid the loss arising from the employment of an accomplished mathematician in performing the lowest processes of arithmetic." (ibid.; p. 201). Further, in his description of the organization of the French government's project of calculating logarithmic tables, Babbage draws a hierarchy of three departments of skilled labour for accomplishing computational tasks successfully:

(a) Experienced mathematicians who carry out analytical investigations provide recipes and formulae to solve computational problems,
(b) workers with intermediate skills who interpret the formulae, substitute the variables with numerical expressions and organize the inputs from the manual computers in a format of calculated tables, and
(c) labour with basic skills that carries out simple calculations.

Skilled mathematicians were the most knowledgeable and innovative sector of this organization and significantly contributed to the advance of the work process by forming new methods for solving problems and simplifying computations. Additional workers that were added to the first two sections of the organization strengthened the pool of problem solving competences. Babbage suggested that by substituting the clerks in the third department with mechanical apparatus that could perform simple arithmetic calculations (such as addition, subtraction and multiplication of two numbers), skilled labour could become more useful by developing new computational methods.

[12] "Computers" is used here in its historical meaning, that is, clerks who were employed by firms to carry out manual calculations, mainly in administrative activities.

One of the results of Babbage's attempts to refine the quality of mathematical calculations was the *Difference Engine*, a mechanical device that automatically calculates astronomical tables. The Engine simplified the work of astronomers and eliminated human errors, thereby improving the accuracy of the calculations. Later, Babbage designed the ambitious *Analytical Engine*, a multi–purpose computing device that could address a broader variety of mathematical problems, whose construction was never completed.[13]

A second major event in the history of modern computing was the publication of Turing's seminal work that presented the solution to *Hilbert's tenth problem* (Turing, 1936). Turing solved one of the main problems of modern mathematics in a way that laid the foundations for computer science.[14] His theory served as a basis for computer operating and programming, which has remained virtually unchanged since then. The concept of a Universal Machine, described by Turing, consists of four fundamental operations: storage of digital data, modification of the stored data (instructed by "behaviour tables", that are known today as code–lines), removal of data from the storage array and generation of output. Those basic functions of the Universal Machine were implemented in the design of digital computers and resulted in production of a multi–purpose platform for computational tasks, capable of storing and manipulating massive amounts of data in very short durations.

The controversy around the patentability of mathematical algorithms and business methods points out major disadvantages of protecting basic computational techniques as intellectual property. Had the concept of the Universal Machine been patented, the patent–owners could have dominated virtually every computer technology that was developed in the following decades. Consequently, patent–holders could have been able to preempt others from entering into the evolving field of information technologies.[15] Substantial economic benefits result from disclosure

[13]Babbage's attempts to produce the Difference Engine inspired two Swedish innovators, George and Edward Scheutz, who succeeded in developing and manufacturing a different version of the machine, for which a French patent was granted (patent no. 13480, May 1850) (Buxton, 1988; Lindgren, 1990).

[14]Hilbert's tenth problem inquires as to whether a definite method for solving all mathematical problems exists. Turing's proof, which introduced the new concept of *computable numbers*, was a milestone in the evolution of computer science and was used as a theoretical basis for the development of digital computers after WWII.

[15]Patent applications for a general purpose computer were rejected over the years for different reasons. In 1936, Zuse, a German engineer, submitted a patent application for a general purpose computer to the German Patent Office. However, the Patent Office found

and dissemination of technical and organizational know–how that re–assigns professional labour to advanced undertakings. On a large scale, the know–how that underlies the automation of repetitious and elementary tasks from its workload can remove them from a broad variety of organizations.

Indeed, the use of software products requires hardware – a personal computer or a server. Yet, computations are more efficiently accomplished on digital hardware than on any other application that uses physical machinery. Bresnahan et al. (1999) indicate that "especially if we look at recordkeeping, remembering, simple calculating and comparing, and similar tasks, the result of IT use and the associated reorganization of work has been the systematic substitution of computer decisionmaking for human decisionmaking in clerical (and similar routine) work ... a re–optimized organization will have new opportunities to substitute out of using humans where computers have comparative advantage." A larger IT reservoir and replacement of physical machinery by software applications can produce larger volumes of computations and enhance the productivity gains of the firm (Brynjolfsson and Hitt, 1998). However, users are likely to prefer physical machinery over its digital equivalents if its value surpasses that of software and if the source code has no additional benefits.

Following the functional and "behavioural" prospects of software, one can identify the use of applying the analogy between software applications and their physical equivalents. This analogy builds upon several similarities between those types of commodities. First, accomplishing productive tasks by technical means is a characteristic of software as well as it is typical for machines. Second, computer programs can be constructed as physical machines, with some degree of design efforts, by embedding their internal logic and and sequence of operation in electronic circuits. Third, programming is based on assembling a variety of operational elements of software (including procedures, data structures and algorithms, *inter alia*) and corresponds to construction of machines from physical elements and components. Fourth, programs, like machines, are large and complex products that usually require interoperability with other products in order to fully function.

Some scholars follow the rationale of the *Alappat* decision (1994) and argue

the degree of novelty insufficient and rejected it. Later, the USPTO rejected Eckert and Mauchly's patent application for a general purpose computer, since the same machine was introduced earlier by Atanasoff and von Neumann (but it was not patented by them).

that software and machinery are similar in essence and differ only in the ways in which they are constructed: Machines are built from tangible materials and computer programs from textual mediators, which are later compiled (see for example Kretschmer, 2003). Following this argument, equivalence in software patents can be determined via comparing the efficiency of different algorithms (Chin, 1998), as in comparing the scales of productivity of different machines that perform the same action. However, computer programs operate through a set of instructions (which is not "textual", but mostly operational), applied as building blocks of software products and technologies. Those components can indeed be compared to advanced mechanisms of machinery, but the main difference is in the levels of difficulty of imitating and reproducing them.

Imitation and reproduction of complex technologies, such as drugs and chemicals, is a long process that often requires reverse engineering. In comparison, software development requires decompilation and re–programming of various elements and functionality in relatively rapid and standard ways, such as "black–box testing".[16] In this respect, legislation often confuses between the medium of creation (the source code of the program) and the artifacts that are created by using it (the behaviour of the program). Therefore, while likening software applications to machines, copyright protection for the source code does not make more sense than protecting the raw materials of machines.

Samuelson et al. (1994) propose a legal scheme through which novelty and equivalence of software inventions can be evaluated in patent disputes. Their test is based on the behavioural aspects of programs, which according to them are the main source of value in software applications. The authors define the behaviour of a program as the set of functions, technical features and information processing (inputs, internal sequence and algorithms and outputs) that its operation involves. It is the way in which a program executes its defined tasks via machine language instructions.[17]

The rationale behind the proposed framework is the following: Software ap-

[16] "Black–box testing" is a testing technique in which the internal structure and the organization of a program are not known to the tester and the source code is not accessible. The way of operation is explored by following the ways in which the inputs are processed and by comparing them to the resulting outputs.

[17] This definition can be interpreted as either "functionality", "technical features", "operational features", "instructions", "performance" of a program, a procedure within it or all those elements altogether, and requires further elaboration and clarity before applying it in new legal guidelines and in analyses of the present regime.

plications compete and attract users on the basis of their performed functions, technical and operational features. When two computer programs have the same functionality and "behaviour", both programs seem indistinguishable and perfect substitutes for the end user, although their sources are completely different. Protecting the behaviour of programs within the restricted scope of specific patent claims can maintain the primary sources of value of a software invention and at the same time can make the patented (and disclosed) behaviour available for new contexts and applications. However, this proposal reflects only the value of programs for end users (through the behaviour of the programs), while the source code of those applications generates different types of value for skilled users. A source code that is more organized, well–structured and well–documented enables programmers to adapt it more easily to the needs of the organization, particularly while maintaining programs or while developing subsequent versions of them. It can significantly reduce the expenditure of firms on information systems, despite similarities to other programs in the resultant "behaviour". Consequently, the structure of the code, the methodologies and tools that are employed in the development process can be as valuable as the final product.

However, the unique competitive value of commercial applications is primarily generated via their functionality and not necessarily through their source code. Every version of the source code represents one way in which required functionality can be obtained. The very same functionality can be achieved by a different way of programming. Usually the code–lines of new programs are crafted from scratch. Their structures vary one from the other despite similarities in their features. Variables and declarations are given different names by different programmers. Code–lines provide an important source of learning, and programmers often follow examples from technical recipe–books and code libraries while producing their own programs. Yet, copying large fragments of source code from one program to the source code of another application, rather than programming them, is complex and in many cases not feasible. Hence, the innovative element in software, which is also the most vulnerable to imitation, lies neither in the general purpose of the program nor in its source code, as those elements are easily generated or reproduced. Instead, the unique way in which features and algorithms are incorporated into the source code to perform defined tasks is the main source of value of each computer application.

### 8.3.4 Computer Programs as Industrial Designs

The previous sections highlight the various similarities between machines and computer programs. To a large extent, software programming indeed resembles the industrial design of physical machines. Like their manufacturers who craft materials and assemble mechanical parts into a final product, programmers produce applications with required functionality by combining elements of source code, interfaces and data structures. The different production phases: design, manufacturing and distribution, exist in both technologies.

Understanding the distinction between the design and the manufacturing phases in information technologies is particularly important for policy and law makers, while considering changes in the legal doctrine. The modified legislation has enabled software firms to broaden the variety of software elements that they own as their intellectual property. Therefore, the impact of the changing legislation on the market is not limited only to final products, but also influences their development. Therefore, assessment of the impact of the legal framework on innovation should also include its effects on the development of software products and technologies.

The existing IPR doctrine, which is largely based on the distinction between ideas and expressions, differentiates between provision of legal protection for the final good that is produced and distributed, and provision of property rights for its technical basis, which is usually formed during the design phase. The division between the "design" and the "manufacturing" phases can determine which of the stages of software development should be classified within the design phase, and hence should enjoy patent protection. Other stages should be perceived as elements of the "manufactured" products and be protected as expressions by copyrights.

Samuelson et al. (1994) argue that designing and programming software applications jointly form the "design" phase. Following their argument, once development of a program is completed, the production of additional copies (that is, "software packages") can be considered as the "manufacturing" phase.

We propose a somewhat different categorization in which the "design" phase includes the analysis and the design of programs and the "manufacturing" phase is the programming (either for specific users or for mass distribution). Such a taxonomy represents more adequately the nature of software development, as the analysis and design process is the equivalent of designing physical products in which blueprints are generated and production methods are selected. During the design stage, software analysts identify the needs of users, the aims and operational features of programs and their internal architecture. Then, they define the required "behaviour" and the set of functions that the program performs. This stage involves disintegration of the complex structure of the planned program into numerous programming tasks, instructions, algorithms, interfaces and sub–routines. The programmers are also involved in the "pre–production" of software and assist in choosing development tools, approving the architecture of the program and assessing the technical feasibility of different features. Later, programming begins and closely follows the specifications of the analysts and the chosen configuration of the program.

The novelty of software inventions lies either in the new *results* that programs produce or in the originality of the *processes* that generate them. Some parts of the applications are achieved via imitation, reverse–engineering, decompilation of other applications or by using available source code, whereas others are purely the creation of their programmers. In this respect, patents and copyrights provide a partial solution for protecting computer programs, as some elements are not fully protected by these regimes or by other legal schemes.[18] However, although the process of software design resembles the planning of new machinery, elements of computer programs cannot be protected as industrial designs as they lack the "ornamental or aesthetic aspect of a useful article. Such particular aspect may depend on the shape, pattern or color of the article ... reproducible by industrial means" (WIPO, 2001).

## 8.4 The Use of Metaphors in Juridical Processes

Programs are often created to provide new contexts that simplify or improve the ways existing processes are carried out. The design and functionality of computer programs create conceptual metaphors through which software operates and tasks are accomplished with relative ease. Moreover, real–world metaphors (such as machinery that is substituted for software) serve as convenient references to provide

[18]Similarly, during the 1980s, advances in the design of semiconductor masks challenged the existing IPRs that lacked the appropriate legal instruments to protect them. Finally, the enactment of the Semiconductor Chip Protection Act in 1984 provided the necessary protection for complete designs and embedded elements (Samuelson and Scotchmer, 2002).

users with functions of products that they used before and as a basis for adding advanced features to simplify the use to increase efficiency. To exemplify, a typewriter can be taken as a useful conceptual metaphor of word processors. As the basic functions of typewriters were transformed into and included in word processors, users are able "to migrate" from typewriters to their digital equivalents with little training. Integrated spell checkers and thesauri are additional features that were added to the basic versions of word processors and increased the value of the product for its users.

The coherence of operation of computer programs and their interoperability with other applications is an important source of value in software development. Coherent operation is often based on metaphors and on the ways the functions of the original product interact with the physical world. Similarly, a successful computer program integrates the technical features of its physical equivalents and other processes that involve them. Moreover, the program enhances the performance of users by adding new technical and operational features that were difficult to implement in the physical product. Therefore, software development does not reproduce copies of physical products in a digital form, but also applies them in new environments and contexts.

The course of employing metaphors to constitute IPR policies created two types of inefficiencies. The first source of inefficiencies resulted from the lack of suitable legal guidelines that accommodate the needs of the evolving industry during long periods. The second source of inefficiencies is more complex than the first. It refers to the late application of a legal framework and a certain technological paradigm that satisfy the needs and the unique characteristics of the industry long after they are replaced by a new and more advanced technological environment. In information technologies, the completion of policy changes happens more than a decade after the emergence of new technological paradigms. Therefore, in many cases, legislative changes fail to resolve conflicts between the legal regime and the evolving market (see the historical taxonomy of software IPRs in Chapter 4).

Software should not be legally protected as intellectual property if it simply replicates existing goods and similar contexts. Though digitization enhances the efficiencies of organizations, it encapsulates a significant innovative value only when it contributes new technological or operational features.

The debate on the social and economic value of IPRs within the context of information technologies highlights another related controversy – the patentability of *business methods*. Business methods can be patented in the US since the ruling in the case of *State Street Bank & Trust v. Signature Financial Group* (1998; United States Court of Appeals for the Federal Circuit, 96–1327). Signature produces software for managing financial services. One of its applications is used for pooling fund assets, which monitors allocation of assets, income and expenses on the basis of daily changes in the market. Since 1993, the firm has held a patent for "data processing system for hub [that is, portfolio] and spoke [that is, partner funds] financial services configuration" (US Patent no. 5,193,056). State Street Bank was sued by Signature for infringing its patent rights and in turn State Street Bank sought resolution in Court by arguing that the patent was invalid on several grounds: First, the patent was granted for a business method that was exempted from the scope of patents according to section 101 of the Patent Law.[19] Second, the patent (issued before the publication of the USPTO guidelines) protects mathematical algorithms and formulae that were at the time non–patentable. At the end of the juridical process, the US Court of Appeals for the Federal Circuit concluded that business methods should not be excluded anymore from the patentable subject matter, stating that it "take[s] this opportunity to lay this ill–conceived exception to rest".

The decision, a recent statutory keystone in patenting software and other business services, has widened the scope of patents to business methods and financial software. Yet, the ruling preserves requirements of novelty and utility, but removes the necessary conditions of technical merits and tangible contribution to technology. The ruling states that "patentability does not turn on whether the claimed method does business instead of something else, but on whether the method, viewed as a whole, meets the requirements of patentability", and therefore business–related inventions can be protected by patents. However, the ruling stimulated other controversies and expanded the debate on software patenting. In particular, the degree of novelty necessary to obtain business patents seems to be lower than in other patent classes (Hall, 2003). For example, manual accounting processes that are converted into software can be protected by patents. Consequently, those long–living business practicees applied in information systems or manual procedures of firms can be patented and then be excluded from the public

[19]Section 101 states that "Whoever invents or discovers any new and useful process, machine, manufacture, or composition of matter, or any new and useful improvement thereof, may obtain a patent therefore, subject to the conditions and requirements of this title."

domain, even though their technical and innovative contribution is marginal.

## 8.5 Re–Drawing the Line Between Ideas and Expressions

The economic literature identifies empirically and theoretically the importance of technical knowledge for stimulating innovation. Knowledge is not limited as an input for the development and for the production of goods, but has become a final good of itself in many industrial sectors. In this respect, IPR issues often result from the shift of the dominant technological paradigm from the physical–goods economy towards the "new" economy that is largely based on intangible capital.

Different from physical goods, knowledge is infinitely expansible. Once it is acquired and distributed, it cannot be restricted from others that obtain and simultaneously hold it. Since knowledge–based goods are constructed upon technical know–how, rather than on machinery and industrial processing, firms can imitate and reverse–engineer products that are present in the market with relatively small efforts.

The first foundations of the software IPR legislation were established in the US case of *Diamond v. Diehr* (1981). In this case, Court recognized computer programs as patentable if they were embedded in physical machinery. Later, a series of *ad hoc* rulings expanded the scope of protection and determined that software and algorithms patentable of and by themselves.

While both patents and copyrights are generally criticized as overprotective, as they provide monopoly over technologies and cultural goods for long periods, the unique case of software adds new and complex dimensions to the debate as it can be protected by both patents and copyrights. Hence, while examining the economic effects of patents and copyrights separately rather than evaluating their cumulative impact, those analyses reflect only fragments of the links between the market and the legal regime.

A different issue is the contribution of copyrights to creation of innovative output in software technologies. Computer programs typically contain a source code, which is designed to carry out specific procedures, arithmetic and logical calculations. Those elements serve data processing and manipulation, which is accomplished by compiling the source code into the binary format of machine language. The source code can be rewritten in a variety of programming tools, applied in different technical environments[20] and reverse–engineered. These characteristics are useful while applying computers as basal platforms for a wide range of software applications. However, the same prospects create major challenges in determining the novelty computer programs for legal puroposes. Therefore, apart from setting laws to protect the final products (that is, the compilations), legislators should address the benefits and drawbacks of protecting other software elements, either as inseparable features of the technology or as distinctive legal entities.

Lacking coherent policy guidelines that define and regulate IPRs for the multiple elements of software, this legal discontinuity was fulfilled until the 1990s by Court's *ad hoc* rulings, which later shaped the legislation in the US and worldwide. It was not until 1996 that the USPTO published official policy guidelines for patenting and copy–protecting aspects of computer programs and algorithms. Since their publication, the *Examination Guidelines for Computer–Related Inventions (Final Version)* have influenced software IPR policies worldwide.

Legal allowances for reverse–engineering exemplify important prospects of law and technical learning in firms, as well as the blurring borders between expressions and ideas in recent doctrinal changes. Reverse–engineering has positive effects improving both innovation and interoperability between complimentary technologies.[21] Firms can analyze features of rival products and test the interfaces between their own technologies and market leading applications. By joining new technologies and existing products they can expand the technological realm and add new ways of use. Therefore, reverse–engineering represents another way in which firms can gain knowledge from the experience of rivals – not for the purpose of copying their products, but to improve their own technologies. Nonetheless, the application of reverse–engineering methods is restricted by legal orders. While the Copyright Act does not impose any constraints on reverse–engineering, Patent Law recognizes the application of technical knowledge by means of reverse–engineering infringing if the technology is protected by valid patents. The patent doctrine introduces a major conflict in technological fields where innovation is sequential and learning from rival technologies is essential for future developments. Allowing acquisition of technical know–how by reverse–engineering contradicts the purpose of providing

---

[20]For example, operating systems, data management systems, or hardware such as desktops, "wise" mobile devices and handheld computers.

[21]Interoperability suggests that demand and supply of each component in the system are strongly influenced by technical advances in other elements.

incentives to innovate through monopoly rights over inventions. Yet, this sort of know–how is fundamental for the production of software technologies.

Interrelatedness plays a major role as well: In software and information technologies, technical progress of one component of the technology influences the development of other features and therefore affects the advance of the whole technology (Antonelli, 1993). However, strong interrelatedness exists only when firms can learn from rival technologies how to improve their own products by merging them with the developments of other firms. Nonetheless, this strategy cannot be implemented if major shares of the technology are protected by patents.

A different perspective usually goes beyond the limited definition of information processing is the use of embedded software. These types of applications are integrated into a wide variety of physical apparatus and involve man–machine and machine–machine interfaces, hardware and content. They usually expand to new technological fields (for example navigation devices, new forms of mobile telephony and VOIP). Those new technological contexts require new definitions of intellectual property and doctrinal guidelines that often do not exist when the new technology is introduced.

Ideas and expressions are both significant for utilizing know–how in new products and technologies. However, drawing a fine distinction between these types of innovative outputs is difficult and existing taxonomies that assist this process are often under debate. Research frameworks that analyze the role of knowledge in the economy (for example evaluation of innovation policies) can reflect a broader outlook on the issues and their potential solutions if analyses of the different functions of ideas and their expressions are included in the scope of the discussion.

## 8.6 Conclusions

The approach towards knowledge–based goods and the legal guidelines that regulate their protection as intellectual property were largely shaped by Court's decision in the case of *Whelan v. Jaslow*. The case has reshaped the definitions of ***property*** by including intangibles within the scope of IPR protection. Moreover, it revolutionized long–living perspectives on the borderlines between expressions and ideas, which had become solid establishments in "traditional" technologies. This case is a keystone in the chain of jurisdiction and IPR policies that largely built upon it and, hence, secured its position in forming future legislation. The case led to the formation of new classifications of ideas and expressions, where new borderlines that separate them are drawn on a case–by–case basis, rather than through coherent and more versatile regulative efforts. Consequently, the legal doctrine that was later established has significantly extended the scope of copyrights for computer programs. The modified IPR doctrine includes components of operability and design that are intrinsic to the technology in the scope of copyrights, while other rulings have meanwhile strengthened software IPRs by recognizing algorithms as patentable.

# 9

# Conclusions

Appropriation and intellectual property policies are far from being static. They constantly develop with the frequent changes in markets, institutions and technologies. Policy makers prefer to form generic legislative guidelines for the filing and enforcement of patents, since a general legal framework and extended scope of traditional IPR regimes typically reduce regulation costs (which is desirable from a social standpoint). However, knowledge–based industries present diverse needs that are loosely met by a general and simplified legal framework. High degrees of technological diversity and complex market mechanisms favour the constitution of "tailor–made" regimes, uniquely formed to fit the peculiar nature of each technology, its patterns of innovation and technological diffusion over enactment of general frameworks.

The case of software is unique as a single product is protected by two major legal mechanisms, that is, patents and copyrights. Software IPRs illustrate how the borderline between ideas and expressions has blurred. Previously, a product was recognized as either encompassing *ideas* or being an *expression* of creativity, while in the case of software the product appears to be both. Although the case of software is currently a unique one, the juridical and technological trajectories have already paved the way for frequent application of loosely–related and remote doctrines to resolve issues of IPRs in information products and technologies and to draw new precedents.[1]

[1]One example is the protection of databases in the EU by a *sui generis* law, which grants a status of property to non–copyrightable facts and data. Another example is the US case of eBay, in which data stored in the company's servers and presented over

Constitution of a proper legal doctrine of equivalence and robust rulings by drawing analogies between physical machines to their digital counterfeits largely depends on acknowledging both the utility in following this course of action and the possible restrictions that emerge from doing so. Although source code, sequence, structure and organization and compilations of programs fundamentally differ from each other in their technical and economic properties, as well as from artistic and literary works, they are granted a similar form of protection by copyrights. The uniform legal scheme that protects those elements for long periods can produce an overprotective regime that may have a substantial and negative impact on innovation and on anti-competitive behaviour of firms. Yet, other valuable elements of software do not enjoy copyright protection and can be easily imitated without infringing the rights of their creators.

The agenda for analysis of intellectual property rights presented in this book serves as a reference to identify overprotective legislation in recent issues, such as business methods patenting. Further, as computer applications are slightly modified and applied on different platforms and hardware, and software ("ideas") and online contents ("expressions") converge, the existing regimes may lead to economic inefficiencies and hinder innovation. Analyses of potential risks caused by overprotective legislation is a recommended practice in evaluating policies of innovation and technical change.

Following the evolution of computer technologies, software patents do not contradict the general purpose of the patent regime, that is, nourishing innovation by providing monopoly over technology. Software patents typically follow the conceptual guidelines by which patents were granted to physical machines that performed (albeit less efficiently) computational tasks and information processing.[2] However, copyright protection granted to the internal organization of computer programs and to operational components of them seems to go far beyond its original aim of protecting artistic and literary works. Consequently, exclusive rights of reproduction are provided to quasi-technical features, such as interfaces and graphical design of computer applications, rather than limiting the scope of copyrights to final outputs (that is, compiled versions of computer programs). The protection of software products and technologies as intellectual property blurred the tradi-

the Internet were protected from extensive browsing by applying the *trespass-to-chatters* doctrine.

[2]Chapter 6 discusses whether the present design of patents is optimal in terms of length and breadth and whether it should be modified.

tional dichotomy between ideas and expressions and reshaped the borders between patents and copyrights. The resulting overlap between both regimes may lead to economic inefficiencies that rise from indefinite guidelines for the protection of ideas and expressions as intellectual assets. Further, the extended doctrine, by which software technology can be patented and copy–protected at the same time, can be regarded as an overprotective policy.

Essentially, the legal protection of software and algorithms as intellectual property is very much doubted. The emergence of the Open Source model has amplified some of the existing concerns. In the Open Source model self–organizing groups operate as online communities of developers and offer a different system of incentives to their innovative members. However, the Open Source model does not necessarily address the majority of concerns that can be resolved within the present institutional and economic environment of IPRs by introducing a new *sui generis* law to protect information technologies. Rather, advocates of Open Source and Free Software promote an alternative model that targets segments of the software market that are based on voluntary participation in development, provision of complementary services for free software implementations as a source of revenues, home–grown applications and academic software and do not address the needs of the majority of firms in the industry for means of appropriation. Should innovation policies be completely based on the Open Source model and abolish IPR regimes, the result is expected to be an under–protective regime in which knowledge disclosure and R&D investments (primarily those made by large firms) will decrease.

Enquiries on the optimal level of protection of computer programs often arise in this context. Campaigns by the Open Source community promote complete or partial removal of intellectual property claims from the source code and its compilations to foster technical advance and freely accessible standards (Lerner and Tirole, 2000; von Krogh et al., 2003). At the other extreme, others suggest that the present regime provides incentives to inventors and innovative SMEs (Heckel, 1992). In between those poles lie variants of the traditional IP doctrines that involve elements from copyrights and patents and are mostly proposed as *sui generis* laws.

From a historical standpoint, the significance of the Universal Machine approach, pioneered by Babbage and later furthered by Turing, and the development of the digital computer emphasize the benefits of producing multi–task platforms that support massive volumes of computations. One set of instructions can be easily modified or replaced by another, rather than constructing new machinery for every arithmetical task. Nevertheless, although the construction of new physical devices to perform computational tasks is far more costly and less efficient than carrying them out by computer programming, physical machines could be easily patented since the introduction of the Patent Law, whereas patent applications in which novel functions were implemented by more efficient means, that is, by computer programs and algorithms, were rejected before the 1980s by the USPTO. However, while software patents are at the core of a continuous debate, the physical equivalents of computer programs (that is, equipment that was built to carry out computational tasks in the pre–era of digital computers) were granted patents with little public opposition.[3] From an economic standpoint, computational machines fulfilled the measures of technical utility and novelty and, hence, obtained monopoly rights for fostering innovation and social welfare. On the other hand, patentability of their digital equivalents, mathematical algorithms applied in computer programs, is often criticized as impeding progress in information technologies.[4] Therefore, drawing parallels between both cases implies that patents issued for physical machinery that carry out informational and computational tasks could have also been regarded as overprotective at the time, if similar juridical judgement were applied.

The outcomes of misapplying an inappropriate regime may vary from hindrance in the pace of innovation to slower diffusion of evolving technologies and emergence of monopolistic structure of ownership over information technologies. The negative effects are significant particularly in initial stages of development, adoption and use of new technologies.

A coherent legal framework is necessary to address the factors of potential market failures and to prevent the lack of R&D investments, which results from reproduction of different software elements by competitors. Doing so, legislation

[3] Patents in general were the subject of various public debates. However, no particular remonstration was particularly aiming at patents that were granted to "computational machines".

[4] Lessig (1999) distinguishes between the aims of coordinating and regulating new technologies: while coordination limits the liberty to enable certain activities (for example through the formation of common standards), regulation limits liberty within the activities themselves in order to achieve desirable outcomes. As in the case of other recent laws in information technologies, the benefits of enacting regulative guidelines over establishing coordinative standards are also being questioned.

has to consider the type and the consequences of imitation, the copied elements of computer programs (that is, software entities) and whether introduction of (partially) equivalent products by second comers threatens to remove substantial shares of revenues and hence lowers the propensity of firms to invest in R&D. However, even when competitors imitate the functionality of a program but distribute it in adjacent markets, far from the inventor's marketplace, or apply it in new and different ways beyond the use that was envisioned by the inventor, the invention has a value of novelty and does not harm the commercial activities of the inventor.

While legislators and Court aim at resolving conflicts between the legal regime and the attributes of software products and technologies, the solutions (provided by statutory rulings and regulatory guidelines) may contradict the needs of developers and may create further conflicts. Therefore, the regime should also consider that a legal scheme devised to protect a specific software element may be in conflict with the best interests of other software entities.

Establishment of legislation on the basis of the Copyright Act, Patent Law and a numerous number of juridical precedents and the consequent hybrid regime can yield negative and undesirable outcomes, as described above. Comparing the level of protection provided to the various entities of software by legal means, the present regime exemplifies some of the problems that are associated with an imbalance between public and private interests, resulting in over– and under–protective legal schemes. The regime provides extensive protection to some elements of software for long periods, in comparison to the average lifetime of computer programs. At the same time, other elements are left almost unprotected and can be freely imitated by competitors without violating the Law (for example the functions and the ways in which particular sub–routines operate). An alternative solution that encompasses the various characteristics of computer programs with a minimal degree of overlap between the legal means of protection can be accomplished through enactment of a *sui generis* law. A new regime, especially designed to meet the unique needs and merits of software technologies and the dynamics of innovation in the software industry, should incorporate elements of existing legislative regimes to guarantee an appropriate degree of certainty to new entrants and the ability to predict and to avoid possible legal disputes. Implementation of a particular IPR regime, as described above, will recover the balance between public and private interests and ensure terms for competition and entry of innovative firms to the market.

# 10

# References


Abi-Saad P., David C., Gandon M. and Weisenburger E. (2001), *Recherche & Developpement en France: Resultats 1999, Estimations 2000, Objectifs Socio-Economiques du BCRD 2001*, Paris, Ministere de l'Education Nationale.

Aboody D. and Lev B. (1998), "The Value Relevance of Intangibles: The Case of Software Capitalization", *Journal of Accounting Research*, Vol. 36, pp. 161–191.

Aghion P. and Howitt P. (1992), "A Model of Growth through Creative Destruction", *Econometrica*, Vol. 60, No. 2, pp. 323–351.

Akerlof G.A. et al. (2002), *Amici Curiae in Eric Eldred et al. v. John D. Ashcroft*, No. 01–618, Submitted to the US Supreme Court, May 2002.

Allison J. and Lemley M. (2000), "Whos Patenting What? An Empirical Exploration of Patent Prosecution", *Vanderbilt Law Review*, Vol. 53, No. 6, pp. 2099–2148.

Anderson P. and Tushman M.L. (1990), "Technological Discontinuities and Dominant Designs: A Cyclical Model of Technological Change", *Administrative Science Quarterly*, Vol. 35, pp. 604–633.

Antonelli C. (1993), "The Dynamics of Technological Interrelatedness: The Case of Information and Communication Technologies", in: Foray D. and Freeman C. (eds), *Technology and the Wealth of Nations: The Dynamics of Constructed Advantage*, London, Pinter Publishers and OECD.

Arditti F.D. and Sandor R.L. (1973), "A Note on Variable Patent Life", *Journal of Industrial Economics*, Vol. 21, No. 2, pp. 177–183.

Arora A., Ceccagnoli M. and Cohen W.M. (2003), "R&D and the Patent Premium", NBER Working Paper, No. 9431, Cambridge, NBER.

Arrow K.J. (1962), "Economic Welfare and the Allocation of Resources for Invention", in: Nelson R.R. (ed.), *The Rate and Direction of Inventive Activity*, Princeton University Press.

Arthur W.B. (1987), "Competing Technologies, Increasing Returns and Lock–in by Historical Events", *Economic Journal*, Vol. 99, No. 394, pp. 116–131.

Arthur W.B. (1996), "Increasing Returns and the New World of Business", *Harvard Business Review*, Vol. 74, No. 4, pp. 100–109.

Arundel A. (2000), "Patent – the Viagra of Innovation Policy?", *Internal Report to the Expert Group in the Project "Innovation Policy in a Knowledge–Based Economy"*, Maastricht, MERIT.

Arundel A. (2001), "The Relative Effectiveness of Patents and Secrecy for Appropriation", *Research Policy*, Vol. 30, No. 4, pp. 611–624.

Babbage C. (1835), *On the Economy of Machinery and Manufactures*, 4th edition, London, Charles Knight.

Barzel Y. (1997), *Economic Analysis of Property Rights*, 2nd edition, Cambridge, Cambridge University Press.

Beck R.L. (1983), "The Prospect Theory of the Patent System and Unproductive Competition", *Research in Law and Economics*, Vol. 5, pp. 193–209.

Besen S.M. and Raskind L.J. (1991), "An Introduction to the Law and Economics of Intellectual Property", *Journal of Economic Perspectives*, Vol. 5, No. 1, pp. 3–27.

Bessen J. and Hunt R.M. (2007), "An Empirical Look at Software Patents", Journal of Economics and Management Strategy, Volume 16, No. 1, pp. 157–189.

Bessen J. and Maskin E. (2000), "Sequential Innovation, Patents and Imitation", Working Paper No. 00–01, Massachusetts Institute of Technology.

Bessy C. and Brousseau E. (1998), "Technology Licensing Contracts: Features and Diversity", *International Review of Law and Economics*, Vol. 18, pp. 451–489.

Bonaccorsi A. and Rossi C. (2003), "Why Open Source Software Can Succeed", *Research Policy*, Vol. 32, No. 7, pp. 1243-1258.

Bowman A.W. and Azzalini A. (1997), *Applied Smoothing Techniques for Data Analysis*, Oxford, Oxford University Press.

Branscomb A.W. (1990), "Computer Software – Protecting the Crown Jewels of the Information Economy", in: Rushing F.W. and Brown C.G. (eds).

Bresnahan T.F., Brynjolfsson E. and Hitt L.M. (1999), "Information Technology, Workplace Organization and the Demand for Skilled Labor: Firm–Level Evidence", *NBER Working Paper*, No. 7136, Washington DC, NBER.

Brueckman W. (1990), "Intellectual Property Protection in the European Community", in: Rushing F.W. and Brown C.G. (eds).

Brynjolfsson E. and Hitt L.M. (1998), "Beyond the Productivity Paradox: Computers are the Catalyst for Bigger Changes", *Communications of the ACM*, Vol. 41, No. 8, pp. 49–55.

Buxton H.W. (1988), *Memoir of the Life and Labours of the Late Charles Babbbage Esq., F.R.S.*, Cambridge, MIT Press, Charles Babbage Institute Reprint Series, vol. 13.

Chin A. (1998), "Computational Complexity and the Scope of Software Patents", *Jurimetrics*, Vol. 39.

Chou C.F. and Shy O. (1993), "The Crowding–Out Effects of Long Duration of Patents", *RAND Journal of Economics*, Vol. 24, No. 2, pp. 304–312.

Clapes A. (1993), *Softwars: The Legal Battles for Control of the Global Software Industry*, Westport, Quorom.

Cohen J.E. and Lemley M.A. (2001), "Patent Scope and Innovation in the Software Industry", *California Law Review*, Vol. 89, No. 1, pp. 1–57.

Cohen, S.A. (1999), "To Innovate or not to Innovate, That is the Question: The Functions, Failures, and Foibles of the Reward Function Theory of Patent Law in Relation to Computer Software Platforms", *Michigan Telecommunications, Technology and Law Review*, Vol. 5, No. 1.

Cohen W.M. and Levinthal D. (1990), "Absorptive Capacity: A New Perspective on Learning and Innovation", *Administrative Science Quarterly*, Vol. 35, No. 1, pp. 128–152.

Cohen W.M., Nelson R.R. and Walsh J.P. (2000), "Protecting Their Intellectual Assets: Appropriability Conditions and Why US Manufacturing Firms Patent (or Not)", *NBER Working Paper*, No. 7552, Washington DC, NBER.

Cohendet P. and Meyer–Krahmer F. (2001), "The Theoretical and Policy Implications of Knowledge Codification", *Research Policy*, Vol. 30, pp. 1563–1591.

Conner K.R. and Rumelt K.P. (1991), "Software Piracy: An Analysis in Protection Strategies", *Management Science*, Vol. 37, No. 2, pp. 125–139.

Cowan R. and Foray D. (1997), "The Economics of Codification and the Diffusion of Knowledge", *Industrial and Corporate Change*, Vol. 6, No. 3, pp. 595–622.

Cowan R. and Harison E. (2001), "Intellectual Property Rights in a Knowledge–Based Economy", *MERIT Study for the Dutch Advisory Council for Science and Technology Policy (AWT)*, AWT Background Study No. 21, May 2001, Maastricht.

Cowan R. and Jonard N. (2003), "The Dynamics of Collective Invention", *Journal of Economic Behavior and Organization*, Vol. 52, No. 4, pp. 513–532.

Cowan R., David P.A. and Foray D. (2000), "The Explicit Economics of Knowledge Codification and Tacitness" , *Industrial and Corporate Change*, Vol. 9, No. 2, pp. 211–253.

Dasgupta P. (1988), "Patents, Priority and Imitation or, the Economics of Races and Waiting Games", *Economic Journal*, Vol. 98, No. 389, pp. 66–80.

Dasgupta P. and David P.A. (1994), "Towards a New Economics of Science", *Research Policy*, Vol. 23, pp. 487–521.

David P.A. (1993), "Intellectual Property Institutions and the Panda's Thumb: Patents, Copyrights and Trade Secrets in Economic Theory and History", in: Wallerstein M.B., Mogee M.E. and Schoen R.A. (eds), *Global Dimensions of Intellectual Property Rights in Science and Technology*, Washington DC, National Academy Press.

David P.A. (2000), "A Tragedy of the Public Knowledge 'Commons'? Global Science, Intellectual Property and the Digital Technology Boomerang", *SIEPR Discussion Paper*, No. 00–02, Stanford Institute for Economic Policy Research, September 2000.

David P.A. and Greenstein S. (1990), "The Economics of Compatibility Standards: An Introduction to Recent Research", *Economics of Innovation and New Technologies*, Vol. 1, pp. 3–41.

Davis L. (2004), "Should We Consider Alternative Incentives for Basic Research? Patents vs. Prizes", *Economics of Innovation and New Technologies*, Vol. 13, No. 5.

Davis R., Samuelson P., Kapor M.D. and Reichman J.H. (1996), "A New View of Intellectual Property and Software", *Communications of the ACM*, Vol.

39, No. 3, pp. 21–30.

Denicoló V. and Zanchettin P. (2002), "How should Forward Patent Protection be Provided?", *International Journal of Industrial Organization*, Vol. 20, No. 6, pp. 801–827.

DiBona C., Ockman S. and Stone M. (eds) (1999), *Open Sources: Voices from the Open Sources Revolution*, Sebastopol, O'Reilly and Associates.

Diotalevi R.N. (1998), "Copyrighting Cyberspace: Unweaving a Tangled Web", *Computer Law Review and Technology Journal*, Spring 1998.

Dosi G. (1988), "Sources, Procedures and Microeconomic Effects of Innovation", *Journal of Economic Literature*, Vol. 26, pp. 1120–1171.

Eisenberg R.S. (2000), "Analyze This: A Law and Economics Agenda for the Patent System", *Vanderbilt Law Review*, Vol. 53, No. 6, pp. 2081–2098.

European Commission (1991), *Council Directive on the Legal Protection of Computer Programs (91/250/EEC)*, Council of the European Communities, Brussels, May 1991.

European Commission (1995), *Green Paper: Copyright and Related Rights in the Information Society.*

European Commission (2000), *Report from the Commission to the Council, the European Parliament and the Economic and the Social Committee on the Implementation and Effects of Directive 91/250/EEC on the Legal Protection of Computer Programs*, COM (2000)199, Brussels, April 2000.

European Patent Office (2001), *Annual Report 2001*, Munich, EPO.

Evans D.S., Nichols A.L. and Reddy B. (2002), "The Rise and Fall of Leaders in Personal Computer Software", in: Evans D.S. (ed.), *Microsoft, Antitrust and the New Economy: Selected Essays*, Amsterdam, Kluwer Academic Publishers.

Farrell J. and Saloner G. (1985), "Standardization, Compatibility and Innovation", *Rand Journal of Economics*, Vol. 16.

Farrell J. and Saloner, G. (1992), "Converters, Compatibility and the Control of Interfaces", *Journal of Industrial Economics*, Vol. 40, No. 1.

Freeman C. and Soete L. (1997), *The Economics of Industrial Innovation*, 3rd edition, Cambridge, MIT Press.

Friedman D.D., Landes W.M. and Posner R.A. (1991), "Some Economics of Trade Secret Law", *Journal of Economic Perspectives*, Vol. 5, No. 1, pp. 61–72.

Gallini N.T. (1992), "Patent Policy and Costly Imitation", *RAND Journal of*

*Economics*, Vol. 23, No. 1, pp. 52–63.

Gallini N.T. (2002), "The Economics of Patents: Lessons from Recent US Patent Reform", *Journal of Economic Perspectives*, Vol. 16, No. 2, pp. 131–154.

Gallini N.T. and Trebilcock M.J. (1998), "Intellectual Property Rights and Competition Policy: A Framework for the Analysis of Economic and Legal Issues", in: Anderson R.D. and Gallini N.T. (eds), *Competition Policy and Intellectual Property Rights in the Knowledge-based Economy*, Industry Canada Research Series, Vol. 9, Calgary, University of Calgary Press.

Ghosh R.A., Glott R., Krieger B. and Robles G. (2002), "Free/Libre and Open Source Software: Survey and Study FLOSS; Part IV: Survey of Developers", *Final Report*, available in: http://www.infonomics.nl/FLOSS/.

Gilbert R.J. and Newbery D.M.G. (1982), "Preemptive Patenting and the Persistence of Monopoly", *American Economic Review*, Vol. 72, No. 3, pp. 514–526.

Gilbert R. and Shapiro C. (1990), "Optimal Patent Length and Breadth", *RAND Journal of Economics*, Vol. 21, No. 1, pp. 106–112.

Ginarte J.C. and Park W.G. (1997), "Determinants of Patent Rights: A Cross–National Study", *Research Policy*, Vol. 26, No. 3, pp. 283–301.

Givon M., Mahajan V. and Muller E. (1995), "Software Piracy: Estimation of Lost Sales and the Impact on Software Diffusion", *Journal of Marketing*, Vol. 59, No. 1, pp. 29–37.

Graham S.J.H. and Mowery D.C. (2002), "Intellectual Property Protection in the US Software Industry", in: Cohen W.M. and Merrill S.A. (eds), *Patents in the Knowledge-Based Economy*, Washington DC, National Academy Press.

Graham S.J.H., Hall B.H., Harhoff D. and Mowery D.C. (2002), "Post-Issue Patent 'Quality Control': A Comparative Study of US Patent Re-exam. and European Patent Oppositions", *NBER Working Paper*, No. 8807, Washington DC, NBER.

Granstrand O. (1999), *The Economics and Management of Intellectual Property: Towards Intellectual Capital*, Cheltenham, UK and Northampton, MA, Edward Elgar.

Granstrand O. (2000), "The Shift Towards Intellectual Capitalism – The Role of Infocom Technologies", *Research Policy*, Vol. 29, No. 9, pp. 1061–1080.

Green J. and Scotchmer S. (1995), "On the Division of Profit in Sequential Innovation", *Rand Journal of Economics*, Vol. 26, No. 1, pp. 20–33.

Grossman G.M. and Helpman E. (1991), *Innovation and Growth in the Global Economy*, Cambridge, MIT Press.

Grossman S.J. (1990), "Experimental Use or Fair Use as a Defense to Patent Infringement", *IDEA: Journal of Law and Technology*, Vol. 30, pp. 243–264.

Hagedoorn J. (2002), "Inter–firm R&D Partnerships: an Overview of Major Trends and Patterns since 1960", *Research Policy*, Vol. 31, No. 4, pp. 477-492.

Hall B.H. (2003), "Business Method Patents, Innovation and Policy", EPIP conference on New Challenges to the Patent System, Munich, April 2003.

Hall B.H. and Ziedonis R.H. (2001), "The Determinants of Patenting in the US Semiconductor Industry, 1980–94", *Rand Journal of Economics*, Vol. 32, No. 1, pp. 101–128.

Hall B.H., Jaffe A.B. and Trajtenberg M. (2001), "The NBER Patent Citations Data File: Lessons, Insights and Methodological Tools", *NBER Working Paper*, No. 8498, October 2001.

Hanel P. (2002), "IP Protection Practices by Manufacturing Firms", *Statistics Canada: Innovation Analysis Bulletin*, Vol. 4, No. 1, pp. 7–10.

Hannan M.T. and Freeman J. (1989), *Organizational Ecology*, Cambridge, Harvard University Press.

Heckel P. (1992), "Debunking the Software Patent Myths", *Communications of the ACM*, Vol. 35, No. 6, pp. 121–140.

Heller M.A. and Eisenberg R.S. (1998), "Can Patents Deter Innovation? The Anticommons in Biomedical Research", *Science*, Vol. 280, pp. 698-701.

Hertel G., Niedner S. and Herrmann S. (2003), "Motivation of Software Developers in Open Source Projects: An Internet–based Survey of Contributors to the Linux Kernel", *Research Policy*, Vol. 32, No. 7, pp. 1159–1177.

Holderness M. (1998), "Moral Rights and Authors' Rights: The Keys to the Information Age", *Journal of Information, Law and Technology*, Vol. 1.

Horowitz A.W. and Lai E.L.C. (1996), "Patent Length and Rate of Innovation", *International Economic Review*, Vol. 37, No. 4, pp. 785–801.

Horstmann I., MacDonald G.M. and Slivinski M. (1985), "Patents as Information Transfer Mechanisms: To Patent or (Maybe) not to Patent", *Journal of Political Economy*, Vol. 93, No. 5, pp. 837–858.

Jaffe A.B. (2000), "The US Patent System in Transition: Policy Innovation and the Innovation Process", *Research Policy*, Vol. 29, No. 4–5, pp. 531–557.

Jaffe A.B. and Trajtenberg M. (2002), *Patents, Citations, and Innovations: A Window on the Knowledge Economy*, Massachusetts, MIT Press.

Jaffe A.B., Trajtenberg M. and Henderson R. (1993), "Geographic Localization of Knowledge Spillovers as Evidenced by Patent Citations", *Quarterly Journal of Economics*, Vol. 108, No. 3, pp. 577–598.

Jeppesen L.B. and Molin M.J. (2003), "Consumers as Co–developers: Learning and Innovation Outside the Firm", *Technology Analysis & Strategic Management*, Vol. 15, No. 3, pp. 363–384.

Kamien M.I. and Schwartz N.L. (1974), "Patent Life and R&D Rivalry", *American Economic Review*, Vol. 64, No. 1, pp. 183–187.

Karjala D.S. (1990), "Intellectual Property Rights in Japan and the Protection of Computer Software", in: Rushing F.W. and Brown C.G. (eds).

Khan B.Z. (1995), "Property Rights and Patent Litigation in Early Nineteenth–Century America", *Journal of Economic History*, Vol. 55, No. 1, pp. 58–97.

Kim L. (1998), "Crisis Construction and Organizational Learning: Capability Building in Catching–up at Hyundai Motors", *Organization Science*, Vol. 9, No. 4, pp. 506–521.

Kitch E.W. (1977), "The Nature and Function of the Patent System", *Journal of Law and Economics*, Vol. 20, pp. 265–290.

Klemperer P. (1990), "How Broad Should the Scope of Patent Be?", *RAND Journal of Economics*, Vol. 21, No. 1, pp. 113–130.

Klette T.J. and Griliches Z. (1998), "Empirical Patterns of Firm Growth and R&D Investment: A Quality Ladder Model Interpretation", *NBER Working Paper*, No. 6753, Cambridge, NBER.

Kretschmer M. (2003), "Software as Text and Machine: The Legal Capture of Digital Innovation", *Journal of Information, Law and Technology*, Vol. 3, No. 1.

Kuester J.R. and Thompson L.E. (2001), "Risks Associated with Restricting Business Method and E–Commerce Patents", *Georgia State University Law Review*, Vol. 17, No. 3, pp. 657–689.

Laffont J.J., Rey P. and Tirole, J. (1998), "Network Competition: Overview and Nondiscriminatory Pricing", *RAND Journal of Economics*, Vol. 29, No.

1, pp. 1–37.

Lakhani K. and von Hippel E. (2003), "How Open Source Software Works: 'Free' User to User Assistance", *Research Policy*, Vol. 32, No. 6, pp. 923–943.

Landes W.M. and Posner R.A. (1989), "An Economic Analysis of Copyright Law", *Journal of Legal Studies*, Vol. 18, pp. 325–363.

Lerner J. (1994), "The Importance of Patent Scope: An Empirical Analysis", *RAND Journal of Economics*, Vol. 25, No. 2, pp. 319–333.

Lerner J. (2000), "Patent Policy Innovation: A Clinical Examination", *Vanderbilt Law Review*, Vol. 53, No. 6, pp. 1841–1856.

Lerner J. and Tirole J. (2002), "Some Simple Economics of Open Source", *Journal of Industrial Economics*, Vol. 50.

Lessig L. (1999), "The Limits in Open Code: Regulatory Standards and the Future of the Net", *Berkeley Technology Law Journal*, Vol. 14, No. 2.

Lessig L. (2002), "Open Source Baselines: Compared to What?", in: Hahn R.W. (ed.), *Government Policy toward Open Source Software*, Washington DC, AEI–Brookings Joint Center for Regulatory Studies.

Levin R.C., Klevorick A.K., Nelson R.R. and Winter S.G. (1987), "Appropriating the Returns from Industrial Research and Development", *Brooking Papers on Economic Activity*, Vol. 3, pp. 783–831.

Lindgren M. (1990), *Glory and Failure: The Difference Engines of Johann Muller, Charles Babbage and Georg and Edvard Scheutz*, Massachusetts, MIT Press.

Machlup F. (1958), *An Economic Review of the Patent System*, Study No. 15, Subcommittee on Patents, Trademarks and Copyrights of the US Senate Judiciary Committee, Washington DC, US Government Printing Office.

Machlup F. and Penrose E. (1950), "The Patent Controversy in the Nineteenth Century", *Journal of Economic History*, Vol. 10, No. 1, pp. 1–29.

Mackaay E. (1994), "Legal Hybrids: Beyond Property and Monopoly?", *Columbia Law Review*, Vol. 94, No. 8, pp. 2630–2643.

Mairesse J. and Turner L. (2005), "Measurement and Explanation of the Intensity of Co–publication in Scientific Research: An Analysis at the Laboratory Level",*NBER Working Paper*, No. 11172, Cambridge, NBER.

Maloney M.T. and McCormick R.E. (1995), "Realignment in Telecommunications", *Managerial and Decision Economics*, Vol. 16, No. 4, pp. 401–425.

Mansell R. and Steinmueller W.E. (2000), *Mobilizing the Information Society:*

*Strategies for Growth and Opportunity*, Oxford, Oxford University Press.

Mansfield E. (1986), "Patents and Innovation: An Empirical Study", *Management Science*, Vol. 32, No. 2, pp. 173–181.

Mansfield E., Schwartz M. and Wagner S. (1981), "Imitation Costs and Patents: An Empirical Study", *Economic Journal*, Vol. 91, No. 364, pp. 907–918.

Maurseth P.B. and Verspagen B. (2002), "Knowledge Spillovers in Europe: A Patent Citations Analysis", *Scandinavian Journal of Economics*, Vol. 104, No. 4, pp. 531–545.

McFetridge D.G. (1995), "Science and Technology: Perspectives for Public Policy", *Occasional Paper*, No. 9, July 1995, Ontario, Industry Canada.

McKelvey M. (2001), "The Economic Dynamics of Software: Three Competing Business Models Exemplified Through Microsoft, Netscape and Linux", *Economics of Innovation and New Technologies*, Vol. 10, No. 3, pp. 199–236.

Menell P. (1989), "An Analysis of the Scope of Copyright Protection for Computer Programs", *Stanford Law Review*, Vol. 41, 1045–1104.

Merges R.P. (1999), "As Many as Six Impossible Patents Before Breakfast: Property Rights for Business Concepts and Patent System Reform", *Berkeley Technology Law Journal*, Vol. 14, No. 2.

Merges R.P. and Nelson R.R. (1990), "On the Complex Economics of Patent Scope", *Columbia Law Review*, Vol. 90, No. 4, pp. 839–916.

Merges R.P. and Nelson R.R. (1994), "On Limiting or Encouraging Rivalry in Technical Progress: The Effect of Patent Scope Decisions", *Journal of Economic Behavior and Organization*, Vol. 25, No. 1, pp. 1–24.

Morrison A. (1999), "Hijack on the Road to Xanadu: The Infringement of Copyright in HTML Documents via Networked Computers and the Legitimacy of Browsing Hypermedia Documents", *Journal of Information, Law and Technology*, Vol. 1.

National Research Council (1997), *Intellectual Property Rights and Research Tools in Molecular Biology*, Washington DC, National Academy Press.

Nelson R.R. and Winter S.G. (1982), *Evolutionary Theory of Economic Change*, Cambridge, Harvard University Press.

Nelson R.R. (1994), "Intellectual Property Protection for Cumulative Systems Technology", *Columbia Law Review*, Vol. 94, No. 8.

Nichols K. (1998), *Inventing Software: The Rise of "Computer-Related" Patents*,

Westport, Quorum Books.

Nicholson J.S. (1892), "Capital and Labour: Their Relative Strength", *Economic Journal*, Vol. 2, No. 7, pp. 478–490.

Nordhaus W.D. (1969), *Invention, Growth and Welfare: A Theoretical Treatment of Technological Change*, Massachusetts, MIT Press.

Nordhaus W.D. (1972), "The Optimum Life of a Patent: Reply", *American Economic Review*, Vol. 62, No. 3, pp. 428–431.

O'Donoghue T., Scotchmer S. and Thisse J.F. (1998), "Patent Breadth, Patent Life and the Pace of Technological Progress", *Journal of Economics and Management Strategy*, Vol. 7, No. 1, pp. 1–32.

OECD (1998a), *21st Century Technologies: Promises and Perils of a Dynamic Future*, Paris, OECD Publication Service.

OECD (1998b), *Measuring Intangible Investment: The Treatment of the Components of Intangible Investment in the UN model Survey of Computer Services*, Paris, OECD Publication Service.

OECD (1998c), *Measuring Electronic Commerce: International Trade in Software*, Committee for Information, Computer and Communications Policy, Directorate for Science, Technology and Industry, Paris, OECD Publication Service.

OECD (2000), *Information Technology Outlook 2000*, Paris, OECD Publication Service.

OECD (2002), *Information Technology Outlook 2002*, Paris, OECD Publication Service.

Ordover J.A. (1991), "A Patent System for Both Diffusion and Exclusion", *Journal of Economic Perspectives*, Vol. 5, No. 1, pp. 43–60.

Ostergard R.L. (2000), "The Measurement of Intellectual Property Rights Protection", *Journal of International Business Studies*, Vol. 31, No. 2, pp. 349–360.

*PC Magazine* (2001), "Performance Tests: File Server Throughput and Response Times", November 2001.

*PC Magazine* (2002), "Samba Runs Rings Around Win2000", April 2002, Available at: http://www.vnunet.com/News/1131114.

Penrose E. (1951), *The Economics of the International Patent System*, Baltimore, John Hopkins University Press.

Perens B. (1999), "The Open Source Definition", in: DiBona et al. (eds).

Raymond E.S. (1999), *The Cathedral and the Bazaar*, Sebastopol, O'Reilly and Associates.

Reese B. and Stenberg D. (2001), "Working Without Copyleft", *O'Reilly Network*, Available at: http://www.oreillynet.com.

Reichman J.H. (1994), "Legal Hybrids Between the Patent and Copyright Paradigms", *Columbia Law Review*, Vol. 94, No. 8, pp. 2432–2558.

Reinganum J. (1983), "Uncertain Innovation and the Persistence of Monopoly", *American Economic Review*, Vol. 73, No. 4, pp. 741–748.

Rice J. (2003), "Collaborative Production Strategies for Technological Innovation and Leadership in Network Industries: The Case of Bluetooth", Presented at the DRUID Winter Conference, Klarskovgaard.

Rosenberg N. (1982), *Inside the Black Box: Technology and Economics*, Cambridge, Cambridge University Press.

Rothman J.B. and Buckman J. (2001), "Which OS is Fastest for High-Performance Network Applications?", *Sys Admin*, Vol. 10, No. 7.

Rushing F.W. and Brown C.G. (eds) (1990), *Intellectual Property Rights in Science, Technology and Economic Performance: International Comparisons*, Boulder, Westview Press.

Samuelson P. (1993), "A Case Study on Computer Programs", in: Wallerstein M.B., Mogee M.E. and Schoen R.A. (eds), *Global Dimensions of Intellectual Property Rights in Science and Technology*, Washington DC, National Academy Press.

Samuelson P. (1999), "Intellectual Property and the Digital Economy: Why the Anti-Circumvention Regulations Need to be Revised", *Berkeley Technology Law Journal*, Vol. 14, No. 2.

Samuelson P. and Scotchmer S. (2002), "The Law and Economics of Reverse Engineering", *Yale Law Journal*, Vol. 111, pp. 1575–1663.

Samuelson P., Davis R., Kapor M.D. and Reichman J.H. (1994), "A Manifesto Concerning the Legal Protection of Computer Programs", *Columbia Law Review*, Vol. 94, No. 8.

Scherer F. (1972), "Nordhaus' Theory of Optimal Patent Life: A Geometric Interpretation", *American Economic Review*, Vol. 62, pp. 422–427.

Schmookler J. (1950), "The Interpretation of Patent Statistics", *Journal of the Patent Office Society*, Vol. 32, No. 2, pp. 123–146.

Schonfeld M. and Restaino L. (2002), "Bioinformatics Patent Litigation Strategy:

A Heightened Role For Experts", *Mealey's Litigation Report: Patents*, available at: www.brownraysman.com/pubs/articles/

Schumm B. (1996), "Escaping the World of 'I Know It When I See It': A New Test for Software Patentability", *Michigan Telecommunication and Technology Law Review*, Vol. 2.

Schumpeter J.A. (1975), *Capitalism, Socialism and Democracy*, New York, Harper (orig. pub. 1942).

Scotchmer S. (1991), "Standing on the Shoulders of Giants: Cumulative Research and the Patent Law", *Journal of Economic Perspectives*, Vol. 5, No. 1, pp. 29–41.

Scotchmer S. (1996), "Protecting Early Innovators: Should Second–Generation Products be Patentable?", *RAND Journal of Economics*, Vol. 27, No. 2, pp. 322–331.

Scotchmer S. (2005), *Innovation and Incentives*, Massachusetts, MIT Press.

Shy O. and Thisse J.F. (1999), "A Strategic Approach to Software Protection", *Journal of Economics and Management Strategy*, Vol. 8, No. 2, pp. 163–190.

SIIA (1999), *1999 "Special 301" Review – Comments of the Computer Software Industry on Policies and Practices of Foreign Countries Regarding Intellectual Property Rights*, Software and Information Industry Association.

SIIA (2001), "1997–2001 Piracy Rates and Losses", Report, Software and Information Industry Association.

Silverberg G. and Verspagen B. (1994), "Collective Learning, Innovation and Growth in a Boundedly Rational, Evolutionary World", *Journal of Evolutionary Economics*, Vol. 4, No. 3, pp. 207–226.

Smith B.L. (2002), "The Future of Software: Enabling the Marketplace to Decide", in: Hahn R.W. (ed), *Government Policy toward Open Source Software*, Washington DC, AEI–Brookings Joint Center for Regulatory Studies.

SPA (1997), *1997 Global Software Piracy Report*, Business Software Alliance and Software Publishers Association.

SPA (1998), *1998 Global Software Piracy Report*, Software Publishers Association.

SPA (2002), *Seventh Annual BSA Piracy Study*, Software Publishers Association.

Stallman R. (1999), "The GNU Operating System and the Free Software Movement", in: DiBona et al. (eds).

Steinmueller W.E. (1996), "The US Software Industry: An Analysis and Interpretive History", in: Mowery D.C. (ed.), *The International Computer Software Industry: A Comparative Study of Industry Evolution and Structure*, New York, Oxford University Press.

Stolpe M. (2000), "Protection Against Software Piracy: A Study of Technology Adoption for the Enforcement of Intellectual Property Rights", *Economics of Innovation and New Technology*, Vol. 9, No. 1.

Syrowik D.R. (1996), "Software Patents – Just Make a Good Thing Better", *Michigan Telecommunication and Technology Law Review*, Vol. 2.

Tandon P. (1982), "Optimal Patents with Compulsory Licensing", *Journal of Political Economy*, Vol. 90, No. 3, pp. 470–486.

Tirole J. (1988), *The Theory of Industrial Organization*, Cambridge, MIT Press.

Tom W.K. (1998), Background Note, in: *Competition Policy and Intellectual Property Rights*, Committee on Competition Law and Policy, Directorate for Financial, Fiscal and Enterprise Affairs, Paris, OECD Publication Service.

Trajtenberg M. (1989), "The Welfare Analysis of Product Innovations, with an Application to Computed Tomography Scanners", *Journal of Political Economy*, Vol. 97, No. 2, pp. 444–479.

Trajtenberg M. (1990), "A Penny for Your Quotes: Patent Citations and the Value of Innovations", *RAND Journal of Economics*, Vol. 21, No. 1, pp. 172–187.

Towse R. (1999), "Copyright and Economic Incentives: an Application to Performers' Rights in the Music Industry", *Kyklos*, Vol. 52, No. 3, pp. 369–390.

Turing A.M. (1936), "On Computable Numbers, with an Application to the Entscheidungsproblem", *Proceedings of the London Mathematical Society*, Series 2, Vol. 2, November 1936.

USPTO (1996), *Examination Guidelines for Computer-Related Inventions – Final Version*, Washington DC, US Patent and Trademark Office.

USPTO (2003), *Performance and Accountability Report – Fiscal Year 2003*, Washington, US Patent and Trademark Office.

USPTO (2004), "Patenting in Technology Classes, Breakout by Geographic Origin (State and Country): Count of 1999–2003 Utility Patent Grants, By Calendar Year of Grant With Patent Counts Based on Primary Patent Classification", Washington, US Patent and Trademark Office.

Van Dijk T. (1996), "Patent Height and Competition in Product Improvements", *Journal of Industrial Economics*, Vol. 44, No. 2, pp. 151–167.

Verspagen B. and Caniëls M.C.J. (2001), "Barriers to Knowledge Spillovers and Regional Convergence in an Evolutionary Model", *Journal of Evolutionary Economics*, Vol. 11, No. 3, pp. 307–329.

Verspagen B. and De Loo I. (1999), "Technology Spillovers Between Sectors and Over Time", *Technological Forecasting and Social Change*, Vol. 60, pp. 215–235.

Vosselman W. (1998), *Measuring Intangible Investment: Initial Guidelines for the Collection and Comparison of Data on Intangible Investment*, Paris, OECD Publication Service.

Von Hippel E. (1982), "Appropriability of Innovation Benefit as a Predictor of the Source of Innovation", *Research Policy*, Vol. 11, pp. 95–115.

Von Krogh G., Spaeth S. and Lakhani K. (2003), "Community, Joining, and Specialization in Open Source Software Innovation: A Case Study", *Research Policy*, Vol. 32, No. 7, pp. 1217–1241.

Wade J. (1995), "Dynamics of Organizational Communities and Technological Bandwagons: An Empirical Investigation of Community Evolution in the Microprocessor Market", *Strategic Management Journal*, Vol. 16, pp. 111–133.

Waterson M. (1990), "The Economics of Product Patents", *American Economic Review*, Vol. 80, No. 4, pp. 860–869.

White K.E. (2002), "*FESTO*: A Case Contravening the Convergence of Doctrine of Equivalents Jurisprudence in Germany, The United Kingdom, and the United States", *Michigan Telecommunications and Technology Law Review*, Vol. 8, No. 1, pp. 1–37.

WIPO (1998), *Introduction to Intellectual Property Theory and Practice*, London, Kluwer Law International.

WIPO (2001), *Collection of Papers on Intellectual Property*, WIPO Publication No. 773(E), Geneva, WIPO Worldwide Academy.

Witek K.E. (1996), "Developing a Comprehensive Software Claim Drafting Strategy for US Software Patents", *Berkeley Technology Law Journal*, Vol. 11, No. 2.

World Trade Organization (1995), *Agreement on Trade-Related Aspects of Intellectual Property Rights*, WTO.

Wright B.D. (1983), "The Economics of Invention Incentives: Patents, Prizes and Research Contracts", *American Economic Review*, Vol. 73, No. 4, pp. 691–707.

Young R. (1999), "Giving It Away: How Red Hat Software Stumbled Across a New Economic Model and Helped Improve an Industry", in: DiBona et al. (eds).

# A

# Appendix: Proof of Propositions 5 and 6

**Proof of Proposition 5**:

From Equation 5.13, we receive:

$$\frac{\partial \pi}{\partial \alpha} = \frac{-\Psi(\alpha)c_1}{(\alpha c_1 + (1-\alpha)\bar{c})^2} + \frac{(1-\alpha)\frac{\partial \Psi}{\partial \alpha}}{(\alpha c_1 + (1-\alpha)\bar{c})} = 0 \tag{A.1}$$

Solving for $\Psi(\alpha)$:

$$\Psi(\alpha) = \frac{(1-\alpha)(\alpha c_1 + (1-\alpha)\bar{c})}{c_1} \cdot \frac{\partial \Psi}{\partial \alpha} \tag{A.2}$$

(a) If $\left.\frac{\partial \pi}{\partial \alpha}\right|_{\alpha=0} \leq 0$, then from Equation A.1:

$$\frac{-\Psi(0)c_1}{\bar{c}^2} + \frac{1}{\bar{c}} \cdot \frac{\partial \Psi(0)}{\partial \alpha} \leq 0 \tag{A.3}$$

and

$$\Psi(0) \geq \frac{\partial \Psi(0)}{\partial \alpha} \cdot \frac{\bar{c}}{c_1} \tag{A.4}$$

As revenue is positive and decreasing with $\alpha$, the firm would choose $\alpha^* = 0$. Consider also the case $\left.\frac{\partial \pi}{\partial \alpha}\right|_{\alpha=1} \geq 0$. Then, from Equation A.1:

$$\frac{-\Psi(1)c_1}{c_1^2} \geq 0 \tag{A.5}$$

Hence, $\Psi(1) \leq 0$. Since $\bar{c} > c_1 > 0$ and no positive revenue is generated at $\alpha = 1$, the firm would choose full opennes to minimize costs.

(b) If $\left.\frac{\partial\pi}{\partial\alpha}\right|_{\alpha=0} \geq 0$ and $\left.\frac{\partial\pi}{\partial\alpha}\right|_{\alpha=1} \leq 0$, then we look for an interim value of $\alpha$, $0 < \alpha^* < 1$, in which profits are maximized.

Simplifying Equation A.1:

$$\frac{\Psi(\alpha)c_1}{\frac{\partial\Psi}{\partial\alpha}} = \alpha(c_1 - 2\bar{c}) - \alpha^2(c_1 - \bar{c}) + \bar{c} \tag{A.6}$$

Solving Equation A.6 for $\alpha$, we receive:

$$\alpha = \frac{-(c_1 - 2\bar{c}) \pm \sqrt{(c_1 - 2\bar{c})^2 + 4[(c_1 - \bar{c}) + \bar{c} - c_1 \cdot \frac{\Psi}{(}\partial\Psi/\partial\alpha)]}}{2(\bar{c} - c_1 \cdot \frac{\Psi}{(}\partial\Psi/\partial\alpha))} \tag{A.7}$$

■

# B

# Appendix: Distribution of Software, Cryptography and Image Analysis Patents

| Patent Class | 1980 | 1981 | 1982 | 1983 | 1984 | 1985 | 1986 | 1987 | 1988 | 1989 | 1990 | 1991 |
|---|---|---|---|---|---|---|---|---|---|---|---|---|
| 380 | 14 | 52 | 43 | 23 | 78 | 87 | 159 | 180 | 144 | 210 | 253 | 227 |
| 382 | 1 | 1 | 18 | 21 | 39 | 53 | 41 | 72 | 75 | 101 | 110 | 150 |
| 703 | 2 | 15 | 21 | 22 | 30 | 27 | 33 | 48 | 55 | 91 | 88 | 96 |
| 704 | 25 | 87 | 105 | 131 | 150 | 146 | 186 | 177 | 228 | 352 | 272 | 248 |
| 705 | 14 | 39 | 68 | 63 | 63 | 95 | 96 | 146 | 142 | 257 | 210 | 207 |
| 706 | | 3 | 3 | 7 | 4 | 4 | 22 | 37 | 53 | 133 | 214 | 205 |
| 707 | 1 | 10 | 11 | 13 | 32 | 33 | 38 | 44 | 41 | 91 | 85 | 87 |
| 709 | 8 | 8 | 21 | 46 | 75 | 50 | 56 | 65 | 90 | 87 | 96 | 103 |
| 710 | 28 | 93 | 79 | 133 | 181 | 136 | 121 | 163 | 150 | 228 | 192 | 215 |
| 715 | 7 | 9 | 17 | 24 | 58 | 54 | 47 | 57 | 80 | 103 | 97 | 96 |
| 717 | | 3 | 2 | 1 | 8 | 8 | 17 | 21 | 26 | 46 | 33 | 28 |
| 718 | 5 | 7 | 11 | 16 | 23 | 19 | 17 | 27 | 27 | 33 | 38 | 33 |

| *Patent Class* | 1992 | 1993 | 1994 | 1995 | 1996 | 1997 | 1998 | 1999 | 2000 | 2001 | 2002 | 2003 |
|---|---|---|---|---|---|---|---|---|---|---|---|---|
| 266 | 365 | 374 | 385 | 380 | 389 | 422 | 571 | 530 | 776 | 652 | 509 | 419 |
| 129 | 175 | 167 | 134 | 382 | 253 | 290 | 502 | 529 | 573 | 652 | 639 | 717 |
| 97 | 135 | 200 | 237 | 703 | 338 | 321 | 497 | 517 | 556 | 703 | 505 | 636 |
| 290 | 359 | 463 | 502 | 704 | 710 | 1,123 | 1,974 | 1,637 | 1,304 | 1,640 | 1,375 | 1,100 |
| 204 | 347 | 334 | 282 | 705 | 394 | 589 | 1,303 | 1,932 | 1,953 | 1,616 | 1,555 | 1,575 |
| 344 | 432 | 366 | 446 | 706 | 429 | 472 | 881 | 378 | 437 | 463 | 485 | 641 |
| 157 | 232 | 293 | 447 | 707 | 538 | 929 | 2,738 | 3,328 | 2,805 | 3,439 | 3,968 | 3,941 |
| 178 | 258 | 326 | 444 | 709 | 759 | 871 | 2,591 | 3,071 | 4,163 | 4,253 | 4,454 | 4,582 |
| 291 | 467 | 554 | 881 | 710 | 1,662 | 1,974 | 3,049 | 2,821 | 3,249 | 3,087 | 3,071 | 3,597 |
| 169 | 195 | 239 | 279 | 715 | 370 | 492 | 758 | 835 | 734 | 852 | 669 | 700 |
| 85 | 108 | 193 | 256 | 717 | 270 | 285 | 795 | 938 | 814 | 1066 | 899 | 1,212 |
| 64 | 83 | 135 | 162 | 718 | 125 | 185 | 377 | 358 | 380 | 432 | 452 | 436 |

**Table B.1.** Distribution of patents by year and by class.

# Index

Printed and bound by CPI Group (UK) Ltd, Croydon, CR0 4YY

23/04/2025

14660979-0005